NEW BABYLON
RISING

RON RHODES

HARVEST HOUSE PUBLISHERS
EUGENE, OREGON

Cover by Bryce Williamson

Cover photo © ivan-96, eugenesergeev, Ig0rZh, loops7 / Getty Images; KevinCarden / Light Stock

New Babylon Rising
Copyright © 2019 Ron Rhodes
Published by Harvest House Publishers
Eugene, Oregon 97408
www.harvesthousepublishers.com

ISBN 978-0-7369-7173-7 (pbk.)
ISBN 978-0-7369-7174-4 (eBook)

Library of Congress Cataloging-in-Publication Data

Names: Rhodes, Ron, author.
Title: New Babylon rising / Ron Rhodes.
Description: Eugene : Harvest House Publishers, 2019. | Includes
   bibliographical references.
Identifiers: LCCN 2018054820 (print) | LCCN 2019012082 (ebook) | ISBN
   9780736971744 (ebook) | ISBN 9780736971737 (pbk.)
Subjects: LCSH: Bible--Prophecies--Babylon (Extinct city) | Babylon (Extinct
   city)--In the Bible. | End of the world.
Classification: LCC BS649.B3 (ebook) | LCC BS649.B3 R46 2019 (print) | DDC
   236/.9--dc23
LC record available at https://lccn.loc.gov/2018054820

Printed in the United States of America
19 20 21 22 23 24 25 26 27 / BP-GL / 10 9 8 7 6 5 4 3 2 1

Written in fond memory of the late Drs.
John F. Walvoord,
J. Dwight Pentecost,
and Charles C. Ryrie

Acknowledgments

Heartfelt thanks go to the late Drs. John F. Walvoord, J. Dwight Pentecost, and Charles C. Ryrie, all of whom were my mentors at Dallas Theological Seminary in the early 1980s. (*Seems like just yesterday!*) Their insights played a significant role in shaping my views on biblical prophecy and other areas of theology.

I continue to be grateful beyond words for my amazing family. My heart overflows with appreciation for my wife, Kerri, and my two grown children, David and Kylie. What awesome gifts God has given me.

I'm also appreciative of Harvest House Publishers, whose staff of committed Christians are true professionals at what they do. A special thanks goes to Harvest House's president, Bob Hawkins Jr., with whom I have shared countless breakfasts and dinners through several decades, during which we hammered out new book projects. What a fruitful relationship we have been blessed with through the years.

Most importantly, I remain ever grateful to the Lord Jesus Christ, not only for His wondrous gift of salvation, but also for the opportunity He has given me to serve Him during this short earthly life. *Come soon, Lord!*

Contents

Introduction:
New Babylon Rising

B abylon plays a critically important role in the Bible—particularly as related to Bible prophecy. I say this because…

- the Bible mentions Babylon more than 280 times.
- the book of Revelation contains 404 verses, and out of those,
  44 deal specifically with Babylon.[1]
- about 11 percent of the book of Revelation deals with Babylon.
  That's a bit over one-tenth of the book.[2]
- while Jerusalem is the most-often-mentioned city in the Bible,
  Babylon is the second-most-often-mentioned city. *That means
  Babylon is an important city for us to know about.*
- while *Jerusalem* literally means "city of peace," *Babylon* means
  "city of confusion and war." They are antithetical to each other.
- while Jerusalem is portrayed as God's city (Revelation 21:2-3),
  Babylon is portrayed as a demonic city (18:2).
- while God's temple was built (and will one day be rebuilt) in
  Jerusalem, the Tower of Babel—a paganized effort of human
  beings to observe and worship the heavens (Genesis 11:1-9)—
  was built in Babylon.
- the book of Revelation describes the New Jerusalem as a

chaste bride (Revelation 21:9-10). New Babylon is described as a great prostitute (17:1,3).

• while the New Jerusalem is portrayed as an eternal city (Revelation 21:1-4), New Babylon is portrayed as a temporal city that will be destroyed by God Himself toward the end of the seven-year tribulation period (18:8).

In view of such facts, I believe Bible expositor David Jeremiah is correct when he says,

> The Bible could be termed a tale of two cities: Jerusalem and Babylon. Jerusalem, of course, is the historical capital of God's chosen nation, Israel, and the future capital of His eternal Kingdom. Babylon, on the other hand, is the city the Bible uses as a recurring symbol for the world's evils—decadence, cruelty, abuse of power, and especially rebellion against God.[3]

Because Babylon plays such a crucial role in Bible prophecy, you and I ought to pay a careful attention to it. The very fact that 11 percent of the book of Revelation deals specifically with Babylon indicates that God wants us to know about the rise of New Babylon in the end times.

In case you're unaware of it, the term *end times* embraces a broad spectrum of events that will take place during the last days. These events include the rapture; the judgment seat of Christ (for Christians); the seven-year tribulation period (and all the events included in that period, such as the emergence of the antichrist and the campaign of Armageddon); the second coming of Christ; Christ's 1,000-year millennial kingdom; the great white throne judgment (for the wicked); a destiny in hell for unbelievers, and a destiny in heaven for believers. Some of these terms may be unfamiliar to you. They might even seem like a foreign language to you. Don't be concerned—I'll explain them all in this book. The important fact I want to empha-size at this early juncture is that the rise of New Babylon is not an iso-lated end-times event; rather, it is intimately related to other aspects of the end times, especially the tribulation period, the antichrist, and Armageddon. I'll address all this in detail in chapter 1.

Ancient Babylon and New Babylon

Ancient Babylon lay in the land of Shinar (Genesis 10:10). This influential civilization, ruled by kings and priests, was situated on the banks of the Euphrates River, a little more than 50 miles south of modern Baghdad in Iraq. Because of its ideal location, Babylon was an important commercial and trade center in the ancient world. It became a powerful kingdom under the leadership of Hammurabi (1792–1750 BC).

Archeologists have discovered a variety of ancient Babylonian documents. For example, Babylonian collections of wisdom liter-ature include the Counsels of Wisdom (dated at 1500–1000 BC), the Akkadian Proverbs (1800–1600 BC), and the Words of Ahiqar (700–400 BC). Many of the proverbs contained in these works are secular in nature, and some are even quite crass in their moral tone. Such crassness is not unexpected because Babylon was a thoroughly pagan culture.

Like other pagan nations of the ancient Near East, the Babylo-nians believed in many false gods and goddesses. These gods were thought to control the entire world of nature, and if one sought to be successful in life, he would do well to placate the gods. In Bab-ylonian religion, the behavior of the gods was considered unpre-dictable at best.

Each city in Babylon had a patron god with an accompanying temple. There were also a number of small shrines scattered about each city where people often met to worship various other deities.

The chief of the Babylonian gods was Anu, considered the king of heaven, while the patron god of Babylon was Marduk.

Belief in an afterlife was prevalent among the Babylonians. The dead were thought to live in the underworld and found their sustenance in offerings made by their living descendants. If no offerings of food or drink were made by descendants, the ghosts of the dead would allegedly return to haunt them. Hence, there was strong motivation to make such offerings.

The Babylonians were well known for their practice of divination. Astrology can trace its roots back to Babylon to around 3000 BC. The ancient Babylonians observed how orderly and rhythmically the planets moved across the sky and concluded that the planets were "gods of the night." Thus the planets were assigned godlike powers and character and were worshipped. These gods were believed to control the fate of human beings on Earth in a broad sense—that is, they controlled the destiny of nations (see Daniel 1:20; 2:2,10,27; 4:7; 5:7,11,15). In view of this, the priests of Babylon sought to understand and predict the movements of these planets so that perhaps they could use this knowledge beneficially on their nation's behalf. With a view to studying and worshipping these deities, the Babylonians built towers called ziggurats. Apparently, the Tower of Babel was one such ziggurat.

It is important to understand the significance of the Tower of Babel, which we find documented in Genesis 11. Bible scholar Charles Dyer provides this insight:

> Babel was humanity's first united attempt to short-circuit God's purpose. This first post-Flood city was designed expressly to thwart God's plan for humankind. The people wanted unity and power, and Babel was to be the seat of that power. Babylon, the city of man trying to rise to heaven, was built in direct opposition to God's plan.[4]

Moreover, the Tower of Babel was constructed so that it would be immune from any possible flood the Lord might send in judgment. Chuck Swindoll explains:

> The ancient Jewish historian, Josephus, pointed out that the Jews built the tower out of "burnt brick, cemented together with mortar, made of bitumen, that it might not be liable to admit water." In other words, they apparently disbelieved God's promise that He would never again send a global flood, and they made their tower waterproof to keep from drowning! Furthermore, the entire project was projected heavenward, an attempt to construct a physical means to earn what only God can freely grant—access to heaven.[5]

These Jewish rebels were clearly trying to short-circuit God! Likewise, during the future tribulation period, we will see that New Babylon will seek to short-circuit God's purposes. In fact, New Babylon will be the seat of the antichrist's power.

Ancient Babylon—an expansionist empire—is often represented in Scripture as being arrayed against God and His people (2 Kings 24:10). In 597 BC, for example, some 3,000 Jews were forced into exile in Babylon under Nebuchadnezzar's leadership. Jerusalem and the temple were obliterated (Lamentations 1:1-7). Though God sovereignly used Babylon as His powerful whipping rod in chastening Israel, Babylon would later be destroyed by God's hand of judgment for its continual standing against His people (Isaiah 13:1-16).

Based upon a literal approach to interpreting prophetic Scripture, it is clear there will be a revived Babylon—a New Babylon—that will rise in the end times during the future seven-year tribulation period. That New Babylon, like its ancient counterpart, will be characterized by paganism, false religion, immorality, a strong anti-God sentiment, and will also be heavily commercialized and politically dominant.

How Do We Know Babylon's Future?

In this book I will provide a great deal of information about Babylon's future, and I will do so with a strong sense of certainty. It is quite natural and understandable to wonder how I can possibly speak with such conviction about events that have not yet transpired. This is especially so for readers who may not be Christians.

While I personally have no ability to predict the future, Scripture reveals that God does. God's ability to foretell future events separates Him from all the false gods of paganism (including those of Babylon). Addressing the polytheism (or belief in many gods) of Isaiah's time, God Himself affirmed in no uncertain terms:

- "Who is like me? Let him step forward and prove to you his power. Let him do as I have done since ancient times when I established a people and explained its future" (Isaiah 44:7).

- "Do not tremble; do not be afraid. Did I not proclaim my purposes for you long ago? You are my witnesses—is there any other God? No! There is no other Rock—not one!" (Isaiah 44:8).

- "Who made these things known so long ago? What idol ever told you they would happen? Was it not I, the LORD? For there is no other God but me" (Isaiah 45:21).

- "I am God, and there is none like me. Only I can tell you the future before it even happens. Everything I plan will come to pass, for I do whatever I wish" (Isaiah 46:9-10).

- "Long ago I told you what was going to happen. Then suddenly I took action, and all my predictions came true...I told you beforehand what I was going to do" (Isaiah 48:3,5).

Of course, anyone can make predictions—that is easy. But having them fulfilled is another story altogether. The more statements you make about the future and the greater the detail, the better the chances are that you will be proven wrong. But God has *never* been wrong.

God's accuracy when it comes to the fulfillment of His prophetic statements relates directly to the fact that He is *all-knowing* (or, using theological terminology, *omniscient*). Because God transcends time—because He is *above* time—He can see the past, present, and future as a single intuitive act. God's knowledge of all things is from the vantage point of eternity. In view of this, we can infer that the past, present, and future are all encompassed in one ever-present "now" to Him.

Scripture reveals that God knows all things, both actual and possible (Matthew 11:21-23). He knows all things past (Isaiah 41:22), present (Hebrews 4:13), and future (Isaiah 46:10). That is why there can be no increase or decrease in His knowledge. Psalm 147:5 affirms that God's understanding "is beyond measure." In fact, His knowledge is infinite (Psalms 33:13-15; 139:11-12; 147:5; Proverbs 15:3; Isaiah 40:14; 46:10; Acts 15:18; Hebrews 4:13; 1 John 3:20).

There are plenty of examples in Scripture where Jesus, as God, indicates He knows *in advance* the freewill decisions human beings will make. One is John 13:38, where Jesus indicated to Peter that before the cock crows, Peter would disown Jesus three times. Notice the specificity of Jesus's prediction. He did not say Peter would disown Jesus a few times, or many times, or even two times or four times, but *three* times. Of course, things unfolded exactly as Jesus predicted.

Jesus also knew that Judas would make the freewill decision to betray Him (John 13:18-19). This was not a mere educated guess on Jesus's part. Jesus omnisciently knew what Judas intended to do.

Jesus's omniscience is also illustrated in the fact that in John 11:7,11, He pronounced to His disciples that Lazarus had died. No one came up to Him and told Him this. Rather, Jesus, in His divine all-knowingness—His omniscience—simply knew that Lazarus had died, even though He was geographically separated from Lazarus and his family.

We further observe that Jesus, as God, could read the hearts of every man and woman (Mark 2:8; John 1:48; 2:24,25; 4:16-19; Acts 1:24; 1 Corinthians 4:5; Revelation 2:18-23). Jesus knew where the fish were swimming in the water (Luke 5:4,6; John 21:6-11), and He knew which fish contained the coin in its mouth (Matthew 17:27). There are many other examples I could provide, but the point is clear: *Jesus is omniscient!*

You may be wondering why I am placing such great emphasis on Jesus and His omniscience. The answer is simple. First Peter 1:11 reveals that the spirit of Christ spoke through the biblical prophets. As well, the prophecies in the book of Revelation—including those that deal with the rise of New Babylon—*come directly from Jesus Christ* (see Revelation 1:1-2). Because Christ is all-knowing—because He is omniscient—*His prophecies of Babylon's future are laser-accurate*. Count on it.

The Ongoing Pattern of Literally Fulfilled Prophecy

There are more than 100 messianic prophecies that were fulfilled literally in the first coming of Jesus Christ. From the book of Genesis to the book of Malachi, the Old Testament abounds with anticipations of the coming Messiah. Numerous predictions fulfilled to the "crossing of the *t*" and the "dotting of the *i*" in the New Testament relate to His birth, life, ministry, death, resurrection, and glory.

Among the literally fulfilled prophecies are that the Messiah would be born of a virgin (Isaiah 7:14), from the line of Abraham (Genesis 12:1-2), from the line of David (2 Samuel 7:12-16), in the city of Bethlehem (Micah 5:2); would be betrayed for 30 shekels of silver (Zechariah 11:12), be pierced for our sins (Zechariah 12:10) by being crucified between thieves (Isaiah 53:12); and would rise from the dead (Psalms 16:10; 22:22). Jesus *literally* fulfilled these and many other messianic prophecies in the Old Testament.

All of this gives us strong confidence to expect that those prophetic utterances that are not yet fulfilled—or not yet completely fulfilled—will also come to pass just as literally as the earlier prophecies. God's track record with past prophecies establishes an unbroken pattern of literal fulfillment. I like to tell people that if they want to understand how God will fulfill prophecies in the future, just take a look at how He has fulfilled prophecies in the past. *The precedent has been set!*

This means that the many prophecies in Scripture that deal with New Babylon should not be taken metaphorically or allegorically, but rather, literally. It is my conviction that there will be a literal city—*New Babylon*—in the Middle East, along the Euphrates River, that plays a crucial role in both religion and commerce in end-times prophecy.

Not "Newspaper Exegesis"

Whenever someone relates certain current events to biblical prophecy, there are naysayers and mockers who like to claim that all this is nothing but "newspaper exegesis." Preterist Gary DeMar, for example, says that we are "reading the Bible through the lens of current events."[6] This is a common accusation.

Addressing this issue, scholar Arnold Fruchtenbaum—in his helpful book *The Footsteps of the Messiah*—commented that "current events must never be the means of interpreting the Scriptures, but the Scriptures must interpret current events."[7] Fruchtenbaum is correct. It is wrong to take a newspaper's headlines and then force them into biblical prophecies. Such forced exegesis is unworthy of serious Bible students. The proper approach is to first study the Scriptures to find out what God has revealed about the future. Then we can measure current events against what the Bible reveals about the future in order to give thoughtful consideration as to whether there is a legitimate correlation (see Matthew 16:1-3; Luke 21:29-33).

Thomas Ice has written many helpful books on Bible prophecy and has this to say about those who make charges of "newspaper exegesis":

> For many years the literal interpreters of Bible prophecy have taught that Israel must return to the land before the tribulation, based upon their understanding of the prophetic timetable. That has come to pass with the founding of the present state of Israel in 1948. The Jews are back in their land and poised to fulfill their destiny when the tribulation begins. Believers in the past, before 1948, did not believe this based upon what the newspapers said. Instead, they believed it because the Bible said so...If this belief had been a function of "newspaper exegesis" then we would not have begun proclaiming our view of a reconstituted Israel until that time. Instead, Bible students were proclaiming it as a future event for hundreds of years before it occurred...In the same way, prophecy students have also taught for many years that there will be a Revived Roman Empire and the need for a rebuilding of the city of Babylon since these entities will play a specific role during the future time of great tribulation.[8]

Whenever we witness events of prophetic significance, we can rejoice in God's sovereign control of human history while at the same time resist the temptation to set dates regarding end-time events, recognizing that God forbids us from doing this (Acts 1:7). All the while, we avoid sensationalism, recognizing that Christ calls

His followers to live soberly and alertly as they await His coming (Mark 13:32-37).

Accurate Observers of the Signs of the Times

Jesus's words to a group of Jewish leaders in Matthew 16 gives us an important insight:

> The Pharisees and Sadducees came, and to test him they asked him to show them a sign from heaven. He answered them, "When it is evening, you say, 'It will be fair weather, for the sky is red.' And in the morning, 'It will be stormy today, for the sky is red and threatening.' You know how to interpret the appearance of the sky, but you cannot interpret the signs of the times" (verses 1-3 ESV).

Jesus was rebuking these Jewish leaders. They were the religious elite of their day and were supposed to know the teachings of Old Testament Scripture—including the *prophetic* portions. Yet they were completely blind to properly discerning the signs of the times.

More specifically, the Pharisees and Sadducees were blind to the reality that the Messiah was in their midst. The miracles Jesus wrought were just as clear a sign to His divine identity as dark clouds in the sky are a sign of impending rain. Specific kinds of miracles had been prophesied of the Messiah in multiple Old Testament passages—for example, the blind will see, the deaf will hear, and the lame will walk (see Isaiah 35:5-6). The Pharisees and Sadducees—experts in the Old Testament—should have seen Jesus as being the fulfillment of these messianic verses. In their blindness, however, they could not "interpret the signs of the times."

The lesson we learn is simple: *Don't make the same mistake made by the Pharisees and Sadducees*. We ought to be educated in the prophetic Scriptures so that we can discern whether the stage is being set for the fulfillment of end-time prophecies.

Jesus also urged, "From the fig tree learn its lesson: as soon as its branch becomes tender and puts out its leaves, you know that summer is near. So also, when you see all these things, you know that he is near, at the very gates" (Matthew 24:32-33 ESV). Jesus indicates in this verse that there are certain things God has revealed via prophecy that ought to cause people who know the Bible to understand that a fulfillment of prophecy is taking place—or perhaps the stage is being set for a prophecy to be fulfilled. Jesus is thus informing His followers to seek to be accurate observers of the times so that when biblical prophecies come to pass, they will recognize it (see also Luke 21:25-28).

Our focus in this book will be on prophecies of New Babylon—or, more specifically, *religious* New Babylon and *commercial* New Babylon. It's all quite controversial because Christians hold to a number of different views about the identity of New Babylon. Even the apostle John seemed a bit stunned to learn about this place: "I stared at her in complete amazement" (Revelation 17:6). We'll try to make sense of all the various views as we proceed.

Of course, no prophecy stands by itself. Prophecies about New Babylon necessarily relate to numerous other end-times prophecies. Don't let this overwhelm you. I'll address all this in chapter 1 and give you a good feel for the big picture of how New Babylon fits in to God's overall end-times prophetic plan.

> *Lord, by the power of Your Spirit, please enable the reader to understand the prophetic Scriptures relating to New Babylon and other end-time events. Please excite him or her with Your Word and instill a sense of awe for the person of our Lord Jesus Christ, who controls all things. I thank You in Jesus's name. Amen.*

1

New Babylon and End-Times Chronology

I enjoy taking complex subjects and making them simpler for people to understand. I've tried to do this in all my previous books on Bible prophecy, and that is my goal for this book.

Toward that end, on the pages that follow I have presented a chronology of the end times that will help you understand precisely where New Babylon—in both its *religious* and *commercial* aspects—fits into God's overall plan. I also want to show how various other prophetic events relate to the emergence of New Babylon. That will enable you to more easily grasp how all the pieces of the prophetic puzzle fit together.

In this chapter I provide a list of 50 short and easy-to-understand summaries of specific prophetic events arranged in what I believe to be a logical and coherent chronology of the end times. That may sound like a lot, but don't be alarmed. All the points are arranged under topical headings, and they flow together quite nicely. Don't assume you need to memorize all this. For now, these summaries are designed to give you a feel for the big picture before you learn more about the specific details. This should help make the entire book smooth sailing for you!

Here's a tidbit of advice to keep mind: If you ever feel the need to, you can always revisit chapter 1 and skim this big-picture survey. The fact that it appears in the first chapter of this book makes this a convenient spot for you to return to.

Let's begin!

Prior to the Tribulation Period

1—God Has a Divine Purpose for the Current Age. Jesus gave us insights on the course of the present age in some of His prophetic parables. For example, in the parable of the great feast, Jesus taught that God offered the kingdom to Israel, but the Jews were indifferent to the offer. God's message of the kingdom is now for all people, including the Gentiles. In the parable of the wheat and weeds, Jesus taught that true and false believers will coexist together until a future time of judgment when they will be separated. In the parable of the mustard seed, Jesus taught that the kingdom started small and will grow immeasurably large.

2—Israel Has Been Reborn as a Nation. Israel's rebirth as a nation in 1948 was a direct fulfillment of biblical prophecies (Ezekiel 36:10,24; 37). Since then, just as prophesied, the Jews have been streaming back to the Holy Land from virtually every nation in the world. God has future plans for Israel! We recall that while Jerusalem is the most oft-mentioned city in the book of Revelation, Babylon is the second-most-mentioned city. Moreover, while Jerusalem is portrayed as God's city (Revelation 21:2-3), Babylon is portrayed as a demonic city (18:2).

3—Apostasy Will Increase as We Near the End Times. First Timothy 4:1 states, "The Holy Spirit tells us clearly that in the last times some will turn away from the true faith; they will follow deceptive spirits and teachings that come from demons" (see also 2 Timothy

3:1-8; 4:3). Apostasy will rise to a fever pitch during the tribulation period (Matthew 24:9-12). This will serve to set the stage for the rise of religious New Babylon during the first half of the tribulation (Revelation 17).

4—*Apparently the United States Will Weaken as We Near the End Times.* The United States of Europe—the revived Roman Empire that will be headed by the antichrist—will initially be the political and economic superpower during the tribulation (see Daniel 2; 7). The antichrist will later shift his headquarters to Jerusalem, and then to commercial New Babylon, which will serve as the economic powerhouse of the end times. It seems logical to infer that for all this to happen, the United States must progressively weaken and may even become an ally of the antichrist's global empire (Daniel 2; 7).

The Rapture and the Resulting Events that Follow

5—*The Church Will Be Raptured Prior to the Tribulation Period.* The rapture is that glorious event in which the dead in Christ will be resurrected, living Christians will be instantly translated into their glorified bodies, and both groups will be caught up to meet Christ in the air and taken to heaven (John 14:1-3; 1 Corinthians 15:51-54; 1 Thessalonians 4:13-17). The rapture apparently occurs prior to the tribulation period. I say this because (1) no New Testament or Old Testament passage on the tribulation period mentions the church; (2) Jesus promised to keep the church from the "hour of trial" coming upon the whole world (Revelation 3:10); (3) Jesus promised to deliver believers from the wrath to come (1 Thessalonians 1:9); (4) the church is not appointed to wrath (Romans 5:9; 1 Thessalonians 5:9); and (5) God typically delivers His people before His judgment falls (see 2 Peter 2:5-9). With no Christians left on earth, it will be all the easier for the false religious system associated with New Babylon to globally rise to power.

6—As a Result of the Rapture, the Divine Restrainer Will Be Removed. Second Thessalonians 2:6 tells us that the antichrist is presently being restrained, and only when the restrainer is removed will the antichrist be revealed. Only one person—the omnipotent God—is powerful enough to restrain Satan, who energizes the antichrist (2 Thessalonians 2:9; 1 John 4:4). We can logically infer that the restrainer is the Holy Spirit, who indwells every believer in the church. When the church is raptured from earth prior to the tribulation, the restrainer (the Holy Spirit) will also be removed from the earth. The antichrist will then manifest himself soon after (see 2 Thessalonians 2:6-7), and religious New Babylon will arise (Revelation 17).

7—As a Result of the Rapture, Christians Are Glorified in Heaven. First Thessalonians 4:13-17 affirms that when the rapture occurs, the dead in Christ will be resurrected and living Christians will be transformed into their glorified bodies. All this will happen instantly. First Corinthians 15:42-43 tells us that the bodies of both groups of believers will be imperishable, glorious, and powerful. Whereas our present bodies are like tents that can be easily knocked down, our glorified bodies will be like sturdy buildings (2 Corinthians 5:1-4). Christians in heaven will be completely unaffected by New Babylon. We will, however, cheer in heaven when New Babylon is finally destroyed at the end of the tribulation (Revelation 18:20).

The Church with Christ in Heaven

8—Sometime Following the Rapture, Christians Will Face Their Lord at the Judgment Seat of Christ in Heaven. All believers will one day stand before the judgment seat of Christ (Greek, the *bema*) (Romans 14:8-10; 1 Corinthians 3:11-15; 9:24-27). At that time, each believer's life will be examined with regard to deeds done while on Earth. Personal motives and intents of the heart will also be weighed.

Note that this judgment has nothing to do with whether Christians will remain saved. Those who have placed faith in Christ are forever saved, and nothing threatens that (John 10:28-30; Romans 8:29-39; Ephesians 1:13; 4:30; Hebrews 7:25). This judgment rather has to do with the reception or loss of rewards for how one has lived on Earth since becoming a Christian (1 Corinthians 3:12-15). Some years after Christians are judged in heaven, New Babylon will face catastrophic judgment on Earth at the end of the tribulation.

9—*The Marriage Between the Church and the Lamb Takes Place in Heaven.* Jesus Christ, the Lamb, frequently referred to Himself as a bridegroom (Matthew 9:15; 22:2-14; 25:1-13; Mark 2:19-20; Luke 5:34-35; 14:15-24; John 3:29). The church is regarded as a virgin bride awaiting the coming of her heavenly bridegroom (2 Corinthians 11:2). Sometime after the rapture, the marriage of the Lamb (bridegroom) and the church (bride) will take place. Unlike the pure bride of Christ (Revelation 19:7), religious New Babylon is described as a great prostitute (17:1,3).

The Invasion of Israel

10—*Meanwhile on the Earth, Israel Will Live at Peace in Her Own Land.* Scripture reveals that in the end times, an all-out invasion of Israel by a massive northern assault force composed of Russia, Iran, Turkey, Sudan, Libya, and other Muslim nations will take place. A precondition for this invasion to occur is that Israel must be living in security and at rest in her homeland (Ezekiel 38:11). Some prophecy scholars believe that Israel is presently living in relative security and rest because of her powerful military, which is able to repel any attack from surrounding enemies. If this view is correct, then the Ezekiel invasion could occur in the not-too-distant future.

11—*Israel Will Be Invaded by a Northern Military Coalition.* The nations that make up this military coalition include Rosh (modern

Russia), Magog (the former southern Soviet republics of Kazakh-stan, Kyrgyzstan, Uzbekistan, Turkmenistan, Tajikistan), Meshech and Tubal (modern Turkey), Persia (the Islamic Republic of Iran), Ethiopia (modern-day Sudan), Put (modern-day Libya), Gomer (another reference to modern-day Turkey), and Beth-togarmah (yet another reference to Turkey) (Ezekiel 38:1-6 NASB). There is good reason to believe that this invasion could take place prior to the trib-ulation period. Apparently New Babylon will not be a part of this invading force. Scripture reveals that God will utterly annihilate these invaders (Ezekiel 38:19-22). Because commercial New Baby-lon will not be destroyed until *the very end* of the tribulation period, we can conclude it is not a part of the invasion (Revelation 18).

The Beginning of the Tribulation

12—The Antichrist Will Sign a Covenant with Israel, and This Will Mark the Beginning of the Tribulation Period. Daniel 9:27 tells us, "The ruler will make a treaty with the people for a period of one set of seven, but after half this time, he will put an end to the sacri-fices and offerings." The antichrist will agree to a seven-year cove-nant with Israel (the entire tribulation period), but he will break the agreement after three-and-one-half years, putting an end to sacri-fices and offerings in the rebuilt Jewish temple. Once the tribulation period begins with the signing of the covenant, people can watch for the rise of religious New Babylon during the first half of the tribu-lation and the rise of commercial New Babylon during the second half. (To clarify, there is one New Babylon that will be a literal city along the Euphrates River, but during the first half of the tribula-tion the religious aspect of New Babylon will be predominant, and the commercial aspect will grow into prominence during the second half. I'll address this in more detail later in the book.)

13—The Antichrist Will Rapidly Rise on the World Scene. He will be a genius in intellect (Daniel 8:23), commerce (Daniel 11:43; Revelation 13:16-17), war (Revelation 6:2; 13:2), speech (Daniel 11:36), and politics (Revelation 17:11-12). This Satan-inspired individual (2 Thessalonians 2:9) will rise to prominence and make a peace treaty with Israel (Daniel 9:27). In his desire to dominate the world, he will double-cross and then seek to destroy the Jews, persecute believers, and set up his own global kingdom (Revelation 13). Initially religious New Babylon will hold sway over the antichrist and his forces (Revelation 17:3), but at the midpoint of the tribulation, the antichrist and his forces will destroy the false religion (verse 16), and he will set himself up as god (2 Thessalonians 2:4). He will then move his headquarters to New Babylon, and instead of promoting false religion, he will focus on developing a global commercial center. (More on all this shortly.)

14—Early in the Tribulation, the Jewish Temple Will Be Rebuilt. We know that the temple must be rebuilt at least by the midpoint of the seven-year tribulation period because Jesus, in His Olivet Discourse, warned that the antichrist will desecrate the temple at that time, setting up an image of himself within the structure (Matthew 24:15-16; see also Daniel 9:27; 12:11). Even today we hear reports that various Jewish individuals and groups have been working behind the scenes to prepare various materials for the future temple, including priestly robes, temple tapestries, and worship utensils. The rebuilding of the temple seems to be on the horizon.

15—The Signs of the Times Will Affirm that the End Times Have Arrived. A "sign of the times" is an event of prophetic significance that points to the end times. We are specifically instructed by Jesus that certain signs will take place as the tribulation period unfolds (Matthew 24). These signs include a great increase in earthquakes, famine, pestilence, signs in the heavens, people who love themselves (humanism), money (materialism), and pleasure (hedonism). There will also be an escalation in false Christs, false prophets and teachers, false apostles, and greatly increased apostasy. These and other such signs will testify that the end times have indeed arrived (see Matthew 24). The increase in false Christs, false prophets, false apostles, and apostasy will smooth the path for the rapid rise of the false religion associated with New Babylon early in the tribulation period.

The First Half of the Tribulation

16—During the First Half of the Tribulation, the Lamb Will Receive the Seven-Sealed Scroll. Christ alone in heaven is found worthy to take this scroll (Revelation 5). This wondrous scene in heaven sets the stage for all that follows—the actual opening of the seven seals. As each seal is opened one by one, we witness judgments falling on those on Earth at the hand of our sovereign and majestic God. Later during the tribulation, judgment will fall on commercial New Babylon (Revelation 18).

17—The 144,000 Jewish Evangelists Will Engage in Ministry. The 144,000 are Jewish men who come to faith in Jesus sometime after the rapture of the church (Revelation 7; 14). They fulfill the mandate originally given to the Jewish nation to share the good news of God with people (Gentiles) all around the world (see Isaiah 42:6; 43:10). These witnesses will be "sealed" (divinely protected) by God as they carry out their service for Him during the tribulation (Revelation 14:1-4; see also 2 Corinthians 1:22; Ephesians 1:13; 4:30). It appears they will begin their work very early in the tribulation period—a work that will be a direct challenge to the false religion associated with New Babylon.

18—God's Two Prophetic Witnesses Will Engage in Ministry. Early during the tribulation, God will raise up two mighty prophets—witnesses who will testify to the one true God with astounding power. The power of these witnesses brings Elijah (1 Kings 17;

Malachi 4:5) and Moses (Exodus 7–11) to mind—the two greatest personalities of the Old Testament. In the Old Testament era, two witnesses were required to confirm a testimony (see Deuteronomy 17:6; 19:15; Matthew 18:16; John 8:17; Hebrews 10:28). Apparently these witnesses will engage in their ministry during the first half of the tribulation, during which time they will directly challenge the false religion connected with New Babylon.

19—The Seven Seal Judgments Will Be Unleashed. Human suffering will steadily escalate during the tribulation period. The first set of judgments to be unleashed on Earth are the seal judgments. These include the rise of the antichrist, the outbreak of war, widespread famine, massive casualties, God's people being killed, a devastating earthquake, and even worse judgments (Revelation 6). Things will go from bad to worse. Many people will seek comfort from the religious system associated with New Babylon. Others will turn to the true God as a result of the 144,000 Jewish evangelists and two prophetic witnesses.

20—Martyrdom Will Increase. While all Christians on Earth will be raptured prior to the tribulation (1 Thessalonians 1:10; 4:13-17; 5:9; Revelation 3:10), large numbers of people will become believers during this seven-year period (Matthew 25:31-46; Revelation 7:9-10), and many of these individuals will be martyred (Revelation 6:9-11). Christ urges His people to stand strong and not fear martyrdom (Revelation 2:10). It is noteworthy that many of these believers will be executed by officials affiliated with New Babylon's false religious system, which is said to be "drunk with the blood of God's holy people who were witnesses for Jesus" (Revelation 17:6).

21—The Trumpet Judgments Will Be Unleashed. Things will continue to go from bad to worse during the tribulation period. The trumpet judgments include hail and fire falling on the earth, a fiery mountain plummeting into the sea, a star (asteroid) falling from heaven and making a deep impact on the earth, various cosmic disturbances, hideous demons torturing humans, fallen angels killing a third of humankind, and even worse judgments. Again, many people will seek comfort from New Babylon's religion. Others will become Christians in response to the ministry of the 144,000 Jewish evangelists and the two prophetic witnesses.

22—Religious Babylon Will Dominate the World. The false religion associated with New Babylon will exercise global influence (Revelation 17:15). It will be utterly unfaithful to the truth and therefore be a spiritual "harlot" (verses 1,5,15-16). It will also exercise powerful political clout among the nations of the world (verses 12-13). It will seem outwardly glorious while being inwardly corrupt (implied in verse 4) and will persecute believers during the tribulation period (verse 6). This false religious system will emerge during the first half of the tribulation and will spew out great deception and apostasy.

The Midpoint of the Tribulation

23—The Little Scroll Will Be Opened. In Revelation 10, we read of an angel with a mysterious little scroll. John obeyed the angel's instruction to eat the scroll, and though it was sweet (like honey) in his mouth, it quickly soured in his stomach. The scroll seems to represent Scripture. God's Word was sweet to John. However, it was also bitter because it included stern warnings of woe and judgment for unbelievers. The book of Revelation records much of this woe and judgment—including that which will eventually fall upon New Babylon (Revelation 18).

24—The Antichrist Will Be Wounded and Will Be Seemingly Resurrected (Revelation 13:1-3). Some Bible expositors believe the antichrist will suffer a mortal head wound, die, and then be literally resurrected. Others believe he will be wounded, though not mortally, and will feign a resurrection from the dead. Either way, the world will believe he has literally resurrected from the dead and therefore will worship him. At this point, one can almost see the writing on the wall that the days of religious New Babylon are numbered, for the antichrist will become the sole object of worship during the second half of the tribulation.

25—Satan Will Be Cast Out of Heaven. In Revelation 12:12-13 we find a sobering description of Satan's ousting from heaven, after which he will indwell—or, at the very least, fully energize—the antichrist (2 Thessalonians 2:9). Satan will be filled with fury because he knows his time is short—a mere 1,260 days, or the last three-and-a-half years of the tribulation. Satan's fury will be expressed through the person of the antichrist, and things will go from bad to *much* worse on the earth.

26—The False Religion Associated with New Babylon Will Be Destroyed. At the midpoint of the tribulation, the antichrist, along with the ten kings who are under his authority, will destroy the false religious system associated with New Babylon. The antichrist will then come into global dominion both *politically* and *religiously*, demanding to be worshipped as God (Daniel 11:36-38; 2 Thessalonians 2:4; Revelation 13:8,15). The final world religion will involve worship of the antichrist alone. No competing religious systems will be allowed—including the one associated with New Babylon.

27—God's Two Prophetic Witnesses Will Be Executed and Then Will Be Resurrected. The miracles performed by God's two prophetic witnesses are reminiscent of Elijah (1 Kings 17; Malachi 4:5) and Moses (Exodus 7–11). They will minister during the first half of the tribulation, and, once their ministry is complete, they will be martyred by the antichrist. All the unbelievers on Earth will celebrate their deaths. Three-and-a-half days later, however, the two witnesses will resurrect from the dead, and the people's celebration will turn to dread (Revelation 11:7-12).

28—The Antichrist Will Break His Covenant with Israel. In Daniel 9:27 we read, "The ruler [the antichrist] will make a treaty [covenant] with the people [the Jews] for a period of one set of seven [seven years], but after half this time [after three-and-a-half years], he will put an end to the [Jewish] sacrifices and offerings" (inserts added for clarification). Notice that the covenant was designed to remain in effect for seven years. But at the three-and-a-half-year mark, the antichrist will renege on the covenant and shut down Israel's temple sacrifices. From that point onward, the antichrist will insist that he alone be worshipped.

29—The Abomination of Desolation Will Occur. At the midpoint of the tribulation, the antichrist will desecrate the Jewish temple by putting an image of himself within it. This is the "abomination of desolation" Jesus spoke of in Matthew 24:15 (NASB). The antichrist will start out as Israel's *protector* (with a signed covenant) but will end up becoming Israel's *persecutor.* He will turn from being Israel's *defender* to being its *defiler.*

30—The False Prophet Will Carry Out His Diabolical Ministry. Satan will empower the false prophet to engage in what we might call Grade-B miracles—lesser than God's miracles, but still impressive (see Exodus 7:11; 2 Timothy 3:8). The false prophet will do these miracles to induce people to worship Satan's substitute for Christ—the antichrist (see Daniel 9:27; 11:31; 12:11; Matthew 24:15). The false religion connected with New Babylon will then be rendered obsolete as worship of the antichrist becomes the sole acceptable religion.

31—The Antichrist Will Blaspheme God. At the midpoint of the tribulation, the antichrist will engage in self-exaltation and self-deification. Second Thessalonians 2:4 says he will "exalt himself and defy everything that people call god and every object of worship. He will even sit in the temple of God, claiming that he himself is God."

There is no greater blasphemy than this. The antichrist truly is *anti-Christ*, putting himself in Christ's place. As Revelation 13:5-6 puts it, "The beast [will] speak great blasphemies against God...terrible words of blasphemy against God, slandering his name and his dwelling—that is, those who dwell in heaven."

32—The Jewish Remnant Will Flee from Israel. Jesus warns the Jews in Jerusalem that when these horrific circumstances unfold, they should forget about gathering their personal belongings and get out of town immediately. They are to literally run for their lives. Time spent gathering things might mean the difference between life and death. Jesus indicates that distress will escalate dramatically and rapidly for the Jews (Matthew 24:16-22; see also Revelation 12:5-6). Jeremiah 30:7 describes this period as "a time of trouble for my people Israel."

33—The Antichrist Will Make War on the Saints. Scripture reveals that the antichrist will engage in great persecution against not only the Jews but also the saints of God: "The beast was allowed to wage war against God's holy people and to conquer them. And he was given authority to rule over every tribe and people and language and nation" (Revelation 13:7-8). A parallel passage is Daniel 7:21, which, speaking of the antichrist, tells us that he was "waging war against God's holy people and was defeating them." Notice that while religious New Babylon persecuted and martyred God's people during the first half of the tribulation (Revelation 17:6), the antichrist will persecute and martyr them during the second half. God's people will have a tough time during the entire tribulation!

34—Midtribulational Announcements Will Be Uttered from Heaven. We can view Revelation 14 as a connecting link between the events that take place midway through the tribulation period (Revelation 10–13) and those that transpire during the second half (15–16). These divine announcements include details about the impending bowl judgments (the worse judgments of all) as well as words of assurance, encouragement, and comfort for God's people in the midst of the tribulation.

The Second Half of the Tribulation

35—The Great Tribulation Begins. The second half of the tribulation period—that is, the last three-and-a-half years—is called the "great tribulation" (Matthew 24:15-21; see also Daniel 9:27). It is during this time that the antichrist will act as "god on Earth," enforcing both political and religious supremacy and setting up his headquarters in commercial New Babylon. This will be the worst time in all human history.

36—The Good News Is that the Great Tribulation Will Be Limited to Three-and-a-Half Years. Revelation 13:5 tell us that the antichrist will make claims to deity, blaspheme the one true God, and demand to be worshipped, and these activities will continue for precisely 42 months—which is three-and-a-half years. Daniel 7:25 also reveals that the antichrist will oppress God's people "for a time, times, and half a time." A "time" is one year, "times" is two years, and "half a time" is half a year. This comes to a total of three-and-a-half years.

37—The Mark of the Beast Will Be Enforced. Revelation 13 reveals that the antichrist and the false prophet will subjugate the entire world so that no one who fails to receive the mark of the beast can buy or sell. This mark will literally be a passport to commerce. There will be the "haves" and the "have nots." This means that those who refuse the mark of the beast will find it very hard to acquire food. Because commercial New Babylon will be the commerce center of the world during the second half of the tribulation, it is logical to infer that a key component to the success of New Babylon is the antichrist's mark of the beast. The only people who will be allowed to sell their products to super-rich New Babylon will be those who have received the mark (Revelation 18:11-15).

38—Deception Will Continue to Escalate. Jesus warns that during the tribulation period there will be many false prophets who lead people astray (Matthew 24:11). The apostle Paul speaks of end-times "evil deception" rooted in "lies" (2 Thessalonians 2:9-11). Revelation 12:9 tells us that Satan—"the one deceiving the whole world"—will be very active during this period. The antichrist's first lieutenant, the false prophet, will deceive "all the people who belong to this world" (Revelation 13:14). Certainly deception will play a significant role in the success of commercial New Babylon, for when God indicts this place in judgment, He will affirm, "Your merchants were the greatest in the world, and you deceived the nations with your sorceries" (Revelation 18:23).

39—The Bowl Judgments Will Be Unleashed. By this time, the seal judgments and trumpet judgments will have already been inflicted upon the earth. Next the bowl judgments will be unleashed (Revelation 16:1-21). People will be inflicted with harmful and painful sores, the sea will become like blood, the rivers and springs of water will also become like blood, the sun will scorch people with fire, the world will be plunged into utter darkness, the Euphrates River will dry up (preparing the way for the outbreak of Armageddon), and more. Woe to those who are upon the earth at this time!

40—The Gospel of the Kingdom Will Be Proclaimed. In Matthew 24:14, Jesus prophesies that "the Good News about the Kingdom will be preached throughout the whole world, so that all nations will hear it; and then the end will come." Contrary to the deceptions associated with commercial New Babylon (Revelation 18:23), the truth will also be proclaimed. God's light will continue to shine in the darkness.

The End of the Tribulation

41—The Campaign of Armageddon Will Begin. Armageddon— a catastrophic war campaign—will take place at the end of the tribulation (Revelation 16:14-16; see also Daniel 11:40-45; Joel 3:9-17; Zechariah 14:1-3). Millions of people will perish in the worst escalation of conflict ever to hit planet Earth. There are eight key stages that unfold during this ongoing campaign:

42—Stage One of Armageddon: The Antichrist's Allies Will Assemble for War. These allies will gather for one purpose—the final destruction of the Jews (Revelation 16:12-16). This attack will be demonically inspired.

43—Stage Two of Armageddon: Commercial Babylon Will Be Destroyed. During the second half of the tribulation period the antichrist will set up his headquarters in New Babylon, and it will become a global commercial center. It is this center that will be annihilated during stage two of Armageddon. This destruction will be an expression of God's mighty wrath (Jeremiah 50:13-14). Babylon will become a desert wasteland. It will be "devastated like Sodom and Gomorrah" (Isaiah 13:19; Jeremiah 50:40)—the destruction will be all-encompassing and permanent.

44—Stage Three of Armageddon: Jerusalem Will Fall and Be Ravaged. The destruction of the antichrist's headquarters in New Babylon will not lessen his resolve to destroy the Jewish people. He will then instruct his military forces to attack Jerusalem. Zechariah 14:1-2 reveals that "all the nations" will be gathered to "fight against Jerusalem." I hate to say it, but this must mean that the United States will be a part of the invading force. Jerusalem will fall and be ravaged in the face of this overwhelming attack.

45—Stage Four of Armageddon: The Antichrist Will Move South Against the Jewish Remnant. Following the destruction of Jerusalem, the antichrist will then move south against the Jewish remnant that escaped from Jerusalem at the midpoint of the tribulation when the antichrist put an image of himself in the Jewish temple. These Jews will be hiding in the deserts and mountains (see Matthew

24:16)—perhaps in the area of Bozrah/Petra, about 80 miles south of Jerusalem. From an earthly perspective, this remnant of Jews will be helpless—they will be utterly defenseless against the overwhelming forces of the antichrist.

46—Stage Five of Armageddon: Israel Will Be Endangered and Will Experience National Regeneration. Endangered by the overwhelming forces of the antichrist, the Jewish remnant will supernaturally experience national regeneration by turning to their Messiah, Jesus Christ (Hosea 6:1-3; see also Joel 2:28-29; Zechariah 12:2–13:1). They will finally recognize their former blindness; their spiritual eyes will be opened and they will see the truth. They will see Jesus for who He truly is and cry out to Messiah Jesus for deliverance.

47—Stage Six of Armageddon: Jesus Christ Will Return in Glory. Jesus will promptly answer the prayers of the Jewish remnant. The divine Messiah will return personally to rescue His people from danger. Every eye will see Him (Revelation 1:7; see also Matthew 24:30). Christ will come as the King of kings and Lord of lords, and none will be able to withstand Him (Revelation 19:11-16).

48—Stage Seven of Armageddon: The Final Battle Will Erupt. Jesus will confront the antichrist and his military forces and will slay them with the "breath" of His mouth: "The Lord Jesus will slay him with the breath of his mouth and destroy him by the splendor of his coming" (2 Thessalonians 2:8). What this means, in popular vernacular, is that Jesus will essentially say "drop dead," and the forces of the antichrist will experience instant death. They will be no match for the King of kings and Lord of lords (Revelation 19:16). The Jewish Messiah will obliterate all who oppose Him.

49—Stage Eight of Armageddon: Christ Will Victoriously Ascend to the Mount of Olives. "On that day his feet will stand on the Mount of Olives, east of Jerusalem. And the Mount of Olives will split apart, making a wide valley running from east to west. Half the mountain will move toward the north and half toward the south" (Zechariah 14:4). We can observe in Scripture that topographical upheavals often accompany God's great acts of judgment (see Micah 1:2-4; Nahum 1:5; Revelation 16:18-21).

50—The Prophetic Saga Continues. Christ will establish His 1,000-year millennial kingdom on earth (Revelation 20:2-7; see also Isaiah 65:18-23; Jeremiah 31:12-14,31-37). This will be followed by the eternal state, in which God's people will dwell with Him face to face forever and ever and ever. Scripture reveals that believers will forever dwell in an eternal city called the New Jerusalem, which will rest upon a new earth (Revelation 21–22). How fitting that while New Babylon is described as a great prostitute (Revelation 17:1,3), the New Jerusalem is likened to a chaste bride (Revelation 21:9-10). Moreover, while New Babylon is portrayed as a temporal city that will be destroyed by God Himself toward the end of the tribulation (Revelation 18:8), the New Jerusalem is portrayed as an eternal city (Revelation 21:1-4).

My friend, it will be glorious!

2

A Sampling of Interpretations

A question some Christians love to debate relates to the word "mystery" as used in connection with the false religious system rooted in New Babylon. The primary verse in this discussion is Revelation 17:5, which, in the King James Version, reads, "Upon her forehead was a name written, Mystery, Babylon the Great, the Mother of harlots and abominations of the earth." In this translation, the word "mystery" is part of the title given to the "woman." As a result, many people wonder what might be meant by the term *mystery Babylon*. It is typically assumed that the word "mystery" as used in Revelation 17:5 means mystical, or symbolical, or allegorical.[1] This has resulted in a variety of interesting theories about the identity of Babylon in Revelation 17.

What Is Mystery Babylon?

In the next chapter I'll address why this understanding of "mystery" is incorrect. For now, I want to zero in on some of the interesting theories about New Babylon that people have come up with—all of them mystical, symbolical, or allegorical. In the process,

I'll point to why these theories fall short of what Revelation 17–18 is really communicating. We'll begin with one of the most popular theories—mystery Babylon is Rome.

Rome

A popular view is that Babylon, in Revelation 17–18, is first-century Rome. This interpretive view is essentially a historicist approach, arguing that the prophecies about Babylon, as stated in Revelation, point to the city of Rome until its historical destruction about AD 476.

Advocates of this view note that long after Revelation was written, Lactantius, Tertullian, Irenaeus, and Jerome all held that Rome was the Babylon of chapters 17 and 18. This view is also held by many modern Bible commentators.

Some proponents of this position suggest that when John wrote Revelation, he was a Roman prisoner. As such, he could not make disparaging references to Rome in his writings. He therefore used the nickname "Babylon" in place of Rome when writing Revelation. He also used the term "prostitute" when speaking of Babylon.

Arguments typically offered in favor of this position include the facts that Rome—like the "Babylon" or "prostitute" in Revelation—was engulfed in paganism, was full of rampant idolatry, relentlessly persecuted the early believers, and was certainly a "great city" inasmuch as it ruled over multiple geographical territories. It is also suggested that mention of the seven mountains or seven hills clearly points to Rome (Revelation 17:9).

This view, however, is not without problems, the most significant being the relationship between the "prostitute" of Revelation 17 and the "beast." More specifically, many who believe that the prostitute (or Babylon) is Rome also believe that the beast is Rome. How can the prostitute be Rome if the beast is also Rome? The book of

Revelation distinguishes between these two. The prostitute is said to "ride" the beast, thus controlling the beast, thereby proving that they are distinct from each other (Revelation 17:3). How can Rome ride upon Rome? Also, in Revelation 17:16, the beast destroys the prostitute. How can Rome destroy Rome? For these reasons the prostitute and the beast must be viewed as distinct. Both cannot refer to Rome at the same time.

Beyond this, ancient Rome did not fall suddenly, dramatically, completely, or permanently, as is true of Babylon in Revelation 18. Rome's decline was a very slow process. Moreover, Rome is not located in a desert or a wilderness, nor is it a seaport city, as is true of the Babylon described in Revelation 17–18.

Initially, the seven-hills argument might sound convincing. However, Bible scholar Andy Woods points us to some significant problems with this idea:

> It seems odd that the seven hills should be equated with the well-known topography of Rome because 17:9 indicates that the identification of the hills calls for *special wisdom*. Why should such a well-known geographical locale to John's first century audience require special theological and symbolic insight for proper identification?
>
> It is unclear that John's audience would have automatically understood the reference in 17:9 to the seven hills of Rome. Although Rome was known as the city on the seven hills, it is interesting to note that eight and possibly nine hills could be counted for Rome.
>
> If the reference to the city on the seven hills was universally well-known in John's day as a reference to Rome, how would the use of this reference insulate John or his readers from Roman persecution? Those found with a copy of the document within their possession would be immediately

suspected of advocating the overthrow of the capital of the Roman Empire.

The reference to the seven mountains (17:9) which are seven heads (17:8) actually belong to the beast (17:3, 7; 13:1) and not the woman named Babylon. Thus, these seven heads or mountains really have nothing to do with the entity Babylon at all. The reference to the seven hills is better understood as referring to seven kingdoms.[2]

All things considered, the Rome view—quite obviously an allegorical view—has too many problems to do justice to Revelation 17–18.

The Roman Catholic Church

Another view that has been quite popular is that references to Babylon in Revelation refer to the Roman Catholic Church. This view first surfaced during and following the days of the Reformation period and continues to be held today. Proponents included such notables as Jonathan Edwards, Adam Clarke, and E.B. Elliott.[3]

Three of the more controversial promoters of this viewpoint in church history are

- Alexander Hislop, author of the highly provocative book *The Two Babylons: The Papal Worship Proved to Be the Worship of Nimrod and His Wife*.
- William Tyndale, who referred to "that great idol, the Whore of Babylon, antichrist of Rome, whom they call the pope."
- Ellen G. White, the founder and prophet of the Seventh-Day Adventist Church, a group considered by many to be a cult.

My old friend Dave Hunt—now with the Lord in heaven—held

this view. He wrote a book titled *A Woman Rides the Beast: The Roman Catholic Church and the Last Days.* While I strongly disagree with his position, I must admit that there are many who continue to agree with his view today.

This theory is typically built on the prostitute motif (Revelation 17:1). Just as a prostitute is sexually unfaithful, so, it is alleged, the Roman Catholic Church is unfaithful and has fallen away from the truth of Christianity. Roman Catholicism is viewed as a corruption of Christianity, and thus the term "Babylon" is fitting.

Some also believe the adornment of the adulterous woman (prostitute) supports this viewpoint: "The woman wore purple and scarlet clothing and beautiful jewelry made of gold and precious gems and pearls" (verse 4). Some suggest this fits the colors of the robes of both popes and cardinals. As well, the affirmation that the "woman" was drunk from the blood of the saints is said to point to Roman Catholicism's persecution and even martyrdom of countless Protestant Christians throughout church history.

As convincing as all this may sound, critics note there are significant problems with this view. First, many who hold that the prostitute is Roman Catholicism also say that the beast of Revelation is Roman Catholicism. This is problematic, for the prostitute and the beast are portrayed in Revelation as distinct from each other. Early in Revelation 17 we read that the woman controls the beast. How can Roman Catholicism control Roman Catholicism? By the end of Revelation 17, we find that the beast destroys the prostitute. How can Roman Catholicism destroy Roman Catholicism? Clearly, the prostitute and the beast must be viewed as distinct from each other.

Beyond this, the Roman Catholic interpretation requires that Bible commentators read their own current historical experiences into the text of Scripture. This view emerged and became prominent during Reformation times, when men like John Calvin and Martin Luther were taking a stand against Roman Catholicism. It is easy to see how, in such a context, Roman Catholicism could be "read into" the prostitute and/or beast of Revelation.

Another problem with this view is the fact that the Roman Catholic Church—though a wealthy church—is certainly not the global economic and commercial powerhouse described in Revelation 18. Further, Roman Catholicism has never ruled over the political leaders and people of the nations of the earth. And should Roman Catholicism be destroyed, we would not expect merchants around the world to woefully lament that loss, as they do when New Babylon is destroyed. Nor does Roman Catholicism engage in the slave trade, as New Babylon will.

It is also worth noting that in recent years, officials of the Roman Catholic Church—the pope included—have issued statements of repentance over some of the church's past acts, including sexual abuse among priests. This hardly sounds like the New Babylon of Revelation 17–18.

There is yet another problem: One must wonder how a theory involving an ecclesiastical institution virtually centuries after the book of Revelation was written could have had any immediate relevance to the original readers of the book of Revelation. Would they have understood the text this way? Many expositors think not. Such a view would seemingly bring more comfort to sixteenth-century Protestants who were facing persecution than to first-century Christians who were being persecuted. (This criticism applies to a number of the other views as well.)

Having said all this, a number of prophecy students believe that while Roman Catholicism is not New Babylon, it is entirely possible that Roman Catholicism might be a part of the religious system rooted in New Babylon. *More on this later.*

Apostate Christianity

As was true with the Roman Catholic theory, the view that Babylon is apostate Christianity relies heavily on the prostitute motif (Revelation 17:1). As mentioned earlier, just as a prostitute is sexually unfaithful, apostate Christianity is unfaithful for having fallen away from the truth of Christianity.

Some describe apostate Christianity in terms of adultery. This implies that at one time there was faithfulness, but this has been replaced by infidelity. Apostate Christianity was once *not* apostate but has since *become* apostate. According to this theory, many of those left behind after the rapture will be a part of this apostate Christianity.

The major problem with this view is it doesn't fit the specific details of New Babylon as described in both Revelation 17 and 18. New Babylon is described as...

- an actual city,
- in the desert or wilderness,
- having a seaport,
- being involved in slave trade,
- ruling over the political leaders and people of the nations of the earth,
- and being a commercial powerhouse, which, when destroyed, causes the merchants of the world to lament.

Those are not characteristics of apostate Christianity. There is also the question of relevance for the original readers of the book of Revelation. Would they have understood the text this way? It's hard to imagine they would have.

As with Roman Catholicism, a number of prophecy students believe that while apostate Christianity is not New Babylon, it is entirely possible that apostate Christianity might be a part of the religious system rooted in New Babylon. *More on this a bit later.*

The Evil World System

Another view that has cropped up from time to time is that Babylon refers in a general way to the evil world system. Taken in this light, the text refers not to a specific period of time—such as the tribulation period—but could refer to any time in church history during which the evil world system stood strong against God. This view is common among those who hold to the idealist interpretation of the book of Revelation. This interpretive school views Revelation as a general description of the struggle between good and evil, between God and the devil, throughout history. In the end, God will defeat evil (Babylon).

Those who take a futurist approach to the book of Revelation see this viewpoint as deficient in multiple ways. Revelation 17–18 seems to describe something much more specific than a generalized evil world system. Too many details are provided in the biblical text. Futurists remind idealists that Babylon is said to be an actual city in the wilderness with a seaport (Revelation 17:18) that has global political power (17:15-18). This city is closely connected with the antichrist, a real person alive during the end times (17:3). The city of Babylon, along the Euphrates, is viewed as a bastion of global commerce (18:9-19). It is also involved in the persecution of end-time believers (17:6; 18:20,24). Such details go far beyond a general evil world system.

New York City

Some Bible interpreters claim there are significant parallels between Babylon the Great in the book of Revelation and New York City. Recent books that have argued for the New York position include *The Fall of America: Babylon the Great* and *The Judgment of Babylon: The Fall of America.* It is reasoned that both Babylon and New York City are excessively rich and dominant economic powers (Revelation 18:11-20), both are a source of global immorality (18:2-9), and both have sins "piled as high as heaven" (18:5). Moreover, New York is a "great city" as well as a port city.

This scenario is not given much credence among serious Bible interpreters. There are multiple doctrinal arguments one could raise against this view. For example, it can hardly be said of New York, as it can be said of New Babylon, that "in your streets flowed the blood of the prophets and of God's holy people and the blood of people slaughtered all over the world" (Revelation 18:24). Moreover, New York does not represent a global religion, nor is it in any way a religious system (17:1-6). It's also not located in a desert or wilderness (verse 3). One would have to ignore multiple details in Revelation 17 and 18 to hold to the New York City view.

Jerusalem

Preterists argue that Babylon the prostitute refers to the city of Jerusalem in the first century.[4] Because of Israel's covenant unfaithfulness, Israel was often described as a prostitute in Old Testament times (Isaiah 1:21; Jeremiah 2:20-24,30-33; 3:1-3,8; Ezekiel 16; 23; Hosea 9:1). Moreover, Jerusalem was responsible for killing Old Testament prophets as well as New Testament apostles and saints (Matthew 23:35; Luke 1:50-51; Acts 7:52).

It is said that Jerusalem ("Babylon") was destroyed by God using the whipping rod of the Roman Empire ("the beast") in the first century. This view is obviously popular among preterists who argue that most of the prophecies in the book of Revelation were fulfilled when Rome overran Jerusalem and the Jewish temple in AD 70.[5] Those who have held to this view include Kenneth Gentry, Hank

Hanegraaff, Philip Carrington, J.S. Russell, Milton Terry, David Chilton, Massyngberde Ford, and R.C. Sproul.

Proponents of this view observe that Revelation itself indicates that its prophecies are "near" (Revelation 1:3; 22:10). Hence, to them, a fulfillment in AD 70 makes good sense.

Furthermore, in Revelation 11:8 and 16:19, Jerusalem is called "the great city." They reason this must mean that Babylon—also called "the great city" in Revelation 17:18—must be Jerusalem.

At first glance some of the arguments for this position appear convincing. However, the careful interpreter uncovers numerous problems with it. Foundationally, there is a strong case that the book of Revelation was written in the 90s, far after Rome destroyed Jerusalem in AD 70. Irenaeus, in the second century, declared that Revelation had been written toward the end of the reign of Domitian (AD 81–96). Later writers, such as Clement of Alexandria, Origen, Victorinus, Eusebius, and Jerome affirmed the Domitian date. This being the case, the book of Revelation must refer to events that are yet future from the vantage point of AD 90.

Further, there are details about the prostitute (the false religion associated with New Babylon) that simply do not fit Jerusalem. For example, in Revelation 17:1, the great prostitute is said to "rule over many waters," meaning that it exercises control over many nations around the world. The idea that Jerusalem ever ruled over many nations is preposterous. (It is more accurate to say that during the extended "times of the Gentiles" [Luke 21:24], Gentile powers rule over Jerusalem, and will continue to do so until Christ comes again at the second coming.)

The prostitute is also said to influence not just world leaders, but the general population of the world (Revelation 17:15; see also 13:8,14). When has Jerusalem done this?

Revelation 17:3 tells us that the prostitute controlled the antichrist and his forces for a time. How could Jerusalem possibly control the antichrist and his military forces?

I could go on. But the point I want to make is that meek and humble Jerusalem cannot possibly be construed as doing any of these things, in ancient times or the end times. Preterists have to engage in a lot of interpretive gymnastics to arrive at this position. (See Appendix B: "Why a Literal Approach is Best.")

As for the idea that the events in the book of Revelation are "near," one must consider the context. Revelation is a book of prophecy (Revelation 1:3) and focuses on the future tribulation period (chapters 4–18), the second coming (19), the millennial kingdom (20), and the eternal state (21–22). The term "near" simply indicates that when the predicted events in Revelation first start to occur, all the events described in the book are "near" and will transpire quickly.

One of the biggest problems for the Babylon=Jerusalem view relates to Revelation 18:21-23. This passage tells us that New Babylon will be so utterly and completely destroyed that it will never rise again—just like Sodom and Gomorrah. If AD 70 represents the fulfillment of this passage, then Revelation 18:21-23 means that Jerusalem *can never be rebuilt again.* Therein lies the problem: *Jerusalem has already been rebuilt.* Not only that, Jerusalem will rise to great prominence during Christ's future millennial kingdom (see Isaiah 2:3; Zechariah 14:16; Revelation 20:9). Jeremiah 17:25 affirms, "There will always be a descendant of David sitting on the throne here in Jerusalem. Kings and their officials will always ride in and out among the people of Judah in chariots and on horses, and this city will remain forever."

It is also worth noting that there is no example in Jewish literature of the use of the term *Babylon* to mean Jerusalem. No church father taught this view. For nearly 2,000 years this view never breathed. It is a recent view.

What about the claim that Babylon "the great city" (Revelation 17:18) must be Jerusalem, because earlier mentions of the "great city" in Revelation refer to Jerusalem (Revelation 11:8; 16:19)? This is a classic example of what is called an "illegitimate totality transfer":

> The argument that "the great city" of Revelation 17–18 is identical to "the great city" of Jerusalem found earlier in Revelation 11:8 represents a hermeneutical error known as "illegitimate totality transfer." This error arises when the meaning of a word or phrase as derived from its use elsewhere is then automatically read into the same word or phrase in a foreign context. Jerusalem advocates commit such an error when they define "the great city" in Revelation 17–18 from how the same phrase is used in totally different contexts elsewhere in Revelation.[6]

There are yet more arguments against the Babylon=Jerusalem view. For example, Jerusalem is not a city of tremendous wealth, as is the New Babylon in Revelation 18. Certainly merchants around the world will not weep and wail should Jerusalem ever be destroyed. All things considered, there is very little to commend this view.

Mecca and Saudi Arabia (Islamic Kingdom)

A very recent view, championed by my friend Joel Richardson—author of *Mystery Babylon: Unlocking the Bible's Greatest Prophetic Mystery*—is that mystery Babylon is Mecca, the city that represents the heart and soul of Islam. Because of the relevance of this recent view, I will devote a bit more space in describing and critiquing it.

Richardson suggests that Mecca fulfills the biblical descriptions of Babylon in Revelation 17–18. To cite a few examples:

- Mecca is a real city (Revelation 17:18; 18:2).
- Mecca fits the requirement of being in a desert or wilderness terrain.

- While Mecca is not a seaport city, it is said to be within a reasonable/drivable distance of a seaport (within an hour).

- Because Mecca is the center of spiritual gravity for the Islamic world—more specifically, for 1.6 billion Muslims—it is a "great city" with far-reaching influence (Revelation 17:18; 18:2). Richardson reminds his readers that multitudes of Muslims pray in the direction of the great city of Mecca five times daily.

- The antichrist—whom Richardson believes will be a Muslim—will lead a Middle Eastern empire centered in Mecca.

- The city of Mecca should be seen as including and representing the much larger Saudi Arabia, much like Moscow represents Russia, and Washington, DC represents the United States.

- Saudi Arabia supports violent and extremist Islam. The enemies of Islam—including Jews and Christians—are "infidels" who are targeted for beheading. Islam will be the single force responsible for countless deaths of God's people in future years (Revelation 18:24). Mecca and Saudi Arabia will be "drunk on the blood of saints." Both the antichrist (13:7) and a revived Islamic Empire (17:6) will war with the saints.

- The kings of luxury mentioned in the Revelation account are a part of the Saudi family (Revelation 18:3,9).

- Saudi Arabia is a corrupter of kings in the sense that Saudi money buys influence—including among American presidents of the past (Revelation 18:3,9,10).

- Religious practices of Islam include those associated with the Kaaba, which is thoroughly pagan in nature and venerated by Muslims worldwide.

- Richardson believes that the Islamic antichrist will eventually turn on Mecca/Saudi Arabia because of corruption and friendliness shown toward the United States. This allegedly fulfills what Revelation says about the antichrist destroying religious Babylon at the midpoint of the tribulation.

While I personally do not agree with Joel Richardson's interpretation of Revelation 17–18, I do commend him for original thinking. He has constructed a new model for understanding this passage that is quite thought-provoking and is certainly more viable than some of the other positions that have surfaced through the ages.

Despite the arguments for this position—some of which are impressive—there are problems as well. Foundationally, I do not believe the Babylon=Mecca view sufficiently appreciates the Ezekiel invasion. Some 2,600 years ago, the ancient prophet Ezekiel prophesied that the Jews would be regathered from "many nations" to the land of Israel in the end times (Ezekiel 36–37). He then prophesied that, sometime later, there would be an all-out invasion into Israel by a massive northern assault force, with Russia heading up a coalition of Muslim nations, including modern Iran, Sudan, Turkey, Libya, and other Islamic nations (38–39). Their goal will be to utterly obliterate the Jews.

Why attack the Jews? Not only do Muslims hate the Jewish people because they believe the land of Israel belongs to them by divine right (Allah allegedly gave it them), they also want Israel's wealth (see Ezekiel 38:11-12). Ezekiel states that the invaders want Israel's "silver and gold," livestock, various goods, and plunder (verse 13).

This plunder might take a number of forms. There are certainly a lot of wealthy people who live in Israel—more than 6,600 millionaires with total assets exceeding $24 billion. Moreover, the mineral resources of the Dead Sea—including 45 billion tons of sodium, chlorine, sulfur, potassium, calcium, magnesium, and bromide—are worth virtually trillions of dollars. There is also the possibility that gas and oil discoveries in Israel will be part of the spoil. All in all, whoever controls the land of Israel can look forward to an incalculably large economic boost.

Scripture reveals that when Israel is attacked by this overwhelming Islamic force, not a single nation will come to her rescue. Israel will stand alone. We must not forget, however, the teaching of Psalm 121:4-5: "He who watches over Israel never slumbers or sleeps. The Lord himself watches over you! The Lord stands beside you as your protective shade." God also promised Israel, "No weapon turned against you will succeed" (Isaiah 54:17).

God will use four means to destroy—to utterly annihilate—the Muslim forces.

1. God will cause a catastrophic earthquake (Ezekiel 38:19-20). Aside from massive casualties, transportation will be disrupted, and apparently the surviving armies of the multinational forces will be thrown into utter chaos (verse 20).

2. Infighting will break out on a massive scale among the invading troops (Ezekiel 38:21). God will sovereignly induce the armies of the various nations in the invading force to turn against and kill each other. This may be at least partially due to the chaos that results following the massive earthquake. Fear and panic will sweep through the forces so each army will shoot indiscriminately at the others. Adding to the confusion is the fact that the armies of the various nations speak different languages—including Russian, Farsi, Arabic, and Turkic. This means communication will be difficult at best. It may also be that the Russians and Muslim nations turn on each other. Perhaps in the midst of the chaos, they will mutually suspect that the other is double-crossing them, and they will respond by opening fire on each other. In any event, there will be immeasurable casualties.

3. There will then be a massive outbreak of disease (Ezekiel 38:22a). Following the earthquake, and after the infighting between the invading troops, there will be countless dead bodies lying everywhere. Transportation will be disrupted to the point it will be difficult, if not impossible, to take the wounded to hospitals or bring in supplies like food and medicine. Meanwhile, myriad birds and other predatory animals will have a feast on this unburied flesh. All this will serve as a recipe for the outbreak of pandemic disease—disease which, according to Ezekiel, will take many more lives.

4. Finally, there will be torrential rain, hailstones, fire, and burning sulfur (Ezekiel 38:22b). It is possible that the powerful earthquake may set off volcanic deposits in the region, thrusting into the atmosphere a hail of molten rock and burning sulfur (volcanic ash) which then falls upon the enemy troops, utterly destroying them.

That won't be all. After God destroys the ground invaders, He says, "I will rain down fire on Magog and on all your allies who live safely on the coasts" (Ezekiel 39:6). The term "Magog" seems to refer to the geographical area in the southern part of the former Soviet Union—perhaps including the former southern Soviet republics of Kazakhstan, Kyrgyzstan, Uzbekistan, Turkmenistan, Tajikistan, and possibly even northern parts of modern Afghanistan. We are told in this prophetic verse that God will rain fire upon this area of the world, as well as Magog's "allies who live safely on the coasts." The destruction will likely include not only military targets like bases, missile silos, radar installations, and the like, but also religious centers, mosques, madrassas, Islamic schools and universities, and other facilities that preach hatred against the Jews. This may be a direct infliction of fire by God Himself, or God could cause this fire through Israel's (or some other nation's) nuclear weaponry. The blow to Islamic nations will be catastrophic.

As the Protector of Israel, God's primary purpose in destroying this massive military coalition will be to deliver Israel from harm. Ultimately, however, this is an outworking of the ancient covenant God made with His friend Abraham. In Genesis 12:3 (ESV) God promised Abraham, "I will bless those who bless you, and him who dishonors you I will curse." Surely the Muslims who comprise this vast Islamic invading force will dishonor Israel by seeking her destruction. In response, God's curse will fall upon the invaders in the form of an annihilating judgment. God is a promise-keeper.

When will this invasion take place? My belief is that it will likely happen prior to the tribulation period. I document this in my book *Northern Storm Rising* (Harvest House Publishers). There are five variables that are especially persuasive to me:

1. Following the rapture, the world will likely be in a state of chaos. Because the United States has such a large population of Christians, the rapture will have a devastating effect on the country. This being the case, Russia and her Muslim allies may well "seize the moment," considering this the ideal time to launch a massive attack against Israel, which, up until this time, had been protected by the United States.

2. Once God destroys Russia and the Muslim invaders prior to the tribulation period, this may open the door for an easier rise of the antichrist as the leader of a revived Roman Empire—a European super-state. (Muslim dreams of an Islamic global caliphate will be dissolved at God's judgment on the Muslim invaders.)

3. With the Muslim invaders having already been destroyed prior to the beginning of the tribulation, this might make it easier for the antichrist to sign a peace pact with Israel (Daniel 9:27), guaranteeing that Israel will be protected (especially from Muslim attacks).

4. This scenario may account for Israel's ability to construct the Jewish temple on the Temple Mount in Jerusalem in a very short

time. With Muslim forces decimated, Muslim resistance will be greatly minimized.

5. If the invasion takes place after the rapture, and the rapture takes place at least three-and-a-half years prior to the beginning of the tribulation period, then this scenario would allow for the weapons used in the invasion against Israel to be completely burned for seven years (Ezekiel 39:9-10) prior to the midpoint of the tribulation, when the people of Israel are forced to flee from Jerusalem (Matthew 24:15-21). It may well be, then, that there is a significant lapse of time between the rapture and the beginning of the tribulation.

Here is the point I am building up to: *How will it be possible for a Muslim antichrist and a Muslim Babylon (Mecca) to rise from the ashes in the aftermath of the Ezekiel invasion?* I don't think that will be possible.

Nor do I think it is reasonable to argue that the antichrist will be a Muslim. First, Daniel 9:26, addressing the 70 weeks of Daniel, reveals that the antichrist will be a Roman:

> After the sixty-two weeks, an anointed one shall be cut off
> and shall have nothing. And the people of the prince who
> is to come shall destroy the city and the sanctuary. Its end
> shall come with a flood, and to the end there shall be war.
> Desolations are decreed (esv).

This verse prophesies that "the city and the sanctuary" (Jerusalem and its temple) will be destroyed by the "people of the prince who is to come." Who destroyed Jerusalem and its temple in AD 70? Titus and his Roman army. The Roman people are the people of the coming prince, the antichrist. The antichrist will therefore be a Roman.

Further, we know that the tribulation period begins when the antichrist signs a covenant with Israel. It is absolutely inconceivable that Israel would actually trust its security and its future to a Muslim leader, given current Muslim sentiments against Israel. How could Israel possibly enjoy a sense of security under a covenant with a Muslim leader? Also, it seems implausible that the general Muslim population in various Muslim countries around the world would go along with joining into a covenant with Israel.

A major problem for the antichrist=Muslim view is the fact the antichrist will proclaim himself to be deity. "The king will do as he pleases, exalting himself and claiming to be greater than every god, even blaspheming the God of gods" (Daniel 11:36). "He will exalt himself and defy everything that people call god and every object of worship. He will even sit in the temple of God, claiming that he himself is God" (2 Thessalonians 2:4).

For a Muslim antichrist to claim he was God would require a thorough trashing of the Muslim creed, "There is no God but Allah, and Muhammad is his prophet." Any true Muslim who holds to that creed would never say he was God. Just as Muslims would never call Jesus God incarnate or the Son of God, so no Muslim would claim to be God. A Muslim antichrist proclaiming he is God would be an infidel and a candidate for beheading. No true Quran-believing Muslim would allow such an assertion to go unanswered.

Aside from the problems mentioned above, we must keep in mind that Revelation 17–18 specifically speaks of Babylon as a city. *A single city.* Not a city that represents a massive geographical territory such as Saudi Arabia:

- "This woman you saw in your vision represents *the great city* that rules over the kings of the world" (Revelation 17:18).
- "Babylon is fallen—*that great city* is fallen" (Revelation 18:2).

- "How terrible, how terrible for you, O Babylon, *you great city!*" (Revelation 18:10).
- "How terrible, how terrible for *that great city!*" (Revelation 18:16).
- "How terrible, how terrible for *that great city!*" (Revelation 18:19).
- "*The great city* Babylon will be thrown down with violence and will never be found again" (Revelation 18:21).

Let's not forget that all the other cities mentioned in the book of Revelation refer to single cities and do not represent larger geographical territories. This includes Ephesus (Revelation 2:1-7), Smyrna (2:8-11), Pergamum (2:12-17), Thyatira (2:18-29), Sardis (3:1-6), Philadelphia (3:7-13), and Laodicea (3:14-22). The larger territory for these cities is specifically identified, for all seven are said to be "in the province of Asia" (1:4). But the cities themselves do not in any way represent the larger territory. The very fact that "nations" are associated with the "city" of Babylon tells us that the biblical text itself distinguishes between cities and larger territories (18:2-3). Babylon—though very powerful—is just *a city!*

Moreover, this single city is portrayed as a seaport, and Mecca is not a seaport city. Revelation 18:17 mentions merchant ships with their captains and sailors and crews. Verse 19 speaks of "shipowners" who "became wealthy by transporting her great wealth on the seas." There is no clue in the text that one must first engage in a 50-mile ground transport from Mecca to the nearest seaport, as the Babylon=Mecca theory holds.

Perhaps the strongest evidence against the Babylon=Mecca theory is the positive evidence presented in the next chapter that, in the book of Revelation, the references made to Babylon all refer to a revived Babylon along the Euphrates River—*New Babylon*.

Babylon Always Refers to Babylon

Though symbolical and metaphorical theories about Babylon's identity are often interesting, my assessment—based on a straightforward reading of the Bible—is that the term should be interpreted in terms of a revived Babylon in Iraq along the Euphrates River. Both the immediate context of Revelation and the broader context of all of Scripture supports this view. I find myself in agreement with prophecy scholar Thomas Ice, who writes, "I believe that just like Israel always refers to Israel in the Bible, so also Babylon always refers to Babylon."[7] We will take a closer look at this in the next chapter.

3

New Babylon: A Literal City

As we noted in the previous chapter, there are a number of interesting allegorical interpretations regarding the identity of Babylon in Revelation 17–18. All of these are ultimately rooted in the idea that Revelation 17:5 (kjv) speaks of a "Mystery Babylon"—a term typically taken to mean "Mystical Babylon," or "Symbolical Babylon," or "Allegorical Babylon."

In this chapter we will discover why references to Babylon in the book of Revelation should be taken to mean a revived *literal city* of Babylon along the Euphrates River—what we might call New Babylon. Following this, we will see that while there are two different aspects of New Babylon—religious and commercial—there is just *one* New Babylon, not two, as some expositors claim.

Evidences for a Literal City

How do we know that all the appearances of the term "Babylon" in Revelation 17–18 refer to a literal city in Iraq along the Euphrates River during the end times? We find solid clues in the text of Scripture. Foundationally, all the other locations listed in the book of Revelation are *literal* locations. For example:

- Ephesus was a leading commercial and trade center of the ancient world. It was one of the more prominent cities in the province of Asia (Revelation 2:1-7).

- Smyrna was located about 35 miles north of Ephesus and was a seaport city, which made it a prosperous commercial center. Because of its business successes, the city became large and wealthy. It was a center of science and medicine (Revelation 2:8-11).

- Pergamum, located in northwest Asia Minor, featured large buildings and a library with over 200,000 items. In ancient times, this city was the official center of emperor worship in Asia (Revelation 2:12-17).

- Thyatira was located about halfway between Pergamum and Sardis and for centuries had been under Roman rule. This city hosted a large military detachment whose essential role was to guard Pergamum, 40 miles to the northwest. The city was a thriving manufacturing and commercial center during New Testament times (Revelation 2:18-29).

- Sardis, about 30 miles southeast of Thyatira, was located at the foot of Mount Tmolus, on the river Pactolus. The city featured pagan worship, as both the Roman Caesar and Artemis—goddess of fertility—were worshipped there. The primary business of this industrial center was harvesting wool, dying it, and making garments from it. The city also had a strong jewelry trade (Revelation 3:1-6).

- Philadelphia—a term literally meaning "brotherly love"—is a city in Lydia, located in western Asia Minor. This city was a major player in the wine industry. Not surprisingly, its chief deity was the god of wine, Dionysus (Revelation 3:7-13).

- Laodicea was a wealthy and commercially successful city

located east of Ephesus, west of Colossae. It had three primary industries: banking, wool, and medicine. Because of an inadequate water supply, an underground aqueduct was built through which water was piped in from hot springs south of the city, becoming lukewarm in transit to Laodicea (Revelation 3:14-22).

- Asia in Revelation 1:4 and the Euphrates River in Revelation 9:14 and 16:12 are also literal geographical locations.

Here is the point: Because the other locations mentioned in the book of Revelation are literal, and because there is no indication in the immediate context that the term "Babylon" is being used metaphorically, then it makes good sense to take it literally. As Bible expositor Andy Woods puts it, "Why should the name Babylon depicted in Revelation 17–18 not be given the same literal interpretation" as all these other geographical locations in the book of Revelation?[1]

The only time in Revelation when a city is not literal is when the text of Revelation actually tells us it is not literal. I am referring to Revelation 11:8, where Jerusalem is called "the city that is figuratively called 'Sodom' and 'Egypt.'" Since this is the only reference to a city that is said to be figurative, it is reasonable to assume that references to other cities are to be taken literally. (If you're wondering whether the term "Mystery Babylon" justifies an allegorical meaning, I'll address that later in the chapter.)

Further, all the other references to Babylon throughout the rest of the Bible always point to a literal city—that is, a godless, sinful, pagan literal city. That's true about all the mentions of Babylon in the Old Testament, and since the book of Revelation draws heavily from the Old Testament, it stands to reason that the term "Babylon" is used in the same sense as in the Old Testament. Bible scholars note that this is especially so in view of the close connection between Revelation and Daniel:

> This point is particularly noticeable when observing the relationship between Revelation and Daniel. Daniel, perhaps more than any other Old Testament book, influenced Revelation. In Daniel, Babylon always means literal Babylon. Given the similarities between Revelation and Daniel, why should Revelation's treatment of Babylon not be understood literally as well?[2]

Note also that because Babylon is mentioned in connection with the Euphrates River in the book of Revelation, a literal city must be meant. We cannot ignore geographical markers provided for us in the context of Scripture.

It is also worth noting that quite a number of highly respected Bible expositors have firmly held that references to Babylon in the book of Revelation refer to the literal city. This includes such notables as B.W. Newton (1853), Robert Govett (1861), G.H. Pember (1888), J.A. Seiss (1900), Clarence Larkin (1918), E.W. Bullinger (1930), William R. Newell (1935), F.C. Jennings (1937), David L. Cooper (1942), and G.H. Lang (1945).[3]

A Confirmation from Jeremiah 50–51

Jeremiah 50–51 provides us further supportive evidence that Revelation 17–18 are speaking about a literal city of Babylon in the end times. Consider the following facts:

- Jeremiah 50–51 includes prophecies about the literal city of Babylon that have not yet been fulfilled. Because these prophecies have not yet been fulfilled, they await future fulfillment.
- There is a very strong connection between what John writes in Revelation 17–18 and the words in Jeremiah 50–51. There

are many parallels between the two. John was clearly drawing on Old Testament information about literal Babylon when he wrote the book of Revelation.

• If Jeremiah 50–51 is without doubt referring to a literal city of Babylon, and if John drew heavily from this passage when he wrote Revelation 17–18, this logically means that Revelation 17–18 refer to a literal city of Babylon, just as Jeremiah 50–51 does. Consider for a moment some of the parallels between Jeremiah and Revelation[4]:

— Jeremiah 51:7 speaks of a "gold cup" just as Revelation 17:4 refers to "a gold goblet."

— Jeremiah 51:13 speaks of "you who dwell by many waters" (ESV), just as Revelation 17:1 speaks of the great prostitute "who is seated on many waters" (ESV).

— Jeremiah 51:7 says Babylon "made the whole earth drunk. The nations drank Babylon's wine, and it drove them all mad." Revelation 17:2 says, "The people who belong to this world have been made drunk by the wine of her immorality."

— Jeremiah describes Babylon's destruction this way: "Suddenly Babylon...has fallen" (51:8). John describes Babylon's destruction likewise: "Babylon is fallen—that great city is fallen" (18:2).

— Jeremiah 51:30 tells us that "her dwellings are on fire" (ESV). Revelation 17:16 tells us the antichrist's forces "burn her up with fire," and "she will be burned up with fire" (18:8 ESV).

— Jeremiah 50:39 affirms, "Never again will people live there; it will lie desolate forever." Revelation 18:21

affirms that "the great city Babylon will be thrown down with violence and will never be found again."

— Jeremiah 50:29 says, "Do to her as she has done to others." Revelation 18:6 likewise says, "Do to her as she has done to others."

— Jeremiah 51:63-64 affirms, "Tie it to a stone and throw it into the Euphrates River. Then say, 'In this same way Babylon and her people will sink, never again to rise, because of the disasters I will bring upon her.'" Revelation 18:21 affirms, "A mighty angel picked up a boulder the size of a huge millstone. He threw it into the ocean and shouted, 'Just like this, the great city Babylon will be thrown down with violence and will never be found again.'"

— Jeremiah 51:6 warns, "Flee from Babylon! Save yourselves! Don't get trapped in her punishment." Revelation 18:4 warns, "Come away from her, my people. Do not take part in her sins, or you will be punished with her."

— Jeremiah 51:48 affirms, "'Then the heavens and earth will rejoice, for out of the north will come destroying armies against Babylon,' says the LORD." Revelation 18:20 says, "Rejoice over her fate, O heaven and people of God and apostles and prophets! For at last God has judged her for your sakes."

My friend, in these parallel verses, we see that John is speaking of Babylon's judgment using terminology from Jeremiah. Since Jeremiah was undeniably speaking of a yet-future judgment on the literal city of Babylon, we must conclude that John was doing likewise in the book of Revelation.

For those who may be wondering, Jeremiah's passage cannot possibly be interpreted as relating to Babylon's destruction by the Medes and Persians back in Daniel's day. After all, Jeremiah 50–51 speaks of Babylon's sudden destruction. This was not the case when Babylon fell to the Medes and Persians. Cyrus actually helped rebuild portions of the city that were in a state of decay, and it became a provincial capital in the Persian Empire. This destruction of Babylon was a gradual process that took place over several centuries.

Further, Jeremiah's prophecy says that Babylon was to be destroyed completely, *never again to revive* (50:3,13,26,39-40; 51:29). Bible expositors note that this did not happen following Babylon's fall to the Medes and Persians:

> One of the dominant themes throughout these verses is the extent of the judgment God is promising to execute on Babylon. This judgment is to be complete and permanent. When Babylon falls, she shall be "completely desolate" and "will never again be inhabited." God is, in effect, vowing to blot the very existence of Babylon from the earth…Obviously this did not take place when Babylon fell to Medo-Persia. She remained populated and productive for centuries after her initial fall.[5]

There is evidence that Babylon was still inhabited as of the early 1900s. Even today there are occupied villages within the walls of ancient Babylon. This means that the Jeremiah prophecies of complete destruction have not yet been fulfilled and must therefore be future (in line with Revelation 17–18).[6]

Jeremiah's prophecy—which has not yet been fulfilled—is directed to "Babylon, concerning the land of the Chaldeans" (Jeremiah 50:1 ESV). The *literal city of Babylon* was to be destroyed. And since John was clearly speaking of New Babylon's future destruction in obviously similar terms—in some cases, *identical* terms—we must conclude that John's Babylon is the literal city of Babylon on the Euphrates, the same Babylon of which Jeremiah spoke.

A Confirmation from Isaiah 13:19-22

In Isaiah 13:19-22 we read,

> Babylon, the most glorious of kingdoms,
>   the flower of Chaldean pride,
> will be devastated like Sodom and Gomorrah
>   when God destroyed them.
> Babylon will never be inhabited again.
>   It will remain empty for generation after generation.
> Nomads will refuse to camp there,
>   and shepherds will not bed down their sheep.
> Desert animals will move into the ruined city,
>   and the houses will be haunted by howling creatures.
> Owls will live among the ruins,
>   and wild goats will go there to dance.
> Hyenas will howl in its fortresses,
>   and jackals will make dens in its luxurious palaces.
> Babylon's days are numbered.

This passage about the literal city of Babylon has not yet been fulfilled. My former mentor John F. Walvoord observed, "As far as the historic fulfillment is concerned, it is obvious from both Scripture and history that these verses have not been literally fulfilled. The city of Babylon continued to flourish after the Medes conquered it, and though its glory dwindled, especially after the control of the Medes and Persians ended in 323 B.C., the city continued."[7]

For both Jeremiah's and Isaiah's prophecies to be fulfilled, the literal city of Babylon must be rebuilt and then destroyed. This is precisely what the book of Revelation indicates will happen in Revelation 17–18. The close connection of Revelation to both Jeremiah and Isaiah—both of which speak of the once-and-for-all destruction of a *literal city of Babylon*—means that Revelation must also be referring to a literal city of Babylon.

The Day of the Lord

This is further confirmed in Isaiah, where we read that these judgments against Babylon will take place during the eschatological "day of the Lord." In the context of Babylon's destruction, we read, "Scream in terror, for the day of the LORD has arrived—the time for the Almighty to destroy" (Isaiah 13:6). "For see, the day of the LORD is coming—the terrible day of his fury and fierce anger. The land will be made desolate, and all the sinners destroyed with it" (verse 9).

The term "day of the Lord" is used in several senses in Scripture. The Old Testament prophets sometimes used it to describe an event to be fulfilled in the near future. At other times, they referred to an event in the distant eschatological future—that is, the future tribulation period. The immediate context of the term generally indicates which sense is intended.

In both cases, the day of the Lord describes God's supernatural intervention into human history in order to bring judgment against sin in the world. The day of the Lord is a time in which God actively controls and dominates history in a direct way instead of working through secondary causes.

Among the New Testament writers, the term is generally used to speak of the judgment that will climax in the end-time seven-year tribulation period (see 2 Thessalonians 2:2; Revelation 16–18) as well as the judgment that will usher in the new earth after the millennial kingdom (2 Peter 3:10-13; Revelation 20:7–21:1; see also Isaiah 65:17-19; 66:22; Revelation 21:1). This theme of judgment against sin runs like a thread through the Bible's many references to the day of the Lord.

A number of Scripture passages indicate that this aspect of the day of the Lord has not yet taken place but awaits the end times. For example, Isaiah 34:1-8 describes a day of the Lord in which God will judge virtually all the nations of the earth: "The LORD is enraged against the nations. His fury is against all their armies. He will completely destroy them, dooming them to slaughter" (verse 2). None of the past days of the Lord have ever involved divine judgment poured out upon all the nations. This indicates that the day of the Lord mentioned in Isaiah 34 must be yet future—that is, the tribulation period.

Similarly, Joel 3:1-16 and Zechariah 14:1-3,12-15 speak of a day of the Lord that will involve God's judgment upon the armies of all the nations when they gather to wage war against Israel. We are told that the Jewish Messiah will come to war against these nations. This seems to coincide with Revelation 16:12-16, where we find that the armies will not begin to gather until the sixth bowl judgment is poured out during the seventieth week of Daniel 9. Revelation 19:11-21 reveals that Christ will wage war against these armies when He comes from heaven to earth as King of kings and Lord of lords. Such facts force the conclusion that the day of the Lord spoken of in Isaiah 34, Joel 3, and Zechariah 14 *is yet future*.

Likewise, the apostle Paul in 1 Thessalonians 5:1-11 reveals that this eschatological day of the Lord is still future. Paul warned that this day would bring sudden, inescapable destruction upon the unsaved of the world. The context of 1 Thessalonians 5 clearly points to the end-times tribulation period.

Now, because the antichrist's signing of the covenant with Israel marks the beginning of the tribulation period, we can also say that this signing of the covenant begins the eschatological day of the Lord. This being so, the judgments against Babylon that take place during "the day of the Lord" will occur during the future tribulation period. It is during the tribulation that Babylon "will be devastated like Sodom and Gomorrah when God destroyed them. Babylon will never be inhabited again. It will remain empty for generation after generation...Babylon's days are numbered" (Isaiah 13:19-22).

When all the important prophetic passages about Babylon are taken together, it is clearly evident that they await a future fulfillment. As Thomas Ice puts it, "Revelation 17 and 18, which speak extensively about Babylon, have many allusions to Old Testament prophecies about Babylon such as Isaiah 13 and 14, Jeremiah 50 and 51, and Zechariah 5:5-11. The only reasonable interpretation for a literal interpreter to reach is 'it is Babylon on the Euphrates.'"[8]

But What About "Mystery Babylon"?

If New Babylon refers to a literal city along the Euphrates River, then what are we to make of the word "mystery" used in Revelation 17:5? Doesn't this term indicate that some kind of symbolical or allegorical Babylon is intended in the text of Scripture?

In answering this question, I can tell you that it would be very convenient if Bible translations universally rendered Revelation 17:5 the same way, but they do not. Some Bible translations render the text such that it's the name of the woman that is mysterious. Other translations make the word "mystery" a part of the woman's name—"Mystery Babylon."

Let's look at some examples. Notice the italicized words in the following Bible translations:

- "On her forehead was written *a name of mystery*: 'Babylon the great, mother of prostitutes and of earth's abominations'" (ESV).
- "*A mysterious name* was written on her forehead: 'Babylon the Great, Mother of All Prostitutes and Obscenities in the World'" (NLT).
- "On her forehead was written *a name, a mystery*: 'Babylon the

Great, the Mother of prostitutes and of the detestable things of the earth'" (NET).

- "The *name written on her forehead was a mystery*: BABYLON THE GREAT THE MOTHER OF PROSTITUTES AND OF THE ABOMINATIONS OF THE EARTH" (NIV).
- "And on her forehead *a name was written, a mystery*, 'BABYLON THE GREAT, THE MOTHER OF HARLOTS AND OF THE ABOMINATIONS OF THE EARTH'" (NASB).
- "On her forehead *a cryptic name* was written: BABYLON THE GREAT THE MOTHER OF PROSTITUTES AND OF THE VILE THINGS OF THE EARTH" (HCSB).

In each of these translations, the name itself is a mystery. *The Bible Knowledge Commentary* affirms, "The NASB and NIV [among other translations] are probably right in separating the word 'mystery' from the title which follows because the word 'mystery' is not a part of the title itself; it describes the title."[9]

Other translations, however, render the term "mystery" as a part of the name or title. The KJV renders the verse, "And upon her forehead was a name written, Mystery, Babylon the Great, the Mother of harlots and abominations of the earth." The NKJV likewise renders it "On her forehead a name was written: MYSTERY, BABYLON THE GREAT, THE MOTHER OF HARLOTS AND OF THE ABOMINATIONS OF THE EARTH." The ASV similarly renders it "Upon her forehead a name written, MYSTERY, BABYLON THE GREAT, THE MOTHER OF THE HARLOTS AND OF THE ABOMINATIONS OF THE EARTH."

In keeping with this latter approach to translation, *The Expositor's Bible Commentary* states, "The first word in the woman's title is 'MYSTERY'...It seems best to see this word as a prefix to the actual name."[10]

I was slightly amused when I consulted the notes in the *NKJV Study Bible*. Despite how the text of the NKJV makes "mystery" a part of the title, the commentary notes in this study Bible say, "MYSTERY may be the first part of the title for BABYLON THE GREAT. But based on the use of the word mystery in v. 7, this verse should probably read, 'On her forehead a mysterious name was written…'"[11] In other words, the scholars who wrote the study notes for the NKJV Study Bible imply that the NKJV translation gets it wrong here.

My understanding of the Greek language tells me that the name is the mystery, not Babylon. That's the most natural way to read the Greek text. I say this because the gender of both "name" and "mystery" are neuter, whereas the gender of "Babylon" is feminine. This strongly suggests that the term "mystery" should be understood as an appositive to the term "name." They belong together. If you're not familiar with what is meant by *appositive*, it simply involves two nouns or noun phrases that are together in a sentence and each one gives more information about the other. In the present case, the neuter term "mystery" gives us more information about the neuter term "name." The identical genders of the two nouns show that one qualifies the other. It would be rather strained to read "mystery" (neuter) as belonging with "Babylon" (feminine).

In light of this, I would like to suggest that the term "mystery" has nothing to do with being mystical, symbolical, or allegorical. I think our best policy is to consider how "mystery" is used elsewhere in the Bible. When we do that, it becomes evident that the word refers to something that was not *previously* revealed but is *now* revealed through divine revelation.

Let's look at a few examples. The word "mystery" is used in 1 Corinthians 15:51 to speak of the rapture: "Behold! I tell you a mystery. We shall not all sleep, but we shall all be changed" (esv). The rapture of the church is categorized as a mystery because it is a doctrine that had never been revealed in Old Testament times. It was mentioned for the first time in the New Testament.

Likewise, Colossians 1:26—which summarizes our riches in Christ—speaks of "the mystery hidden for ages and generations but now revealed to his saints" (esv). In other words, our riches in Christ were not known in Old Testament times but were revealed in the New Testament.

Another example is how the apostle Paul—reflecting on how God's gospel of grace had become available for Gentiles—spoke of "how the mystery was made known to me by revelation" (Ephesians 3:3 esv). Salvation for the Gentiles was not an Old Testament doctrine, but at this time God revealed it to Paul.

Our conclusion is simple and straightforward. The way that the term "mystery" is used throughout Scripture reveals that it refers to something that was not *previously* revealed but is *now* revealed by God through divine revelation.

With this backdrop in mind, it is now easier to properly interpret the meaning of Revelation 17:5: "On her forehead a name was written, a mystery, 'BABYLON THE GREAT, THE MOTHER OF HARLOTS AND OF THE ABOMINATIONS OF THE EARTH'" (nasb). This means that the name given to the woman (who represents false religion rooted in Babylon) is something that was not previously revealed but was now being revealed through divine revelation.

Seen in this light, the use of "mystery" for the woman's name in Revelation 17:5 does not require or even imply a mystical or allegorical understanding of Babylon. Nor does it argue against understanding Babylon as anything other than a literal city along the Euphrates River in the end times. Revelation 17:5 is simply telling us that the name "BABYLON THE GREAT, THE MOTHER

OF HARLOTS AND OF THE ABOMINATIONS OF THE EARTH" was not revealed of Babylon's religion in Old Testament times but more recently has been revealed through divine revelation. (We will explore the meaning of this phrase, in the broader context of Revelation 17, in the next chapter.)

One Literal New Babylon, Two Aspects

Now that we've established that Babylon in Revelation 17–18 is a literal city along the Euphrates, let's look at the two different aspects of this city that are predominant at different times in the tribulation period. The first aspect is the religious system that emanates from New Babylon during the first half of the tribulation. The second aspect is commercial New Babylon, which will become prominent during the second half.

Some prophecy enthusiasts interpret Revelation 17–18 as meaning that in the end times there will be two Babylons—a religious Babylon and a commercial/political Babylon. It is more correct to say that there will be *one* New Babylon in the end times—a literal city along the Euphrates River that will have both a religious and a commercial aspect.

How do we know there will be only one New Babylon in the end times? More precisely, how do we know that the religious New Babylon described in Revelation 17 involves the same city as the commercial New Babylon described in Revelation 18? A detailed comparison of the two chapters points to one New Babylon in the end times:

- Revelation 17 refers to "Babylon the Great" and "the great city" (verses 5 and 18). Revelation 18 refers to "Babylon, you great city" (verse 10).
- Revelation 17 indicates that the great prostitute (referring to the religious system affiliated with New Babylon) will be

burned with fire (verse 16). Revelation 18 likewise says Babylon will be burned with fire (verse 8).

- Revelation 17 indicates that ultimately, it is God who will be behind the great prostitute's destruction (verse 17). Revelation 18 likewise indicates that ultimately, it is God who will be behind New Babylon's destruction (verse 8).

- Revelation 17 reveals that the great prostitute "wore purple and scarlet clothing and beautiful jewelry made of gold and precious gems and pearls" (verse 4). Revelation 18 speaks of the great city of New Babylon that "was clothed in finest purple and scarlet linens, decked out with gold and precious stones and pearls" (verse 16).

- Revelation 17 says the great prostitute "held a gold goblet full of obscenities and the impurities of her immorality" (verse 4). Revelation 18 says Babylon has "brewed a cup of terror for others" (verse 6).

- Revelation 17 reveals that "the kings of the world have committed adultery" with the great prostitute (verse 2). Revelation 18 says "the kings of the world have committed adultery" with New Babylon (verse 3).

- Revelation 17 likewise says, "The people who belong to this world have been made drunk by the wine" of the great prostitute's immorality (verse 2). Revelation 18 says, "The kings of the world have committed adultery" with New Babylon (verse 3).

- Revelation 17 says the great prostitute was "drunk with the blood of God's holy people who were witnesses for Jesus" (verse 6). Revelation 18 says that in New Babylon's streets "flowed the blood of the prophets and of God's holy people and the blood of people slaughtered all over the world" (verse 24).[12]

Because of such precise parallels, it seems clear that both Revelation 17 and 18 are referring to the same New Babylon. Bible expositor Andy Woods summarizes it this way:

> A strong exegetical case can be made to support the proposition that Revelation 17 and 18 should be viewed as a unit speaking of one Babylon rather than two separate units speaking of two Babylons...Both chapters refer to Babylon as having the same name (17:5; 18:2), being a city (17:18; 18:10), wearing the same clothing (17:4; 18:16), holding a cup (17:4; 18:6), fornicating with kings (17:2; 18:3), being drunk with wine of immorality (17:2; 18:3), persecuting believers (17:6; 18:24), experiencing destruction by fire (17:16; 18:8), and experiencing destruction by God (17:17; 18:5, 8).[13]

And yet despite there being a single Babylon, I believe the focus in Revelation 17 is on the false religious system associated with New Babylon (the "great prostitute"), while the focus in Revelation 18 is on commercial New Babylon—which makes the merchants of the world rich.

What justification is there for drawing a distinction between the religious and commercial aspects in Revelation 17 and 18? For starters, we know that chapter 17 describes a different aspect of New Babylon than chapter 18 because the respective revelations for each chapter come from different angels. In Revelation 17:1 we read, "One of the seven angels who had poured out the seven bowls came over and spoke to me." This angel then provided revelation to John about religious New Babylon. Then in Revelation 18:1 we read, "After all this I saw another angel come down from heaven...He gave a mighty shout." This angel then provided revelation about commercial New Babylon (verses 1-2). The most natural way to understand Revelation 17 and 18, then, is that the two different visions from two different angels portray two different aspects of the one literal city that we call New Babylon.

Notice also that whereas the kings in Revelation 17:16 hate and want to destroy religious Babylon at the midpoint of the tribulation period, the kings and rulers in Revelation 18:9 mourn when commercial Babylon is destroyed late in the tribulation period. This confirms a distinction between the two aspects of New Babylon.

I will address both aspects of New Babylon in the next chapter.

4

Religious and *Commercial*
New Babylon

My goal in the previous chapter was to firmly establish two essential facts:

1. In Revelation 17–18, Babylon should be understood as a literal city along the Euphrates River.
2. Though there is a religious aspect to Babylon in Revelation 17 and a commercial aspect in chapter 18, there is but *one* New Babylon. Both aspects are rooted in the one literal city of Babylon along the Euphrates River.

My goal in this chapter is to zero in on the nature of the religious system that emanates from New Babylon, as well as the nature of commercial New Babylon. We will see that both play a critical role during the tribulation period.

The Religious System that Emanates from New Babylon—Revelation 17

In Revelation 17 we find prophecies about the false religion associated with New Babylon. Verses 1-6 describe this false religion, and verses 7-18 interpret it. Such interpretation is necessary because there is a lot of symbolic language involved. We will camp here for a while so that we can unpack the full meaning of John's words.

John's Description of the False Religious System—Revelation 17:1-6

Let's begin by reading Revelation 17:1-6:

> One of the seven angels who had poured out the seven bowls came over and spoke to me. "Come with me," he said, "and I will show you the judgment that is going to come on the great prostitute, who rules over many waters. The kings of the world have committed adultery with her, and the people who belong to this world have been made drunk by the wine of her immorality."
>
> So the angel took me in the Spirit into the wilderness. There I saw a woman sitting on a scarlet beast that had seven heads and ten horns, and blasphemies against God were written all over it. The woman wore purple and scarlet clothing and beautiful jewelry made of gold and precious gems and pearls. In her hand she held a gold goblet full of obscenities and the impurities of her immorality. A mysterious name was written on her forehead: "Babylon the Great, Mother of All Prostitutes and Obscenities in the World." I could see that she was drunk—drunk with the blood of God's holy people who were witnesses for Jesus. I stared at her in complete amazement.

I can imagine you might be scratching your head right now, wondering what such language could possibly mean. But don't be concerned. What you've just read is a good example of apocalyptic literature. (The book of Daniel is another example.) In the upcoming pages I'll share about how we can best understand this type of literature.

First, let me say that with Revelation 17 coming relatively late in the book of Revelation, you might initially get the impression that the false religious system associated with New Babylon emerges quite late in the tribulation period. This is not the case. Try to keep in mind that the book of Revelation was written in the order in which the truth was *revealed* to John, not in the actual order that events will unfold during the tribulation. What God revealed to John in Revelation 17 about the false religious system will transpire during the first half of the seven-year tribulation.

In Revelation 17 we learn that New Babylon—a literal city along the Euphrates River—symbolizes *as well as emanates* a false religious system that has global influence. To illustrate, Wall Street is an actual street in New York City, but it also symbolizes the stock market. The White House is a literal building in Washington, DC, but it also symbolizes the presidency of the United States. In much the same way, New Babylon is an actual city, but it also symbolizes a false religion in Revelation 17 as well as a commercial powerhouse in chapter 18.

I'm not surprised that the term *Babylon* will be used to represent false religion in the end times. After all, in ancient times, the Babylonians believed in many false gods and goddesses and were deeply entrenched in paganism, idolatry, and various forms of divination and occultism. It is hard to even think of Babylon without false religion coming to mind. One of my former mentors, Dr. Charles Ryrie, wrote, "Hammurabi made Babylon a religious power about 1600 BC by making Marduk god of the city of Babylon and head of a pantheon of 1,300 deities."[1]

In Revelation 17:1, the false religious system of the end times is likened to a "great prostitute." Prostitution is often used as a graphic metaphor in Scripture to symbolize unfaithfulness to God. One example of this appears in Jeremiah 3:6-9, where we read about how unfaithful Israel was in Old Testament times:

> During the reign of King Josiah, the LORD said to me,
> "Have you seen what fickle Israel has done? Like a wife
> who commits adultery, Israel has worshiped other gods on
> every hill and under every green tree…Israel treated it all
> so lightly—she thought nothing of committing adultery
> by worshiping idols made of wood and stone. So now the
> land has been polluted."

(For other examples, take a look at Ezekiel 20:30; Hosea 4:15; 5:3; 6:10; 9:1.)

Note that it was not just that Israel turned away from Yahweh, the one true God of the Bible. It was also that Israel worshipped false gods. The people of Israel participated in false religions. It would be comparable to a professed Christian today turning away from the God of the Bible and worshipping Allah, the god of Islam, or worshipping Shiva, one of the gods of Hinduism, or both! Such would be highly offensive to God.

The great prostitute in Revelation 17 symbolizes the false religious system of Babylon—probably some form of apostate and paganized Christendom that embraces all those who will be "left behind" following the rapture (see Romans 5:9; 1 Thessalonians 1:9-10; 5:9; Revelation 3:10). As prophecy scholar Thomas Ice puts it, "All the streams of apostate Christianity—Roman Catholicism, Eastern Orthodoxy, and Liberal Protestantism—will converge into ecclesiastical Babylon (Revelation 17) during the tribulation."[2] Prophecy scholar Mark Hitchcock similarly suggests it is probably "a kind of religious amalgamation or world church that will pull together people of various religious backgrounds into one great ecclesiastical alliance after the disappearance of the true church at the rapture. And this world church will evidently be centered in the rebuilt city of Babylon."[3]

Revelation 17:1 informs us that this prostitute "rules over many waters." The term "waters," as used in the book of Revelation, typically refers to various nations and peoples. This passage, then, symbolically speaks of false religion's control over the various peoples, multitudes, nations, and languages of the world. It will be global in its impact. Charles Ryrie is correct when he says that "when believers are taken to heaven in the Rapture before the tribulation begins, religion does not disappear from the earth. Indeed, it will flourish under this unfaithful Babylon for the first half of the tribulation."[4] He, too, agrees that "the apostate church will be ecumenical, or worldwide."[5]

Revelation 17:2 reveals that "the kings of the world have committed adultery with her." The fornication spoken of here refers not to actual sexual sin, but rather, to being intimately related to—sleeping in bed with—this false religious system. Such "fornication" implies idolatry, which is unfaithfulness to the true God.

We all know that wine can intoxicate a person. Revelation 17:2 tells us that "the people who belong to this world have been made drunk by the wine of her immorality." In other words, many around the globe will become intoxicated by this false religion. Just as wine can have a controlling influence over people, so will this false religion have a controlling influence on the world's population. This false religious system will apparently open the door for people to engage in any kind of immoral lifestyle they want.

Having long specialized in the study of the cults and false religions of our world, I can tell you without hesitation that there is often a close connection between false doctrine and immoral living. For example:

- The Children of God cult has long taught that the Holy Spirit is a sexy, nearly naked woman (the Father's wife); Christ was conceived through sex between the angel Gabriel and Mary; Christ fornicated with his female disciples (Mary, Martha, and Mary Magdalene) and may have contracted venereal disease; Christ has orgies in heaven; family members can fornicate and commit adultery as long as they "do it in love"; and they can engage in "flirty fishing" in order to gain converts.

- We also see immorality manifested in the Unification Church. To undo original sin, the late Reverend Moon engaged in ritual sexual purification practices. The ritual involved a female church member having sexual intercourse with the messianic leader (Reverend Moon) in order to become purified. The sexual rite is believed to "purify the womb" of the woman, enabling her to give birth to children free from original sin. This occurred countless times in the Unification Church.

- Among Wiccans (witches), sex is often used as a sacrament. It is said to be an outward sign of an inward grace. Both heterosexuality and homosexuality are acceptable to witches. Sometimes sex is used in magic rituals. Sex may be used within a ritual or spell-casting session to facilitate or augment the efficacy of a given magical rite. That is, sexual activities are used to accomplish the desired goal of the occultist. Auto-, hetero-, and homosexual expressions are equally valid in sex magic. Some Wiccans suggest that without autoerotic practice it is impossible to achieve anything in sex magic. Sex can allegedly bring one into union with the divine.

- In Mormonism, Joseph Smith—the founder—was a polygamist. The number of wives he had is not known for certain but estimates range from 28 to 84. The likelihood is that there were 33, most of whom were younger than Smith, with one being a mere 14 years of age at the time they married. Smith's first (and true) wife Emma was deeply hurt and angered about it all. Joseph, though, had a word from the Lord for Emma to the effect that the Lord would kill her if she did not submit and cleave to Joseph. Brigham Young took over the Mormon Church after Joseph Smith was killed, and Young himself married some 20 wives by the time he died. He fathered 57 children by 16 of these wives. Though polygamy has been officially outlawed by mainstream Mormonism, it is estimated that there are still some 30,000 polygamists who live clandestinely in Salt Lake City and southern Utah.

• New Agers also set forth false doctrine accompanied by immoral living. New Age leader Matthew Fox is a representative example. Fox completely robs Jesus Christ of His uniqueness; portrays Jesus as merely one of many enlightened individuals who have incarnated the Cosmic Christ; reduces Christianity to one of many viable options in the smorgasbord of world religions; argues that we must move from a "personal Savior" Christianity to a Cosmic Christ Christianity; chastises those who have stood against the goddess religions of the native peoples of the world; maternalizes the nature of God; exalts the cosmos to deity; superimposes New Age interpretations on countless biblical texts; denies humanity's sin problem; proposes a "cosmic redemption" based on a revival of mysticism rather than the work of the historical Jesus; and flatly denies the biblical teaching that homosexual acts are sinful, affirming instead that heterosexuality and homosexuality are equally acceptable to the Cosmic Christ.

This brief sampling should be enough to demonstrate that there is often a connection between false doctrine and immorality. According to Revelation 17:2, that will be true of the false religion of New Babylon. The same devil that inspires false doctrine also motivates immoral living (see 1 Corinthians 7:5).

John then "saw a woman sitting on a scarlet beast that had seven heads and ten horns, and blasphemies against God were written all over it" (Revelation 17:3). The woman is the "great prostitute" mentioned in verses 1 and 2. This woman—this blasphemous religion associated with New Babylon—is said to sit on, *thus controlling*, the scarlet beast, who is the blasphemous antichrist (see Revelation 13:1,6; 16:9,11,21). Clearly, then, Babylon's false religion will control the antichrist for a time.

Notice how "the woman" is described: "The woman wore purple and scarlet clothing and beautiful jewelry made of gold and precious gems and pearls. In her hand she held a gold goblet full of obscenities and the impurities of her immorality" (Revelation 17:4). This imagery indicates that the false religious system associated with New Babylon will be wealthy and have a glorious outer appearance. In ancient times, prostitutes often dressed extravagantly in order to more easily seduce men. Apparently this false religious system will be "adorned" so as to lure the people of the world into her religious web. This system will be outwardly appealing.

The woman—the false religion that is a prostitute—is said to have a "gold goblet," which on the outside looks nice. No matter how beautiful a cup looks on the outside, however, it is deadly if it contains poison. This false religion will appear good on the outside, but on the inside it will be poisonous (see Deuteronomy 18:9; 29:17; 32:16; Jeremiah 51:7). Many will be deceived. It is just like the cults of our day—they look great on the outside but are full of doctrinal poison on the inside.

Revelation 17:5 then tells us, "A mysterious name was written on her forehead: 'Babylon the Great, Mother of All Prostitutes and Obscenities in the World.'" In ancient Rome, prostitutes typically wore a headband with their name imprinted on it (see Jeremiah 3:3). In the case of the great prostitute, the name on her forehead reveals that religious New Babylon is the greatest and most obscene false religion to ever come upon the world. In fact, it is *the source* (the "mother") of all false religion all around the world. This is said to be a "mystery" because this fact had not yet been revealed about Babylonian religion but is now made known by God through divine revelation.

This false religious system will be a dire enemy of God's people. John affirmed, "I could see that she was drunk—drunk with the blood of God's holy people who were witnesses for Jesus. I stared at her in complete amazement" (Revelation 17:6). Christian martyrdom will be commonplace. No wonder Jesus earlier warned that "there will be greater anguish than at any time since the world began. And it will never be so great again" (Matthew 24:21). The blood of the martyrs no doubt includes the blood of God's two prophetic witnesses (Revelation 11:10) and all who stand for Jesus.

The Interpretation of John's Vision about Religious Babylon— Revelation 17:7-17

Having considered the description of John's vision recorded in verses 1-6, we now move on to the interpretation of the vision recorded in verses 7-17. The angel said to John, "Why are you so amazed?...I will tell you the mystery of this woman and of the beast with seven heads and ten horns on which she sits" (verse 7). The angel recognized that John was baffled by what he had just seen, and now provides more information about both the beast (verses 7-14) and the woman (verses 15-18).

The beast is the antichrist, and the revelation given to John about him is quite astounding:

> The beast you saw was once alive but isn't now. And yet he will soon come up out of the bottomless pit and go to eternal destruction. And the people who belong to this world, whose names were not written in the Book of Life before the world was made, will be amazed at the reappearance of this beast who had died (Revelation 17:8).

What does all this mean? Some Christian interpreters believe that the antichrist will in fact die, due to a mortal wound, and will subsequently be resurrected by Satan. Others rebut that Satan doesn't have the power to raise humans from the dead. They suggest that the antichrist will be seriously injured and give the appearance of having died without really doing so. Bible scholar Walter Price is representative of those who hold the view that the antichrist will appear to be dead but not actually be dead:

> The apostle Paul...was stoned in Lystra, and the citizens "dragged him out of the city, supposing that he was dead" (Acts 14:19 ESV). While in an unconscious state, Paul "was caught up into Paradise, and heard unspeakable words, which it is not lawful for a man to utter" (2 Cor. 12:4). Paul had received, as it were, what seemed like a death stroke. At the same time he was thought to be dead, his spirit was caught up into the third heaven and there received a profound revelation from God. This same thing, in reverse, will happen to the Antichrist. The Antichrist, sometime during his career as Caesar, will receive a death stroke. He will be no more dead than was the apostle Paul. But just as the citizens of Lystra thought Paul was dead, so the Antichrist will be thought dead.[6]

Price then raises the possibility that just as Paul's spirit departed from his body and was taken up to God's domain, where he received further revelations (2 Corinthians 12), so the antichrist's spirit may depart from his body (appearing to be dead) and be taken into the abyss by Satan, where Satan will offer the world's kingdoms to him.

> Just as Satan took Jesus up into a high mountain and showed him all the kingdoms of the world, and offered them to him, if he would fall down and worship him; so Satan will take the Antichrist into the depths of the

> Abyss and show him all the kingdoms of the world…Jesus refused to bow down to Satan. The Antichrist will not refuse.[7]

Price suggests that the antichrist's spirit will then return from the abyss, thus fulfilling Revelation 11:7 ("the beast…comes up out of the bottomless pit"), and will reenter what appears to be a dead body. He will give the appearance of rising from the dead, then continue on his satanically inspired mission. Mark Hitchcock suggests that while in the abyss, the "Antichrist probably receives his orders and strategy from Satan, literally selling his soul to the devil, and then comes back to earth with hellish ferocity to establish his world domination over a completely awestruck earth."[8]

The passage tells us that the antichrist will then go to destruction (Revelation 17:8). Fresh from the bottomless pit, and empowered by Satan, the antichrist will take a destructive path in the final years of the tribulation period, which will lead to eternal destruction in the lake of fire (see Matthew 7:13; John 17:12; Philippians 1:28; 3:19; 2 Thessalonians 2:3; Hebrews 10:39; 2 Peter 2:3; 3:7,16; Revelation 19:20).

We are told that "the people who belong to this world…will be amazed at the reappearance of this beast who had died." Based on the original Greek of this text, these people are what we might call *earth-dwellers*, those characterized by the things of the earth. We might also call them *worldlings* or *worldly people*.

They are the ones "whose names have not been written in the Book of Life." The book of life records the names of the redeemed who will inherit heaven (Revelation 3:5; 13:8; 17:8; 20:12,15; 21:27; see also Luke 10:20; Philippians 4:3). The names of the worldlings will not be in this book. These worldlings will marvel that the beast was alive, then died, then will come to life again. They will then worship him.

The angel then tells John something that seems incomprehensible: "This calls for a mind with understanding: The seven heads of the beast represent the seven hills where the woman rules. They also represent seven kings. Five kings have already fallen, the sixth now reigns, and the seventh is yet to come, but his reign will be brief" (Revelation 17:9-10). Wow, that's a lot! Let's try to unpack the meaning.

Without going into excessive detail, the seven mountains symbolize the seven kingdoms and their kings that are mentioned in Revelation 17:10 (verse 10 is a commentary on verse 9). In Scripture, mountains often symbolize kingdoms (Psalm 30:7; 68:15-16; Isaiah 2:2; 41:15; Jeremiah 51:25; Daniel 2:35,44; Habakkuk 3:6,10; Zechariah 4:7).

These seven kingdoms are Egypt, Assyria, Babylon, Medo-Persia, Greece, Rome, and that of the antichrist. False, paganized religion influenced all these empires. After all, the "woman" or prostitute is said to have been "seated" on them all, indicating her influence over them.

As for the kings who rule over these kingdoms (Revelation 17:10), five are said to have fallen, one still exists, and one is yet to come. At the time of John's writing, the Egyptian, Assyrian, Babylonian, Medo-Persian, and Greek empires had fallen. Rome still existed in his day. The antichrist's kingdom was yet to come.

The reign of the seventh king—the antichrist—will be brief (Revelation 17:10). "He was given authority to do whatever he wanted for forty-two months" (13:5)—the last half of the tribulation period, which is three-and-a-half years.

Revelation 17:11 also seems enigmatic: "As for the beast that was and is not, it is an eighth, but it belongs to the seven, and it goes to destruction" (ESV). Contextually, this verse simply means that the antichrist is both the seventh and the eighth king, in view of his apparent death and resurrection. He is the seventh king prior to his serious wound, and the eighth king after his so-called resurrection. This eighth king ultimately "goes to destruction."

John is then informed that the ten horns he had seen earlier were ten kings who don't yet have power (Revelation 17:12). They will receive delegated authority under the antichrist during the tribulation. They are said to reign "for one brief moment," which is not unexpected because the reign of the antichrist will also be short-lived (Revelation 13:5). These kings will be unanimously committed to serving under the antichrist.

These kings will collectively make war on the Lamb (Jesus Christ) (Revelation 17:14). In making war against Him they follow the lead of the antichrist, who has always been against (*anti*) Jesus Christ. This war against the Lamb will be waged at Armageddon. Of course, it will be a futile endeavor, for the Lamb is the King of kings and Lord of lords. He is sovereign over all things (see Revelation 19:16; 1 Timothy 6:15; see also Deuteronomy 10:17; Psalm 136:3). None can defeat Him.

John is then informed that "the waters where the prostitute is ruling represent masses of people of every nation and language" (Revelation 17:15). In Old Testament times, water was a common symbol for people (Psalm 18:4,16; 124:4; Isaiah 8:7; Jeremiah 47:2). This imagery indicates that this single apostate religious system rooted in New Babylon will influence the entire world.

Revelation 17:16 reveals that initially, the antichrist will utilize this false religious system (the "prostitute") to bring unity to the peoples of the world. But once he has accomplished this purpose, he will no longer need the false religion. He will hate it and dispose of it with the help of his ten sub-commanders. Bible commentator Warren Wiersbe notes: "Throughout history, political systems have 'used' religious bodies to further their political causes...When dictators are friendly with religion, it is usually a sign that they want to make use of religion's influence and then destroy it."[9]

There are no textual clues as to the precise timing of the religion's destruction. However, it seems most logical and coherent to place it at the midpoint of the tribulation period, at the same time the antichrist will assume the role of world dictator by proclamation (see Daniel 9:27; Matthew 24:15). It makes sense to infer that at the same basic time, the antichrist will come into both global political dominion and religious dominion, demanding even to be worshipped (Daniel 11:36-38; 2 Thessalonians 2:4; Revelation 13:8,15). Hence, the false religious system that dominated during the first half of the tribulation will be obliterated once the antichrist is on religious center stage. The final world religion will require people to worship the antichrist alone.

Interestingly, we are then informed, "God has put a plan into their minds, a plan that will carry out his purposes. They will agree to give their authority to the scarlet beast, and so the words of God will be fulfilled. And this woman you saw in your vision represents the great city that rules over the kings of the world" (Revelation 17:17-18).

Even though the antichrist and his ten sub-commanders engage in the destruction of the false religious system, God is the One who is bringing about His sovereign purposes through them. Human history in all its details, even the most minute, is but the outworking of the eternal purposes of God. What has happened in the past, what is happening today, and what will happen in the prophetic future is all evidence of the unfolding of a purposeful plan devised by the wondrous personal God of the Bible (Ephesians 3:11; 2 Timothy 1:9). In the present case, God will sovereignly motivate the destruction of the Babylonian false religion, as well as allow the antichrist to come into world dominion—but only for a short time.

Commercial New Babylon—Revelation 18

While Revelation 17 speaks of the false religion associated with New Babylon and the antichrist's role in it, Revelation 18 provides us with important facts about the commercial aspect of New Babylon. This chapter speaks predominantly of the destruction of commercial New Babylon, and I'll discuss that destruction in detail a bit later in the book. For now, allow me to summarize the most pertinent facts we learn about commercial New Babylon from our passage:

1. *The political leaders of the world will play a key role in the global influence and affluence of commercial New Babylon.* Revelation 18:3 tells us, "The kings of the world have committed adultery with her." This refers not to actual sexual immorality but rather to a close and intimate relationship between world leaders and commercial New Babylon. This openness to commercial New Babylon no doubt accounts for its global reach. This anti-God economic and commercial system will thus influence everyone on earth. World leaders will be open to commercial New Babylon because it brings each of them "great luxury" (verse 9).

2. *Business people from around the world will grow rich because of their connection to commercial New Babylon.* Revelation 18:3 affirms, "Because of her desires for extravagant luxury, the merchants of the world have grown rich." Business people all over the globe will accrue incredible wealth by selling their goods to New Babylon (verses 12-13).

3. *Commercial New Babylon will purchase a wide array of products.* Included are such things as

> gold, silver, jewels, and pearls; fine linen, purple, silk, and scarlet cloth; things made of fragrant thyine wood, ivory goods, and objects made of expensive wood; and bronze, iron, and marble...cinnamon, spice, incense, myrrh,

frankincense, wine, olive oil, fine flour, wheat, cattle, sheep, horses, wagons, and bodies—that is, human slaves (Revelation 18:12-13).

This is no doubt just a partial list. Commercial New Babylon—in its thirst for luxury and extravagance—will purchase anything you can think of, and all who sell her products will grow rich.

4. All who are connected to commercial New Babylon will live in luxury and splendor. Because of their connection to commercial New Babylon, "the merchants of the world [will] have grown rich" (Revelation 18:3). World leaders will enjoy "her great luxury" (verse 9) just as business people "became wealthy" (verse 15). Even the "shipowners [will become] wealthy by transporting her great wealth on the seas" (verse 19). We clearly see here that the reason so many people will love commercial New Babylon is that *they love money.*

5. Many of the products purchased by commercial New Babylon will be transported via merchant ships on the ocean. We are told that "the captains of the merchant ships" and their crews—as well as "shipowners"—will serve as channels through which a multitude of commercial goods will reach New Babylon (Revelation 18:17,19).

6. Commercial New Babylon will be headed up by an economic genius—the Satan-inspired antichrist. Starting at the midpoint of the tribulation period, the religious capital of the antichrist will be Jerusalem, where he will set up an image of himself in the Jewish temple. Meanwhile, his economic and public capital will be the city of Babylon, which will become the commercial center of the world.

Let us not forget that the antichrist, through the false prophet, will require "everyone—small and great, rich and poor, free and slave—to be given a mark on the right hand or on the forehead. And no one [will] buy or sell anything without that mark, which [is] either the name of the beast or the number representing his name" (Revelation 13:16-17). We deduce from this that the products purchased by commercial New Babylon will be from merchants who have received the mark of the beast.

Aside from the mark of the beast, there is another indicator of the close connection that will exist between New Babylon and the antichrist. In Revelation 14:8-10 we read:

> Then another angel followed him through the sky, shouting, "Babylon is fallen—that great city is fallen—because she made all the nations of the world drink the wine of her passionate immorality."
>
> Then a third angel followed them, shouting, "Anyone who worships the beast and his statue or who accepts his mark on the forehead or on the hand must drink the wine of God's anger. It has been poured full strength into God's cup of wrath. And they will be tormented with fire and burning sulfur in the presence of the holy angels and the Lamb."

In this passage we witness a close connection between the doom associated with New Babylon and the doom associated with worshipping the beast, the antichrist. *The two belong together.*

The Feasibility of a Rebuilt Babylon

How is it feasible that Babylon will be rebuilt during the end times? To this question, I can offer several observations.

First and foremost, recall that when the late Saddam Hussein was in power, he spent more than one billion dollars in oil money to enhance the city of Babylon. In his case, a billion dollars accomplished the revival of the city in rather rapid fashion.

Second, when the antichrist comes into power during the tribulation period, he will have access not only to unlimited funding, but to an unlimited work force. *What the antichrist wants, the antichrist will get.* He will make Hussein's efforts seem like child's play.

Third, it is quite possible that the oil in Iraq will be the primary source of funds for the rebuilding of Babylon. It seems that an oil-rich Iraq is part of God's blueprint for the end times. As one commentator put it, "It's no accident that Babylon is in Iraq, a nation with such staggering oil reserves. God said that Babylon will be rebuilt as a great commercial center in the end times."[10]

Babylon's appeal to the antichrist may relate to the city's prime location—it is in close proximity to other oil-rich nations, such as Iran, Kuwait, and Saudi Arabia. As prophecy commentator Nathan Jones says, "It would be very smart to have a capital in the oil fields where you can defend it well."[11] The antichrist will be able to control immense wealth and power—up to two-thirds of the remaining oil on the planet. It is hard to think of a better place to establish an economic and commercial center.

Other countries of the world, such as China, may find it difficult to control their lust for the oil treasures associated with this global center. Could it be that China—the kings of the East (Revelation 16:12)—will engage in a direct challenge to the authority of the antichrist, who—headquartered in Babylon at this time—will be in control of the world's oil supply in the Middle East? This control of the world's oil supply will make it easy for him to choke off any nation he chooses. It may be that China will become desperate for fuel and will have no other choice but to move against the Satan-inspired oil czar who rules Babylon.

Whether or not this happens, the antichrist will have the power and resources to easily rebuild Babylon in a quick, efficient manner. It's on the horizon.

5

Historical Insights from Genesis 10–11

We've already learned a lot about New Babylon as described in Revelation 17–18. We can gain even further insights by examining the founding, history, and significance of old Babylon. Toward that end, let's camp for a while in Genesis 10–11 and examine Babylon in its embryonic state.

Nimrod and the Founding of Babylon—Genesis 10:8-10

In Genesis 10:8-10 we read,

> Nimrod...was the first on earth to be a mighty man. He was a mighty hunter before the LORD. Therefore it is said, "Like Nimrod a mighty hunter before the LORD." The beginning of his kingdom was Babel, Erech, Accad, and Calneh, in the land of Shinar (ESV).
>
> Nimrod, a descendant of Cush, had a reputation as a mighty hunter and a powerful leader (Genesis 10:8). His name literally means "rebel." This rebel-warrior was an enemy of Israel. Bible expositor Warren Wiersbe observed that Nimrod "was a mighty tyrant in the sight of God, the

first dictator. The word 'hunter' does not refer to the hunting of animals, but rather to the hunting of men."[1]

We are told that "the beginning of his kingdom was Babel, Erech, Accad, and Calneh, in the land of Shinar" (Genesis 10:10 ESV). Nimrod was the founder of the Babylonian Empire. He also headed up the effort to build the tower of Babel. He was not only a powerful political leader, but—along with his wife—he was very committed to pagan religion.

Babel is an early name for Babylon. The city was situated on the banks of the Euphrates River, a little more than 50 miles south of modern Baghdad. Because of its ideal location—along a major river—Babel/Babylon soon became an important commercial trade center in the ancient world. As we've already learned, New Babylon will also be a commercial trade center.

The ancient Babylonians were thoroughly pagan, believing in many false gods and goddesses. They were deeply engulfed in divination and occultism and became famous for their heavy reliance on astrology. They believed that by observing the planets and stars in the sky they could uncover secret information about the will of the gods and how to defeat their enemies (see Daniel 1:20; 2:2,10,27; 4:7; 5:7,11,15). Babel/Babylon is typically represented in Scripture as being rebelliously arrayed against God and His people, culminating in the New Babylon of Revelation 17–18 (see 2 Kings 24:10).

Nimrod: A Type of the Antichrist

Many Bible students view Nimrod as a type of the antichrist. A *type* may be defined as "a figure or representation of something to come."[2] The late Bible expositor Donald K. Campbell said that a type is "an Old Testament institution, event, person, object, or ceremony which has reality and purpose in biblical history, but which also by divine design foreshadows something yet to be revealed."[3]

Types are therefore prophetic in nature. Many of the types we find in the Old Testament (about 50) speak prophetically of Christ in some way. It is not surprising that there are types of the antichrist as well.

Of course, we must be careful to distinguish types and prophecies in their respective forms. Bible scholar Paul Lee Tan explained that "a type prefigures coming reality; a prophecy verbally delineates the future. One is expressed in events, persons, and acts; the other is couched in words and statements."[4]

Two extremes are to be avoided in the study of typology. There are some interpreters who see too many types in the Old Testament. Directly opposite are those who see all alleged types as cases of forced exegesis. Both extremes are unbalanced and should be avoided. If you are interested in a balanced approach to interpreting types, a number of good sources are available.[5]

Legitimate types in the Old Testament are types not because human beings have said so but because God is sovereign in the revelatory process. The reason some Old Testament persons or things foreshadowed someone or something in the New Testament is that God planned it that way.[6]

How, then, is Nimrod a type of the antichrist?

- Nimrod was the political head of Babylon, just as the antichrist will be the political head of New Babylon.
- He was a promoter of false religion, just as the antichrist will promote the false religion that forces people to worship him.
- His name means "rebel" and foreshadows the antichrist as a rebel against God.
- He was a hunter of human beings, much like the antichrist will hunt down Christians and Jews during the tribulation period and execute them.
- He was an enemy of Israel, just as the antichrist will be.

Aside from Nimrod, many Bible interpreters believe there are other types of the antichrist found in the Old Testament. In brief, these include:

- The devilish serpent in the garden of Eden that sought to corrupt God's paradise, instigating the first man and woman to rebel against God (Genesis 3).
- Amalek, the son of Esau (Genesis 36:12,16), whose descendants opposed Israel during the wilderness sojourn (Exodus 17:8-16; Deuteronomy 25:19; 1 Samuel 15:2-3).
- Balaam, a foreign prophet who stood against Israel (Numbers 22–24).
- The pharaoh of the exodus, who harshly oppressed the Israelites in Egypt and openly defied the one true God (Exodus 1:11,22; 5:2).
- The Assyrian king Sennacherib, who oppressed the northern kingdom and arrogantly sought to capture Jerusalem (2 Kings 18:13–19:37).
- The Babylonian king Nebuchadnezzar, who destroyed and desecrated the temple in Jerusalem, persecuted Israel in exile, and usurped divine prerogatives (2 Kings 24:13-14; Daniel 4:30).
- The Roman Caesars, who ruled the world and promoted emperor worship (see John 19:12,15).
- The Roman general Titus, who destroyed Jerusalem and the temple in AD 70.

By studying these various types of the antichrist, we find evidences that the antichrist in the end times will oppose the divine program, impose a foreign (anti-God) belief system upon people, oppose and oppress the people of God, seek to be worshipped, and desecrate the Jewish temple, among other things.

The Tower of Babel—Genesis 11:1-9

In Genesis 11:1-9 we read:

> At one time all the people of the world spoke the same language and used the same words. As the people migrated to the east, they found a plain in the land of Babylonia and settled there.
>
> They began saying to each other, "Let's make bricks and harden them with fire." (In this region bricks were used instead of stone, and tar was used for mortar.) Then they said, "Come, let's build a great city for ourselves with a tower that reaches into the sky. This will make us famous and keep us from being scattered all over the world."
>
> But the LORD came down to look at the city and the tower the people were building. "Look!" he said. "The people are united, and they all speak the same language. After this, nothing they set out to do will be impossible for them! Come, let's go down and confuse the people with different languages. Then they won't be able to understand each other."
>
> In that way, the LORD scattered them all over the world, and they stopped building the city. That is why the city was called Babel, because that is where the LORD confused the people with different languages. In this way he scattered them all over the world.

Let's consider what these verses are telling us. Genesis 11:1 says that "at one time all the people of the world spoke the same language and used the same words." There is increasing archeological evidence that at one time, all the people of the world had a single language. This is borne out in Sumerian literature, which alludes to this several times. One clay tablet uncovered by archaeologists records remarkable similarities to the Genesis 11 account of the tower of Babel and its destruction.

It's important to keep in mind that God created human language for a purpose. When God made Adam in His own rational image, He gave Adam the gift of intelligible speech. This enabled him to communicate objectively with his creator as well as with other human beings (Genesis 1:26; see also 11:1,7). God sovereignly chose to use human language as His means of giving humans His revelations, often through the "Thus saith the LORD" pronouncements of the prophets (see Isaiah 7:7; 10:24; 22:15; 28:16; 30:15; 49:22; 51:22; 52:4; 65:13).

It wasn't long before language—the gift of communication—was abused by sinful human beings. Whereas a single language was originally intended for blessing, it was now being used for sinful purposes. God thus found it necessary to confuse people by forcing them to speak different languages, thereby steering them off their hell-bent path to destruction.

God had commanded the peoples to be fruitful and multiply and to scatter across the earth, but they decided to move to Nimrod's city of Babel and settle there (11:1-12). This constituted blatant rebellion against God's command that the people scatter. Apparently, Nimrod wanted them in his cities and under his control.

The Building of a Ziggurat

Genesis 11:3-4 tells us that the people made bricks and sought to "build a great city...with a tower that reaches into the sky." They said, "This will make us famous and keep us from being scattered all over the world." Because there were few stones on this Babylonian plain, they had to make bricks. There's nothing wrong with that, but these bricks were to be used for an ungodly purpose. They were made with the intention of directly violating God's will.

The tower the people wanted to build was called a ziggurat, or a seven-staged tower. These ziggurats were considered means by which the gods above could visit the earth below. One Old Testament scholar put it this way:

> Ziggurats were structures designed to provide stairways from the heavens (the gate of the gods) to earth so that the gods could come down into their temple and into the town and bring blessing. It was a convenience provided for the deity and his messengers.[7]

Bible expositor Warren Wiersbe added:

> Archeologists have excavated several of these large structures which were built primarily for religious purposes. A ziggurat was like a pyramid except that the successive levels were recessed so that you could walk to the top on "steps." At the top was a special shrine dedicated to a god or goddess. In building the structure, the people weren't trying to climb up to heaven to dethrone God; rather, they hoped that the god or goddess they worshipped would come down from heaven to meet them. The structure and the city were called "Babel," which means "the gate of the gods."[8]

In ancient times, ziggurats were dedicated to a variety of different deities. In fact, any single deity could have several ziggurats dedicated to him or her in different cities. Even though a given city might have several ziggurats, the main one was always associated with the patron deity of the city.[9] There is some evidence that ziggurats were viewed as an earthly imitation of the heavenly residence of the gods.[10]

Each ziggurat was viewed as a channel of communication between the celestial and terrestrial domains—a meeting point between heaven and earth. A ziggurat was typically viewed as a "sacred mountain" and was "looked upon as the center of the universe," or the "navel of the earth."[11]

More than a few scholars have suggested that Nimrod's ultimate goal was overarching unity, or oneness. The people wanted to live in a city so that they could have political unity, and they wanted to build a tower or ziggurat for religious unity.[12]

One can see obvious parallels to New Babylon in Revelation 17 and 18. Political and commercial unity will be found in the literal city of New Babylon, which will have worldwide influence during the second half of the tribulation period. Religious unity will have already come upon the earth through the religious system associated with New Babylon during the first half of the tribulation.

"Let Us Make a Name for Ourselves"

The people under Nimrod's leadership were motivated to do all this because it "will make us famous" (Genesis 11:4 NLT), or, more literally, "make a name for ourselves" (ESV). Clearly, the people were attempting to usurp divine prerogatives here. After all, it was God alone who made Abram's name great, as well as David's (see Genesis 12:2; 2 Samuel 7:9; 8:13). Elsewhere in Scripture, God makes a name for Himself. Isaiah 63:12,14 speaks of God, saying, "Who caused his glorious arm to go at the right hand of Moses, who divided the waters before them to make for himself an everlasting name...You led your people, to make for yourself a glorious name."

In Jeremiah 32:20 we read of God, "You have shown signs and wonders in the land of Egypt, and to this day in Israel and among all mankind, and have made a name for yourself, as at this day." Nehemiah 9:10 tells us that God "performed signs and wonders against Pharaoh and all his servants and all the people of his land, for you knew that they acted arrogantly against our fathers. And you made a name for yourself, as it is to this day" (ESV). Seen against this context, the people of Babylon were clearly showing incredible arrogance in trying to make a name for themselves.

Bible expositor Charles Dyer gets to the heart of what happened:

> Babel was humanity's first united attempt to short-circuit God's purpose. This first post-Flood city was designed expressly to thwart God's plan for humankind. The people wanted unity and power, and Babel was to be the seat of that power. Babylon, the city of man trying to rise to heaven, was built in direct opposition to God's plan.[13]

Nimrod and his followers were revolting against God:

> This infamous project was an arrogant declaration of war against the Lord, not unlike the revolt described in Psalm 2:1-3. To begin with, the people were resisting God's edict to scatter and repopulate the earth...They decided to build a city and a great ziggurat and stay together. But even more, they wanted to make a name for themselves so that others would admire them and perhaps come and join them. Their purpose statement was the Devil's lie in Eden: "You will be like God" (Gen. 3:5 NIV).[14]

All this reminds us of Lucifer's sin—*pride* (Isaiah 14:14; Ezekiel 28:11-19; 1 Timothy 3:6). In his pride, Lucifer defied the one true God. The result was that he was judged by God. Now, the people at Babel sought to pridefully build a tower and "make a name" for themselves. They did this in defiance of the one true God. Just as God judged Lucifer, so did He judge those who participated in the building of the tower of Babel. We can also observe that New Babylon, and its god (the antichrist), will be judged and destroyed too.

Genesis 11:4 also reminds us of Lucifer. There, we read that the ziggurat "reaches into the sky," or, more literally, has its "top in the heavens" (ESV). We recall that Lucifer sought to "ascend above the heights of the clouds" and "make myself like the Most High" (Isaiah 14:14 ESV). Everything about Babel was devil-driven, just as it will be in the end times with New Babylon.

The Lord Came Down

Genesis 11:5 tells us, "The LORD came down to look at the city and the tower the people were building." Notice the irony here. The people, in their arrogance, wanted to build a high skyscraper. But now the Lord "came down" to see what was, from His perspective, a puny effort.

Bible expositor Kent Hughes observes,

> Here the satire peaks. The tower's top was in the sky where God ostensibly dwelt. But this was Yahweh, the infinitely transcendent and incomparably super-eminent God of the whole Old Testament, of whom Isaiah declared, "It is he who sits above the circle of the earth, and its inhabitants are like grasshoppers; who stretches out the heavens like a curtain, and spreads them like a tent to dwell in" (40:22 ESV). This Yahweh must draw near, not because he is near-sighted, but because he dwells at such tremendous height and their work is so tiny. Their tower was so microscopic that the all-seeing omnipotent God had to come down to see. It was as if God stooped down like a man on his hands and knees and lowered his face to the earth to see the great tower. The psalmist says, "He who sits in the heavens laughs; the Lord holds them in derision" (Psalm 2:4 ESV). Great peals of laughter echoed in the heavens.[15]

Of course, God did not need to investigate the tower of Babel to know what was going on there, for He is omniscient (all-knowing). The language used in Genesis 11:5, however, dramatizes the puniness of the people's efforts.

God Confused Their Languages

God then said, "Look!...The people are united, and they all speak the same language. After this, nothing they set out to do will be impossible for them" (Genesis 11:6). The meaning here is that

God knew that if the people of Babel succeeded here, they would continue their relentless pursuit of glory and fame. There would be no limit to their unrestrained rebellion against Him. They would continue building a human kingdom to the exclusion of God's kingdom. And that was something God could not permit.

As one scholar put it, God was troubled about what might happen to the people in Babel if their efforts went unchecked. "They would build up a delusion of self-sufficiency through their false religion," and they would "throw off God and attempt to rule the universe." It is possible that "their Babylonian hearts would become impenetrable and irredeemable."[16]

That is why God said, "Come, let's go down and confuse the people with different languages. Then they won't be able to understand each other" (Genesis 11:7).

Notice the contrast: The people had earlier said, "Come, let's" build a mighty tower (Genesis 11:4). Then God said, "Come, let's" confuse their languages (11:7). God answered the incredible arrogance of these people.

Ultimately, of course, God did it for their own good. His dispersion of them thwarted their march toward destruction. Church Father Jerome commented, "When the tower was being built up against God, those who were building it were disbanded for their own welfare. The conspiracy was evil. The dispersion was of true benefit even to those who were dispersed."[17]

Some Bible expositors interpret the word "let's" (*"let's* go down and confuse the people with different languages") as an Old Testament reference to the Trinity. In favor of this view is verse 5, which tells us that "the LORD came down to look at the city and the tower the people were building." Because it was the Lord who came down, the "let us" must be a reference to the Lord alone. The great Augustine commented, "It is conceivable that here there may have been an allusion to the Trinity, if we suppose that the Father said to the Son and the Holy Spirit, 'Come, let us descend and confound their tongue.' The supposition is sound."[18] Others believe God was addressing an angelic assembly in heaven, inviting them to participate in the judgment against those involved at the tower of Babel.

Either way, the ultimate goal was the same: Human languages would now be altered so that people could not communicate with each other. These people had sought worldwide fame. Now they would experience worldwide humiliation. They became famous in a very bad way.

The account about the tower of Babel closes with Genesis 11:8-9: "In that way, the LORD scattered them all over the world, and they stopped building the city. That is why the city was called Babel, because that is where the LORD confused the people with different languages. In this way he scattered them all over the world."

These sinful people had been instructed by God to fill the earth. They refused, congregated in one place in the land of Shinar, and defied God. God then forced them to fill the earth by confusing their language and dispersing them. *God had His way in the end*. As God put it in Isaiah 46:10, "Everything I plan will come to pass, for I do whatever I wish."

The Connection of Babel to New Babylon

Genesis 10–11 provides some relevant historical backdrop to what we read about New Babylon in Revelation 17–18. I say this because just as ancient Babel was both a literal city and symbolized a pagan religious system, so New Babylon will be a literal city and symbolize a pagan religious system. The parallels are obvious. As prophecy scholar Mark Hitchcock puts it:

> From the time of Genesis 10–11, the word Babylon has represented both a city and the religious system that arose in

that city. Babylon is a literal geographical location on the Euphrates River. But it is also the false religious system that began at the tower of Babel when, for the first time, men came together and organized their own religion in rebellion against God. That false religion spread out from there to all the other major nations of the earth and still affects us today. For example, how many millions of people still read horoscopes based on Babylonian astrological charts?[19]

After the rapture of the church, and after the tribulation period begins, Babylon will rise again—both the literal city and the pagan religious system that is rooted in it. Humans will again organize in rebellion against the one true God, just as they did at the tower of Babel. The tower and the city represent the two aspects of Babylon that continue today: religious rebellion and apostasy (Revelation 17) balanced against political and commercial power (Revelation 18).

My former prophecy mentor at Dallas Theological Seminary, John F. Walvoord, said, "Babylon was important not only politically but also religiously...From the beginning, then, Babylon was both a town and a tower, a city and a system, a place and a philosophy. We will encounter this same twofold depiction of Babylon later when we look at Babylon in Revelation 17–18."[20]

Closing Insights

Who would have thought we could learn a few life lessons from the historical depiction of Babel and New Babylon in the Bible? One of the key lessons here is the foolishness of human pride and arrogance. Peter said, "Dress yourselves in humility as you relate to one another, for 'God opposes the proud but gives grace to the humble'" (1 Peter 5:5). Pride is self-focused; humility is God-focused. Pride is self-exalting; humility is God-exalting. Pride distances one from God; humility draws one near to God.

We find many examples in Scripture of prideful individuals

who learned the hard way that pride goes before destruction. Consider this description of Satan: "You said to yourself, 'I will ascend to heaven and set my throne above God's stars. I will preside on the mountain of the gods'" (Isaiah 14:13). King Nebuchadnezzar of Babylon boasted, "Look at this great city of Babylon! By my own mighty power, I have built this beautiful city as my royal residence to display my majestic splendor" (Daniel 4:30). Centuries later, after Herod gave a public address, the people shouted, "It's the voice of a god, not of a man," and Herod did not correct them (Acts 12:21-22).

What do these three have in common? They were all judged and humbled by God. They learned the truth of Jesus's words: "Those who exalt themselves will be humbled" (Matthew 23:12). They learned that "pride goes before destruction, and haughtiness before a fall" (Proverbs 16:18). They learned that God does not like pretenders to the divine throne. New Babylon will learn this lesson in a big way at the end of the tribulation period.

6

Historical Insights from Daniel

In chapter 5 we considered key insights from Genesis, and I introduced the subject of typology. I demonstrated that Nimrod was a "type" of the antichrist. We will continue that discussion in this chapter and focus on how King Nebuchadnezzar of Babylon was also a type of the antichrist.

To review, a type may be defined as a figure or representation of something yet to come. More specifically, a type is "an Old Testament institution, event, person, object, or ceremony which has reality and purpose in biblical history, but which also by divine design foreshadows something yet to be revealed."[1] Types are therefore prophetic in nature.

Types do not involve mere coincidences. They occur in the Old Testament because God is sovereign in the revelatory process. The reason some Old Testament persons or things foreshadowed someone or something in the New Testament is that God planned it that way. By studying types, we gain keen insights into God's intended meaning on specific prophetic persons or events.

Babylon's Dominance, Defiance, and Deities

Daniel was taken captive as a youth to Babylon by King Nebu-chadnezzar in 605 BC. He was 15 or 16 years old when this hap-pened and ended up spending the rest of his life there—perhaps 85 years or more. He was assigned to be a governmental official in charge of assisting with the imported Jews taken into captivity.

There were three deportations involved in Babylon's victory over Judah. The first took place in 605 BC and included Daniel and his friends. The second occurred in 597 BC and included the prophet Ezekiel. The third was in 586 BC, when the Babylonians destroyed both Jerusalem and its temple.

We might wonder why God would allow His people—the Jews—to go into captivity in a thoroughly pagan nation like Babylon. In the book of Deuteronomy, God—through Moses—promised great blessings if the nation lived in obedience to the Sinai covenant. God also warned that if the nation disobeyed His commands, it would experience the punishments listed in the covenant—including exile from the land (Deuteronomy 28:15-68).

Old Testament history is brimming with examples of how unfaithful Israel was to God's covenant. And just as God promised, disobedience brought exile to God's people.

Ultimately, the Babylonian captivity was God's chosen means of chastening Judah. This punishment was intended as a corrective. Throughout both the Old and New Testaments, we find that God disciplines His children to purify them. Just as an earthly father dis-ciplines his children, so God the heavenly Father disciplines His children to train and educate them (Hebrews 12:1-5; see also Job 5:17; 33:19; Psalm 118:18; Proverbs 3:11-12). The prophet Daniel, in his book, indicated that God yet has a future for His people. Indeed, that future includes Israel during the tribulation period, when the Jewish people will experience severe persecution by the antichrist.

The biblical text tells us that when King Nebuchadnezzar of Babylon destroyed the Jewish temple, he took "some of the sacred objects from the Temple of God" (Daniel 1:2). These objects would have included the golden altar, the golden table for the Bread of the Presence, the lampstands of pure gold, the tongs of gold, the cups, the snuffers, the basins, the dishes for incense, and the fire pans of pure gold (1 Kings 7:48-51). The seizing of these sacred objects as spoils were believed by the Babylonians to represent the victory of Babylon's gods over the God of Israel.

Like other pagan nations of the ancient Near East, the Babylonians believed in many false gods and goddesses. These gods were thought to control the entire world of nature, and if a person sought to be successful in life, he or she would do well to placate the gods. It was also believed that the military victories of the Babylonians were an indication that their gods were more powerful than any other nation's gods. However, in the Babylonian religious system, the behavior of the gods was considered unpredictable at best.

Each city in Babylon had a patron god with an accompanying temple. There were also a number of small shrines scattered about each city where people often met to worship various other deities.

Given this brief introduction to the book of Daniel and quick survey of Babylon, let's consider some of the typological elements that we've witnessed so far:

- Just as ancient Babylon promoted false religion, so New Babylon will promote false religion.
- Just as ancient Babylon was an important commercial and trade center in the ancient world, so New Babylon will be a commercial powerhouse.
- Just as Nebuchadnezzar and ancient Babylon were dominant over the Jewish people and their temple, so the antichrist and New Babylon in the end times will be dominant over the Jews.

- Just as the ancient Jewish temple was defiled by Nebuchadnezzar and plundered of its sacred objects, so the antichrist
  will defile the Jewish temple of the tribulation period by sitting within it and putting up an image of himself in it.
- Just as God purposefully allowed the Jews to be taken captive
  by Babylon to chastise them, so God will purposefully allow
  Israel to go through the tribulation period, during which New
  Babylon will be dominant. God will use this to prepare a Jewish remnant to repent and turn to Jesus as their Messiah at the
  end of the tribulation period.

Forced Submission to a False Religion

Nebuchadnezzar dreamed of a statue of a man made of gold, silver, bronze, and iron, and Daniel informed him that he was the head
of gold on the statue (Daniel 2:38). In his megalomania, Nebuchadnezzar went on to erect a full golden image of himself—gold from
head to toe—to put an exclamation point on his greatness.

In Daniel 3:1-7 we read,

> King Nebuchadnezzar made a gold statue ninety feet tall
> and nine feet wide and set it up on the plain of Dura in the
> province of Babylon. Then he sent messages to the high
> officers, officials, governors, advisers, treasurers, judges,
> magistrates, and all the provincial officials to come to the
> dedication of the statue he had set up. So all these officials
> came and stood before the statue King Nebuchadnezzar
> had set up.
>
> Then a herald shouted out, "People of all races and
> nations and languages, listen to the king's command!
> When you hear the sound of the horn, flute, zither, lyre,
> harp, pipes, and other musical instruments, bow to the
> ground to worship King Nebuchadnezzar's gold statue.

Anyone who refuses to obey will immediately be thrown into a blazing furnace."

So at the sound of the musical instruments, all the people, whatever their race or nation or language, bowed to the ground and worshiped the gold statue that King Nebuchadnezzar had set up.

There were many varying ranks of Babylonian government officials present at the ceremony, and this golden image served to portray Nebuchadnezzar as the one who was over all of them.

The image was 90 feet tall and only 9 feet wide. This 10-to-1 ratio would make this statue very skinny. (The ratio of a normal human being is more like 5 to 1.) It may be that the image pictured a more normal-looking human figure elevated upon some type of massive base that made him appear high and exalted.

Because of its height and the fact it was made of gold, the statue was no doubt an imposing symbol of Nebuchadnezzar's majesty and authority. Because it was to be worshipped, it was clearly an idol.

All the government officials were required to bow in worship of the image to show their full and unqualified allegiance to Nebuchadnezzar. Daniel would not have been present with this group; the biblical text informs us that he remained in the capital city "in the king's court" (Daniel 2:49). Daniel's three friends, however—Shadrach, Meshach, and Abednego—were called to Dura to show their loyalty.

In obedience to Nebuchadnezzar, the seven classes of government officials all showed up to the dedication ceremony and demonstrated their respect by standing before the statue. The fact that they would be required to bow down and worship the image had both religious and political significance. In other words, their bowing would not only serve as a recognition of Nebuchadnezzar's divine status but would also indicate submission to his political power and authority.

The penalty for refusing to bow down and worship was incineration in what was apparently an industrial-sized oven used for smelting metals and baking bricks. Nebuchadnezzar used this same punishment against two Judean false prophets, Zedekiah and Ahab (Jeremiah 29:22). It appears that this may have been a common Babylonian means of execution, as indicated in the Code of Hammurabi (Sections 25, 110, and 157).

An awesome and formidable image stood before the people. The king had given the command. Now the music started. On cue, all the government officials showed their submission by bowing. Nebuchadnezzar thereby achieved what he wanted—an open display of leaders vowing political and religious submission.

We then read in Daniel 3:8-12 that some of the king's assistants— *astrologers*—brought charges against Daniel's friends:

> Some of the astrologers went to the king and informed on the Jews. They said to King Nebuchadnezzar, "Long live the king! You issued a decree requiring all the people to bow down and worship the gold statue when they hear the sound of the horn, flute, zither, lyre, harp, pipes, and other musical instruments. That decree also states that those who refuse to obey must be thrown into a blazing furnace. But there are some Jews—Shadrach, Meshach, and Abednego—whom you have put in charge of the province of Babylon. They pay no attention to you, Your Majesty. They refuse to serve your gods and do not worship the gold statue you have set up."

When Shadrach, Meshach, and Abednego refused to bow, they were acting under clear instructions from God's law. In Exodus 20:3-5 God commanded: "You must not have any other god but me. You must not make for yourself an idol of any kind or an image of anything in the heavens or on the earth or in the sea. You must not bow down to them or worship them, for I, the LORD your God, am a jealous God who will not tolerate your affection for any other gods." Shadrach, Meshach, and Abednego had to choose between King Nebuchadnezzar and the one true God, who is the King of kings. They chose wisely!

In their refusal to bow, the three Hebrew youths likely recalled some of God's promises. For example, in Isaiah 43:1-2 God promised His people: "Israel, the one who formed you says, 'Do not be afraid, for I have ransomed you. I have called you by name; you are mine. When you go through deep waters, I will be with you. When you go through rivers of difficulty, you will not drown. When you walk through the fire of oppression, you will not be burned up; the flames will not consume you." Based on their faith in the God of promises, Shadrach, Meshach, and Abednego stood tall while all the other leaders bowed low.

This brings up the controversial issue of whether it is ever justified for God's people to disobey civil authorities. Many Christians have concluded that they must obey the government unless the government explicitly orders them to go against one or more of God's commands found in Scripture. When that happens, believers must obey God rather than the government.

An illustration of this principle may be found in the New Testament. After being ordered by the Sanhedrin (the Jewish government) not to preach any further, "Peter and the apostles replied, 'We must obey God rather than any human authority'" (Acts 5:29). God commanded Peter and the others to preach; the Jewish government told them not to preach. They chose to obey God rather than human government. Shadrach, Meshach, and Abednego likewise chose to obey God over men.

It would have been one thing for Shadrach, Meshach, and Abednego to privately refuse to bow before the golden image. But the three youths were public about their refusal. To Nebuchadnezzar, this represented an obvious defiance of his religious and political authority. He was therefore enraged. He immediately ordered that these three be brought before him.

Nebuchadnezzar questioned the lads and told them if they refused to bow down to the image, they'd be thrown into a furnace. He then asked, "What god will be able to rescue you from my power?" (Daniel 3:15). Nebuchadnezzar apparently considered himself as being higher than all other gods, for he said no other gods could turn back his hand or circumvent his authority.

The end result was that they were indeed thrown into the fiery furnace, but God delivered them such that not even a single hair on their heads was singed. God does not always choose this kind of deliverance; sometimes He allows His children to be martyred. Daniel's friends were ready for martyrdom, but God had other plans.

In light of this brief overview of the faithfulness of Daniel's friends, let's consider some of the typological elements that we've witnessed in our Scripture passage:

- Just as idolatry was rampant in ancient Babylon, so idolatry will be rampant in New Babylon.

- Just as Nebuchadnezzar had religious assistants (astrologers and other occultists), so the antichrist will have a religious assistant called the false prophet.

- Just as an image was erected representing the authority and divine status of Nebuchadnezzar, so the antichrist will place an image of himself in the Jewish temple—an image representing his godhood and authority.

- Just as Nebuchadnezzar with his image called for both

religious and political submission, so the antichrist and New Babylon will call for religious and political submission.

- Just as forced submission to a false religion took place in ancient Babylon, so forced submission to a false religion (involving worship of the antichrist)—enforced by the mark of the beast—will take place in New Babylon.

- Just as a death penalty awaited those who refused to bow to Nebuchadnezzar's image, so many who reject the antichrist in the end times will face martyrdom.

- Just as God sovereignly protected three of His servants on earth from death in ancient Babylon, so God in the tribulation period will sovereignly protect His 144,000 Jewish servants who are "marked with the seal of God" (Revelation 7:4).

- Just as Daniel's friends were willing to face death because of the wonderful promises of God, so believers in the tribulation period will be willing to face death because of God's promises.

- Just as Nebuchadnezzar considered himself as god above all other deities, so the antichrist will "exalt himself and defy everything that people call god and every object of worship" (2 Thessalonians 2:4).

Antiochus Epiphanes—Another Type of the Antichrist

In Daniel 8 we find mention of Antiochus Epiphanes, whom many scholars believe also to be a type of the antichrist. In Daniel 8:10 we are told that Antiochus threw "some of the stars to the ground" and trampled them. There is no small controversy among Bible expositors as to what this means. However, a consensus has emerged among many that the term "stars" likely refers to the Jewish people. Hence, this metaphorical language apparently describes Antiochus's relentless persecution of the Jewish people. Keep in mind that in Scripture, the term "stars" is often used in reference to the Jewish people. For example, recall Joseph's dream: "Listen, I have had another dream…The sun, moon, and eleven stars bowed low before me!" (Genesis 37:9). In this dream, the sun (Joseph's father), the moon (Joseph's mother), and the 11 stars (Joseph's 11 brothers) would one day bow before him. These astronomical terms refer to the whole clan of Israel.

Likewise, in Revelation 12:1 we encounter a metaphorical description of Israel as a woman who has a "crown of twelve stars." The 12 stars represent the 12 tribes of Israel. We can conclude, then, that Antiochus's trampling of the stars refers to his trampling of the Jewish people. And history reveals that Antiochus did in fact brutally persecute the Jewish people from 170–164 BC.

Daniel 8:11 then tells us that Antiochus "challenged the Commander of heaven's army." Antiochus, by his actions, was putting himself in the place of God. This, of course, is not the first time in the book of Daniel that a human leader set himself up as God. Recall how Nebuchadnezzar spoke of himself in divine terms (Daniel 3:1-7). Darius, too, was prayed to as a god for a time (6:6-9).

Antiochus then stopped the daily sacrifices in the Jewish temple, thereby halting Israel's religious practices (Daniel 8:11). He also defiled the temple by slaughtering a pig within the Holy of Holies. Apparently he was seeking to destroy the Jewish faith.

Antiochus then trashed the law of Moses, which was communicated to Moses by God (Daniel 8:12). This act essentially amounted to trashing God. Speaking of Antiochus, 1 Maccabees 1:56-57 informs us, "The books of the law which they found they tore in pieces and burned with fire. Where the book of the covenant was found in the possession of anyone, or if anyone adhered to the law, the decree of the king condemned them to death."

This wicked Jew-hater prospered in some of his plans—but only for a time, according to the divine timetable (see Daniel 8:14). One of God's angels—a "holy one"—announced that Antiochus's defiling of Israel and her temple would last only 2,300 evenings and mornings—from 171 BC to 165 BC.

A bit later in Daniel, Antiochus is called "a fierce king, a master of intrigue" (verse 23). History reveals that he took the throne through deceit and guile. Verse 25 tells us, "He will be a master of deception and will become arrogant; he will destroy many without warning." He was not only deceitful, he was also cunning, full of guile, treacherous, and unscrupulous. Many of the people he destroyed were Jewish.

We are also told in verse 25 that Antiochus "will even take on the Prince of princes in battle." Antiochus, a pagan king, raised himself up as a divine being against Israel's king, the most high God, the ruler of heaven and earth.

Not unexpectedly, we are then told that Antiochus "will be broken, though not by human power" (verse 25). Antiochus would be destroyed by God's hand. God sovereignly determines the day a person dies. As Job said to God, "You have decided the length of our lives. You know how many months we will live, and we are not given a minute longer" (Job 14:5; see also Psalm 139:16; Acts 17:26). Scripture also reveals that God sometimes inflicts premature death as a judgment (see Acts 5:1-10; 12:23; 1 Corinthians 11:30; 1 John 5:16).

Given this backdrop, it is easy to see how Antiochus was a type of the antichrist. Just as Antiochus set himself up as God and defiled the Jewish temple, so will the antichrist set himself up as God and defile the Jewish temple. Just as Antiochus was a fierce persecutor of the Jews, so will the antichrist persecute the Jews. Just as Antiochus's power was great, so will the antichrist's power be great. Just as Antiochus operated through deceit and guile, so will the antichrist. Just as Antiochus was destroyed by God, so will the antichrist be destroyed by God—that is, by Jesus Christ at the second coming (Revelation 19:11-21).

All this becomes even more significant when we realize that much of what was true about Antiochus will also be true of New Babylon. Indeed, New Babylon will be a fierce persecutor of the Jews (Revelation 18:24), New Babylon's power will be great (18:3,9), New Babylon will engage in great deception (18:23), and New Babylon will be destroyed by God (18:2,6,8,9).

Prophecies of the Antichrist

The book of Daniel not only speaks typologically about the antichrist, but also provides specific prophecies about his life and character. For example, Daniel 11:36 tells us, "The king will do as he pleases, exalting himself and claiming to be greater than every god, even blaspheming the God of gods." There are two observations we can make here: (1) Instead of seeking God's will, the antichrist will be self-willed. (2) As a qualification, however, Scripture also seems to indicate that the antichrist will do as Satan wills. Second Thessalonians 2:9 tells us that "this man will come to do the work of Satan with counterfeit power and signs and miracles." Of course, Satan himself is self-willed, so it is not surprising that the antichrist will be too.

Notice that just as the antichrist will exalt himself as god and seek to be worshipped (2 Thessalonians 2:4; Revelation 13:5-8), Scripture reveals that Satan earlier sought to exalt himself to deity (Isaiah 14:12-17; Ezekiel 28:11-19). The antichrist will take on the character of the one who controls him.

The fact that the antichrist claims to be greater than any god and blasphemes the "God of gods" is consistent with what we learn from Revelation 13:5-6: "The beast [antichrist] was allowed to speak great blasphemies against God. And he was given authority to do whatever he wanted for forty-two months. And he spoke terrible words of blasphemy against God, slandering his name and his dwelling—that is, those who dwell in heaven" (insert added for clarification). There is no greater blasphemy than this. The antichrist truly is *anti*-Christ, even putting himself in Christ's place. We are also told that the antichrist—the world dictator—will demand that the world worship and pay idolatrous homage to him. Anyone who refuses will be persecuted and even martyred.

Daniel 11:38 tells us that the antichrist "will worship the god of fortresses." The "god of fortresses" is a metaphorical way of describing the antichrist's unquenchable thirst for power. In other words, power will be the antichrist's god. He won't be satisfied until he attains world dominion (see 2 Thessalonians 2:4; Revelation 13:8,15). He will use the incredible material wealth at his disposal (gold, silver, precious stones) to build up his military arsenal. Much of this wealth will no doubt be rooted in New Babylon (Revelation 18).

Daniel 11:45 tells us that "his time will suddenly run out, and no one will help him." The ESV more accurately translates this, "He shall come to his end, with none to help him." Apparently the antichrist meets his end in connection with Israel's conversion to Christ at the end of the tribulation period (Zechariah 12:2–13:1). Scripture reveals that Israel will confess its national sin (Leviticus 26:40-42; Jeremiah 3:11-18; Hosea 5:15), at which time Israel will be saved, thereby fulfilling Paul's prophecy in Romans 11:25-27.

As the forces of antichrist are closing in on the Jewish remnant during Armageddon, Israel will recognize their Messiah and plead for Him to return and deliver them (they will "mourn for him as for an only son"—Zechariah 12:10; Matthew 23:37-39; see also Isaiah 53:1-9), at which point their deliverance will come (see Romans 10:13-14). Israel's leaders will have finally realized the reason that the tribulation has fallen on them—perhaps due to the Holy Spirit's enlightenment of their understanding of Scripture, or the testimony of the 144,000 Jewish evangelists, or perhaps the testimony of the two prophetic witnesses.

We are then told that at the Lord's second coming, "the beast was captured, and with him the false prophet who did mighty miracles on behalf of the beast—miracles that deceived all who had accepted the mark of the beast and who worshiped his statue. Both the beast and his false prophet were thrown alive into the fiery lake of burning sulfur" (Revelation 19:20).

What a turn of events!

- At Armageddon, New Babylon will be destroyed.
- The Jewish remnant will find salvation in the Jewish Messiah, Jesus Christ, who will rescue them from the forces of the antichrist.
- The antichrist and false prophet will be destroyed and cast into the lake of fire.
- Christ will then set up His glorious kingdom. How awesome it will be!

Typology and Babylon's Destruction

During a feast, King Belshazzar of Babylon witnessed a hand writing words on a wall. This writing was a message directly from God: "MENE, MENE, TEKEL, and PARSIN" (Daniel 5:25). Daniel translated the words for Belshazzar:

Mene is an Aramaic word meaning "numbered" or "counted." The word is repeated by God for emphasis. Because of Belshazzar's pride and wickedness, God had numbered his days and his kingdom. Babylon would soon come to its demise due to a siege set up by an invading Medo-Persian force.

Tekel is an Aramaic word meaning "weighed" or "assessed." God is the one who weighs a person's actions and motives (see 1 Samuel 2:3; Psalm 62:9). God, as the divine Judge, evaluates people and gives a verdict. Belshazzar had been weighed, and he and his kingdom were found to be ripe for judgment.

Peres is an Aramaic word meaning "divided." Babylon was soon to be destroyed and taken over by the Medo-Persian Empire.

In short, God's message to Belshazzar was this: "You have grievously sinned. You have been defiant. You have not repented. You are terminated." That very night, King Belshazzar—who had pridefully and arrogantly exalted himself—forfeited his life via divine judgment at the hands of the Medo-Persian invading force (Daniel 5:30).

Scripture reveals that New Babylon will be destroyed toward the very end of the tribulation period. We read of a calamitous war campaign called *Armageddon* (see Daniel 11:40-45; Joel 3:9-17; Zechariah 14:1-3; Revelation 16:14-16). Millions of people will perish in the worst conflict ever to hit the earth.

Armageddon will involve an extended, escalating conflict, and it will be catastrophic. In view of all that occurs at Armageddon, it would be wrong to refer to it as a battle, as if it were a single event. In fact, the campaign of Armageddon will have eight stages.

It is at stage two of Armageddon that New Babylon will be destroyed by an invading force from the north. This northern army will act as God's whipping rod against New Babylon every bit as much as the Medes and Persians were His whipping rod against the Babylonians in Old Testament times. The destruction of New Babylon is documented in Revelation 18, which I will discuss a bit later in the book. For now it is enough to note that ancient Babylon's demise is a "type" of New Babylon's destruction in the end times. I can almost hear God saying to the antichrist and New Babylon,

"You have sinned grievously. You have been defiant. You have not repented. You are terminated."

Typology and God's Kingdom

As Daniel explained to Nebuchadnezzar the meaning of his dream about an image made of gold, silver, bronze, and iron, he noted that a rock had struck the image at its feet (Daniel 2:34). First the feet shattered, then the rest of the body shattered. Then the remaining particles blew away in the wind—like chaff. (Chaff refers to worthless husks that separate from the grain during the process of threshing.) Not a trace of the image could thereafter be found.

In Scripture, the term "rock" is often used in reference to the divine Messiah, Jesus Christ (see Psalm 118:22; Isaiah 8:14; 28:16; 1 Peter 2:6-8). Following the destruction of the image by the rock (Jesus Christ), we are told, "The rock that knocked the statue down became a great mountain that covered the whole earth" (Daniel 2:35). In the Bible, mountains often represent kingdoms. Not only will Christ overthrow the earthly kingdoms, but He will—following His second coming—set up His own millennial kingdom over all the earth, which will last 1,000 years (Revelation 11:15; 19:11-20; 20:4).

The prophesies in the book of Daniel line up perfectly with those in the book of Revelation. We read of New Babylon's destruction in Revelation 18, the second coming of Christ in chapter 19, and the establishment of Christ's millennial kingdom in chapter 20.

Parallels Between the Past and the Future

We learn much about the antichrist and Babylon from the typology found in the book of Daniel and comparing it with Revelation chapters 17 and 18. By studying these various types, we find evidences that the antichrist and/or New Babylon will...

- oppose the divine program
- impose a foreign (anti-God) religious belief system upon people
- require forced submission to a false religion
- blaspheme the one true God
- engage in rampant idolatry
- seek to force the world to engage in various forms of wrongful worship
- oppose and oppress the people of God, even putting them to death
- and be defeated and destroyed by the Lord in the end

We also find these typological references confirmed by and expanded upon by direct end-time prophecies in the book of Daniel:

- The tribulation period will begin when the antichrist signs a covenant with Israel (Daniel 9:27).
- The tribulation period will last precisely seven years (Daniel 9:27).
- The tribulation period will be the worst period ever to come upon humanity (Daniel 12:1).
- During the tribulation period God will resume His special dealings with Israel (Daniel 9:26-27).
- God provides a prophetic timetable for Israel (Daniel 9).
- There will be a revived Roman Empire in the tribulation period, over which the antichrist will rule (Daniel 2; 7).
- Daniel reveals that the antichrist will have a great intellect, be an expert in commerce, and have strong oratorical skills (Daniel 8:23; 11:36,43).
- The antichrist will exalt himself over every god (Daniel 11:36).

- The antichrist will desecrate the Jewish temple (Daniel 11:31).
- The antichrist will persecute the saints for an extended time (Daniel 7:21).

My friends, sobering days lie ahead!

7

The Role of the Antichrist
in New Babylon

The antichrist will emerge into power during the future tribulation period (Daniel 8:9-11; 11:31-38; 12:11; Matthew 24:15; 2 Thessalonians 2:1-12; Revelation 13:1-5; 19:20; 20:10). This individual will be the embodiment of all that is anti-God and anti-Christian. The Greek word translated *anti* means "instead of," "against," and "opposed to." More than any other, the antichrist will position himself as "*instead of* Christ," "*against* Christ," and "*opposed to* Christ." He will set himself up against Christ and the people of God in the last days before the second coming. More than 100 passages of Scripture speak of this diabolical being.

The apostle Paul calls him a "man of lawlessness" (2 Thessalonians 2:3,8,9). The antichrist will perform counterfeit signs and wonders and deceive many people during the tribulation period (2 Thessalonians 2:9-10). The apostle John describes him as "the Beast" (Revelation 13:1-10). This Satan-empowered individual will rise to political prominence in the tribulation period, seek to dominate the world, attempt to destroy the Jews, persecute all true believers in Jesus Christ, set himself up as God in a rebuilt Jewish temple, and set up his own kingdom (Revelation 13).

The antichrist will speak arrogant and boastful words in glorifying himself (2 Thessalonians 2:4). Eventually he will rule the whole world (Revelation 13:7), with his headquarters initially set up in Rome (Revelation 17:8-9), then for a time in Jerusalem (Matthew 24:15-20), and finally in New Babylon (Revelation 18). He will be defeated and destroyed by Jesus at His second coming (Revelation 19:11-16), and is destined for the lake of fire (Revelation 19:20).

The Antichrist Mimics Christ

In the introduction of this book, I noted that Jerusalem is the most-often-mentioned city in the Bible, and Babylon is second. While Jerusalem means "city of peace," Babylon means "city of confusion and war." While Jerusalem is portrayed as God's city in the Bible (Revelation 21:2-3), Babylon is portrayed as a demonic city (18:2). While the New Jerusalem is portrayed as a chaste bride (Revelation 21:9-10), New Babylon is described as a great prostitute (17:1,3). While the New Jerusalem is portrayed as an eternal city (Revelation 21:1-4), New Babylon is portrayed as a temporal city that will be destroyed by God Himself (18:8).

It is highly revealing to compare the true and ultimate ruler of Jerusalem (Jesus Christ) with the ruler of New Babylon (the antichrist). When we do, we find that the antichrist will make every attempt to mimic the true Christ in multiple ways:

- Jesus did miracles, signs, and wonders (Matthew 9:32-33; Mark 6:2). The antichrist will do counterfeit miracles, signs, and wonders (Matthew 24:24; 2 Thessalonians 2:9).
- Jesus will appear in the millennial temple (Ezekiel 43:6-7). The antichrist will sit in the tribulation temple (2 Thessalonians 2:4).

- Jesus is God (John 1:1-2; 10:36). The antichrist will claim to be God (2 Thessalonians 2:4).

- Jesus is the Lion from Judah (Revelation 5:5). The antichrist will have a mouth like a lion (Revelation 13:2).

- Jesus made a peace covenant with Israel (Ezekiel 37:26). The antichrist will make a different kind of peace covenant with Israel (Daniel 9:27).

- Jesus causes human beings to worship God (Revelation 1:6). The antichrist will cause human beings to worship both Satan and himself (Revelation 13:3-4).

- Followers of Jesus will be sealed on their forehead during the tribulation period (Revelation 7:4; 14:1). Followers of the antichrist will be sealed on their forehead or right hand (Revelation 13:16-18).

- Jesus has a worthy name (Revelation 19:16). The antichrist will have blasphemous names (Revelation 13:1).

- Jesus will get married to a virtuous bride (Revelation 19:7-9). The antichrist will be associated with a vile prostitute (Revelation 17:3-5).

- Jesus will be crowned with many crowns (Revelation 19:12). The antichrist will be crowned with ten crowns (Revelation 13:1).

- Jesus is the King of kings (Revelation 19:16). The antichrist will be called "the king" (Daniel 11:36).

- Jesus will sit on a throne (Revelation 3:21; 12:5; 20:11). The antichrist will sit on a throne (Revelation 13:2; 16:10).

- Jesus will have a one-thousand-year worldwide kingdom (Revelation 20:1-6). The antichrist will have a three-and-a-half-year worldwide kingdom (Revelation 13:5-8).

- Jesus is part of the Holy Trinity—Father, Son, and Holy Spirit

(2 Corinthians 13:14). The antichrist will be part of an unholy trinity—Satan, the antichrist, and the false prophet (Revelation 13).

It is not surprising that the antichrist will mimic Christ, for he will be inspired by Satan, and other scriptures reveal that Satan himself is a great counterfeiter. For example, Scripture reveals that Satan has his own church—a synagogue that "belongs to Satan" (Revelation 2:9). Satan has his own ministers—ministers of darkness who proclaim a different Jesus and gospel (2 Corinthians 11:4-5). He has formulated his own system of theology—"teachings that come from demons" (1 Timothy 4:1; Revelation 2:24). His ministers spread a counterfeit gospel—"a different kind of Good News than the one we preached to you" (Galatians 1:7-8). Satan has his own throne (Revelation 13:2) and worshippers (13:4). He inspires false Christs and self-constituted messiahs (Matthew 24:4-5). He employs false teachers who teach "destructive heresies" (2 Peter 2:1). He sends out false prophets (Matthew 24:11) and sponsors false apostles who imitate the true (2 Corinthians 11:13). Satan, the master mimicker, will also inspire the antichrist's mimicking of Christ (2 Thessalonians 2:9).

Dissimilarities Between Christ and the Antichrist

Despite the many ways the antichrist will seek to mimic Christ, Scripture points to many dissimilarities that exist between the two:

- One is called the Christ (Matthew 16:16); the other the antichrist (1 John 4:3).
- One is called the man of sorrows (Isaiah 53:3); the other the man of sin (2 Thessalonians 2:3).
- One is called the Son of God (John 1:34); the other the son of perdition (2 Thessalonians 2:3).

- One is called the Lamb (Isaiah 53:7); the other the beast (Revelation 11:7).

- One is called the Holy One (Mark 1:24); the other the wicked one (2 Thessalonians 2:8).

- Christ came to do the Father's will (John 6:38); the antichrist will do his own will (Daniel 11:36).

- Christ was energized by the Holy Spirit (Luke 4:14); the antichrist will be energized by Satan, the *un*holy spirit (2 Thessalonians 2:9; Revelation 13:4).

- Christ submitted Himself to God (John 5:30); the antichrist will defy God (2 Thessalonians 2:4).

- Christ humbled Himself (Philippians 2:8); the antichrist will exalt himself (Daniel 11:37).

- Christ honored the God of His fathers (Luke 4:16); the antichrist will refuse to do so (Daniel 11:37).

- Christ cleansed the temple (John 2:14,16); the antichrist will defile the temple (Matthew 24:15).

- Christ was rejected by many (Isaiah 53:7); the antichrist will—by force—be accepted by many (Revelation 13:4).

- Christ was slain for the people (John 11:51); the antichrist will be the slayer of people (Isaiah 14:20).

- Christ was received up into heaven (Luke 24:51); the antichrist will go down into the lake of fire (Revelation 19:20).

The Character of the Antichrist

Strong Appearance. Daniel 7:20 reveals that the antichrist will seem "greater than the others," and will be a "fierce king" (8:23). The whole world "will be amazed at" the appearance of the antichrist (see Revelation 17:8; see also 13:3-4). He will decidedly manifest this strength in New Babylon.

Intellectual Genius. The Old Testament speaks of the antichrist as "one who understands riddles" (Daniel 8:23 ESV)—a Jewish idiom indicating great intellect. That which may baffle other humans will be child's play for him. The antichrist's mind will be energized by Satan (2 Thessalonians 2:9), who himself has a far greater intellect than mere human beings (Revelation 13:2).

Oratorical Genius. Daniel 7:8 reveals that the antichrist will have "a mouth speaking great things" (ESV; see also Daniel 7:20). He will have "the mouth of a lion" (Revelation 13:2), which Bible interpreters believe means that his oratorical skills will be awe-producing. The antichrist will apparently have a perfect mastery of language and speak eloquently. His oratory will not only gain widespread attention but command respect from the masses. His oratorical skills will no doubt play a role in the global success of commercial New Babylon in the end times.

Philosophical Genius. The antichrist will be a master at setting forth an anti-God philosophy that will sway the masses. This philosophy will be demon-driven (Revelation 16:13; see also 1 Timothy 4:1), and many will be deceived (see John 8:44; 1 Timothy 4:1; 1 John 4:1-6). The philosophies of hedonism and materialism will especially permeate New Babylon.

Political Genius. The antichrist will emerge from apparent obscurity. By his profound diplomatic skills, however, he will win the admiration of the political world and compel many to follow his lead. Though he will begin his political career as a "little horn" (Daniel 7:8), he will be catapulted into global fame and power by means of brilliant statesmanship. He will quickly ascend to the topmost rung of the political world (Revelation 17:12-13). At the center of this world will be New Babylon.

Governmental Genius. Because of the antichrist's strong governing abilities, other global leaders "will agree to give their authority to the scarlet beast" (Revelation 17:16-17). He will bring unity where there had been conflict, and all the world will marvel at his abilities. His governing abilities will especially shine in New Babylon.

Commercial Genius. During the tribulation period, no one will be able to buy or sell anything without receiving the mark of the antichrist (Revelation 13:17). All commerce will come under his absolute control, with his headquarters in New Babylon. With today's technology—supercomputers, smart cards, RFID chips, biometrics, GPS technology, and the like—this policy will be easy to enforce.

Military Genius. Revelation 6:2 tells us that the antichrist "rode out to win many battles and gain the victory." People living during that time will say, "Who is as great as the beast?…Who is able to fight against him?" (13:4). Fear of the antichrist will motivate obedience to him.

Religious Genius. The antichrist will first use the false religion associated with New Babylon to bring unity to the world. Once that is accomplished, he and his forces will destroy the false religion and he will proclaim himself God (see 2 Thessalonians 2:4). People will readily pay him homage (Revelation 13:14-15).

A Defiant Personality. The antichrist will be the most defiant, arrogant, proud, and self-impressed person the world has ever known. In Daniel 11:36-37 we read that the antichrist "will do as he pleases, exalting himself and claiming to be greater than every god, even blaspheming the God of gods…He will have no respect for the gods of his ancestors…for he will boast that he is greater than them all." Indeed, he "will exalt himself and defy everything that people call god and every object of worship. He will even sit in the temple of God, claiming that he himself is God" (2 Thessalonians 2:3-4).

Full of Religious Deception. There will be massive deception in the end times (1 Timothy 4:1; 2 Timothy 4:3-4). Once the antichrist arrives on the scene, he will fan apostasy into a flame, disseminating deception on a massive, lethal level. He will engage in "evil deception" (2 Thessalonians 2:10) that lies at the heart of commercial New Babylon (Revelation 18:3).

Diabolical at the Core. The antichrist will break the covenant he makes with Israel (Daniel 9:27), persecute the saints (Daniel 7:21-25; Revelation 13:7), kill God's two witnesses (Revelation 11:7), force the world to worship him as god (Revelation 13:8), bring the world into economic bondage to himself (Revelation 13:16-17), cause all the nations to move against Jerusalem (see Zechariah 14:1-3), and much more. There has never been a more diabolic being.

Titles of the Antichrist

We learn a lot about the antichrist by the names and titles ascribed to him in Scripture. Here are three of the more important:

The Beast. Revelation 13:1-3 refers to the antichrist as a "beast." This is the most frequently used title of the antichrist in Revelation, appearing there 32 times. The term portrays the brutal, bloody, uncontrolled, and wild character of the antichrist. It points to his beastly or animal nature. Many Bible interpreters have noted how the term "the beast" contrasts the antichrist from the true Christ as "the Lamb of God." Christ the Lamb was slain for people. The antichrist, who is the beast, will slay people. In Revelation 17, we read of a "woman sitting on a scarlet beast" (verse 3). That the woman—the false religion rooted in New Babylon—sits upon the beast means that the false religion controls the antichrist during the first half of the tribulation period.

Man of Lawlessness. In 2 Thessalonians 2:3 (ESV) we read of the antichrist, "Let no one deceive you in any way. For that day will not come, unless the rebellion comes first, and the man of lawlessness is revealed…" (see also 2 Thessalonians 2:8). This term indicates that the antichrist will be full of sin. Scripture reveals that he "will do as he pleases" (Daniel 11:36), not as God wills. He will therefore be "lawless," for he will stand against the law of God. This "man of lawlessness" will be in his comfort zone in New Babylon, whose "sins are piled as high as heaven" (Revelation 18:5).

The Son of Destruction. Scripture refers to the antichrist as the "son of destruction" (2 Thessalonians 2:3 ESV). The term carries the idea of "one who is utterly lost and given over to evil." The Greek term has been translated variously as "son of destruction," "son of perdition," "the one who is doomed to destruction," "the champion of wickedness...destined to inherit perdition," "the man doomed to perdition," and "the son of hell." Whichever translation is correct, it depicts a horrific person who will head up New Babylon.

Satan's Nature Reflected in the Antichrist's Nature

Satan is pictured in Scripture as being extremely powerful and influential. He is called the "ruler of this world" (John 12:31) and "the god of this world" (2 Corinthians 4:4). He is called "the commander of the powers in the unseen world" (Ephesians 2:2). He is also said to deceive the whole world (Revelation 12:9; 20:3). He is portrayed as having power in the governmental realm (Matthew 4:8-9; 2 Corinthians 4:4), the physical realm (Luke 13:11,16; Acts 10:38), the angelic realm (Ephesians 6:11-12; Jude 9), and the ecclesiastical (church) realm (Revelation 2:9; 3:9).

Earlier in the chapter, I noted how Satan inspires the antichrist to mimic Christ (see 2 Thessalonians 2:9; Revelation 13:2). In similar fashion, there are three key aspects of the antichrist's character that are inspired and motivated by Satan. It is important to note these:

1. The Antichrist Will Be Prideful and Self-Exalting, Just as Satan Is

In Isaiah 14:12-17 and Ezekiel 28:11-19 we read about the fall of Lucifer (Satan). Lucifer, in pride, sought to take God's place:

> You said to yourself,
> "I will ascend to heaven and set my throne above God's stars.

> I will preside on the mountain of the gods…
> I will climb to the highest heavens
>   and be like the Most High"
> (Isaiah 14:13-14).

We see the same characteristic in the antichrist, who will be energized by the devil. "He will exalt himself and defy everything that people call god and every object of worship. He will even sit in the temple of God, claiming that he himself is God" (2 Thessalonians 2:4). The devil's pride and self-exaltation will be reflected in the antichrist.

It is noteworthy that the same pride and self-exaltation evident in Satan and the antichrist will also be evident in New Babylon, who "[will boast] in her heart, 'I am queen on my throne'" (Revelation 18:7).

2. The Antichrist Will Deceive Just Like Satan Deceives

We learn from Scripture that Satan is the "father of lies" (John 8:44). This means that he is an originator and inspirer of lies and deception. In fact, Satan is a master deceiver, and the greatest among all liars. His lies are typically religious in nature, distorting the biblical picture of God, Jesus, and the true gospel. Revelation 12:9 calls Satan "the deceiver of the whole world" (ESV).

Because Satan is the "father of lies" and "deceiver of the whole world," it makes sense that the one whom he energizes—the antichrist—will also be characterized by lies and deception. The antichrist "will come to do the work of Satan with counterfeit power and signs and miracles. He will use every kind of evil deception to fool those on their way to destruction" (2 Thessalonians 2:9-10).

The deception evident in Satan and the antichrist will also be evident in New Babylon, which is said to have "deceived the nations" (Revelation 18:23).

3. The Antichrist Will Persecute Just Like Satan Persecutes

We know that Satan is a diligent persecutor of God's people (Revelation 12:12-17). Likewise, the antichrist—who will be empowered and energized by Satan—will be a diligent persecutor of God's people. Revelation 13:7 tells us that the antichrist will be "allowed to wage war against God's holy people and to conquer them." A parallel passage is Daniel 7:21, which, speaking of the antichrist, tells us that he will "[wage] war against God's holy people and…[defeat] them."

The same persecution evident in Satan and the antichrist will also be evident in New Babylon. Indeed, in New Babylon's streets will flow "the blood of the prophets and of God's holy people and the blood of people slaughtered all over the world" (Revelation 18:24; see also 17:6).

Now, here's something to think about: We know that Satan's character will be reflected in the antichrist. We also know that wicked spirits will be hard at work in New Babylon. After all, we are told that New Babylon will be "a home for demons" and "a hideout for every foul spirit" (Revelation 18:2). It is therefore understandable why Satan, the antichrist, and New Babylon will all possess similar characteristics.

Satan, the antichrist, and New Babylon will also suffer similar fates. Satan will be thrown into the bottomless pit (Revelation 20:3). The great city of New Babylon will be thrown down (18:21). The antichrist will be "thrown alive into the fiery lake of burning sulfur" (19:20).

The Antichrist in New Babylon Will Not Be a Muslim

The city of New Babylon will become the commercial center of the world during the second half of the tribulation period. The antichrist will make his headquarters there during this time.

Some Bible interpreters believe the antichrist will be a Muslim. Those who hold to this view typically claim that he will be a military leader who will subdue the earth, establish a new world order, institute new laws globally, institute a world religion, persecute the Jews, behead troublemakers, and seize and conquer Jerusalem. All these things are parallel, it is said, to what the Muslim Mahdi will do when he comes. Therefore, the antichrist must be the coming Muslim Mahdi.

I have some friends who hold to this view, and while I respect them, I personally do not believe the antichrist will be a Muslim, even though he will take leadership in New Babylon. First and foremost, Scripture reveals that the antichrist will be a Roman. How do we know this? Daniel 9:26, speaking of the seventy weeks of Daniel, tells us: "After the sixty-two weeks, an anointed one shall be cut off and shall have nothing. And the people of the prince who is to come shall destroy the city and the sanctuary. Its end shall come with a flood, and to the end there shall be war. Desolations are decreed" (ESV). This passage tells us that Jerusalem and its temple will be destroyed by the "people of the prince who is to come." Who destroyed Jerusalem and its temple in AD 70? It was Titus and his Roman army. The Romans are the people of "the coming prince," the antichrist. This makes it unlikely that the antichrist will be a Muslim.

Another factor that militates against the possibility of a Muslim antichrist relates to the covenant that the antichrist will sign with Israel. This event will mark the beginning of the tribulation period. In Daniel 9:27 we read that the antichrist "shall make a strong covenant with many for one week"—that is, one week of years, or seven years (ESV). Why would a Muslim leader sign a covenant with Israel guaranteeing protection of the Jewish people? After all, most Muslims today hate the Jewish people, and they want the land of Israel back. They want the Jews out of Israel. It seems inconceivable that a Muslim antichrist would sign a covenant with Israel.

Not only does it stretch credulity to say that a Muslim leader would be willing to sign a covenant protecting Israel, it is positively inconceivable that Israel would trust its security—*its very survival*—to a Muslim leader! This is especially true given today's rhetoric about how Muslims want to "wipe Israel off the face of the earth" and "push Israel into the sea."

Moreover, there is no way that the general Muslim population in various Muslim countries around the world would go along with any Muslim leader who made such a covenant with Israel. The Muslim antichrist hypothesis assumes that Muslims will universally submit to such a covenant. I cannot believe it. Based on a long historical precedent, it is clear that Muslims would strongly react *against* any such covenant made by a Muslim leader.

In addition, Daniel 11:36 says of the antichrist, "The king will do as he pleases, exalting himself and claiming to be greater than every god, even blaspheming the God of gods." We also read in 2 Thessalonians 2:4 that the antichrist "will exalt himself and defy everything that people call god and every object of worship. He will even sit in the temple of God, claiming that he himself is God." For a Muslim antichrist to claim to be God would represent an absolute and heinous trashing of the Muslim creed: "There is one God named Allah, and Muhammad is his prophet." No true Muslim would ever claim that he was God. Just as it is anathema to Muslims to call Jesus "God incarnate" or the "Son of God," so it would be anathema to Muslims for *any* human to claim he was God. (Keep in mind that Muslims are radical monotheists.) A Muslim antichrist would thus be viewed as an infidel among Quran-believing Muslims.

In keeping with this is the Muslim teaching that "God can have no partners." Muslims often say this when they argue against the

Christian doctrine of the Trinity. But that statement is certainly applicable to any human leader on earth who has the audacity to claim he is God.

Muslims teach that Allah is so radically unlike any earthly reality—so utterly transcendent and beyond anything in the finite realm—that he cannot be described using earthly terms. That being so, how could a human Muslim (the antichrist) claim to be God—a God described in earthly terms? All things considered, the Muslim antichrist theory is plagued by insurmountable problems.

A Portrait of the Antichrist

Following are some key takeaways from this chapter:

- The antichrist will mimic Christ in many ways, but he will also have many dissimilarities.
- The antichrist will have a strong appearance and will be a genius in many ways—intellectual, oratorical, philosophical, political, governmental, commercial, military, and religious. He will be a defiant personality, full of religious deception, and will be diabolical to the core. Many of these qualities will also be manifest in New Babylon.
- We learn much about the antichrist by his titles—especially the beast, man of lawlessness, and son of destruction.
- Satan's nature will be reflected in the antichrist.
- New Babylon will show many characteristics that are similar to those of Satan and the antichrist.
- Though the antichrist will rule in New Babylon, he will not be a Muslim.

8

The Mark of the Beast and the Coming Cashless Society

We noted in chapter 6 that Nebuchadnezzar, the king of ancient Babylon, was a "type" of the antichrist. Nebuchadnezzar had many religious assistants, such as astrologers, enchanters, magicians, and sorcerers (see Daniel 2:2). The antichrist will also have a religious assistant—the false prophet.

During the seven-year tribulation period, a supreme false prophet will emerge who will be the right-hand man of the antichrist (Revelation 13). While the antichrist will primarily be a military and political leader, the false prophet will primarily be a religious leader.

This means that the antichrist will not carry out his diabolical plans alone. The false prophet can be viewed as the first lieutenant of the antichrist. The book of Revelation reveals that the false prophet will...

- control religious affairs on earth (Revelation 13:11),
- be motivated by Satan (verse 11),
- promote the worship of the antichrist (verse 12),

- execute those who refuse to worship the antichrist (verse 15),

- control economic commerce on the earth with a view to enforcing worship of the antichrist (verse 17),

- perform apparent signs and miracles (verse 13), and

- bring deception and false doctrine upon the whole world (verse 14).

The apostle John describes the false prophet in Revelation 13:11: "I saw another beast come up out of the earth. He had two horns like those of a lamb, but he spoke with the voice of a dragon." What does this strange imagery mean?

Just as the antichrist will be a beast, so also will the false prophet. The Greek word translated "another" is *allos*, meaning "another of the same kind." Together, this beastly duo will wreak havoc upon the earth for seven years during the tribulation period.

This false prophet will have "two horns" (Revelation 13:11). Recall that the antichrist will have "ten horns" (13:1). Because horns indicate power and authority, we can infer that the false prophet will have less power and authority than the antichrist. The false prophet's "horns" or authority will be lamblike in the sense that he will be meeker and gentler in expressing his authority before others.

The false prophet will speak like a dragon (Revelation 13:11). This means that he will speak words inspired by the dragon, who is Satan. Just as true prophets are inspired by the Holy Spirit, so the false prophet will be inspired by the *un*holy spirit—Satan. Prophecy scholar Ed Hindson comments that "he looks religious, but he talks like the devil."[1] He will speak winsome, deceptive words of praise about the antichrist, seeking to lure the world into worshipping him.

The goal of the false prophet will be to make "all the earth and its people to worship the first beast." He will be the epitome of a false prophet because he will point to a "god" other than the God in the Bible—the antichrist.

To force the people of the earth to worship the antichrist, the false prophet will require that everyone receive the "mark of the beast." Revelation 13:16-18 describes it this way:

> [The false prophet] required everyone—small and great, rich and poor, free and slave—to be given a mark on the right hand or on the forehead. And no one could buy or sell anything without that mark, which was either the name of the beast or the number representing his name. Wisdom is needed here. Let the one with understanding solve the meaning of the number of the beast, for it is the number of a man. His number is 666.

Our passage reveals that the diabolical beastly duo—the antichrist and the false prophet—will subjugate the entire world so that no one who does not first receive the mark of the beast can buy or sell anything. We can infer that every seller on earth will have a distinct account number, as will every buyer on earth. *Only* those buyers who have the mark of the beast will be permitted to make purchases from sellers who have the mark as well. My friend, this becomes particularly relevant regarding people's ability to acquire the necessities of life—*such as food and water*.

The Backdrop of Global Famine

The four horsemen of the apocalypse are connected to the first four seal judgments that are poured out on humankind early in the tribulation period (Revelation 6). First mentioned is the antichrist riding a white horse, with a crown and a bow without an arrow (6:2). The crown suggests he is a ruler. The mention of the bow without an arrow symbolizes that the antichrist's world government will begin without warfare, but war will quickly follow: "He rode out to win many battles and gain the victory" (Revelation 6:2).

The second horse, mentioned in Revelation 6:3-4, is red—a color representing bloodshed, killing with the sword, and war (see also Matthew 24:6-7). This rider carries a large sword. These verses indicate that humankind's efforts at bringing about peace will be frustrated, for peace will be taken from the earth. As bad as this will be, however, it will only represent the initial "birth pains" of what is yet to come upon the earth (Matthew 24:8; Mark 13:7-8; see also Luke 21:9).

The third horse, mentioned in Revelation 6:5-6, is black. The rider is carrying a pair of scales in his hand. This symbolizes famine (with subsequent death) as the prices for wheat and barley are extravagantly high, requiring a full day's wages just to buy a few meals (see Lamentations 5:8-10). A famine of such great magnitude would not be unexpected following global warfare.

There will be runaway inflation during this time. The buying power of money will drop dramatically. As one Bible expositor put it, "The situation would be such that one would have to spend a day's wages for a loaf of bread with no money left to buy anything else. The symbolism therefore indicates a time of economic devastation and famine when life will be reduced to the barest necessities."[2]

Black is an appropriate color here, for it points to the lamentation and sorrow that naturally accompanies extreme deprivation. That black can represent hunger is illustrated for us in Lamentations 4:8-9: "Now their faces are blacker than soot. No one recognizes them in the streets. Their skin sticks to their bones; it is as dry and hard as wood. Those killed by the sword are better off than those who die of hunger. Starving, they waste away for lack of food from the fields."

Such famine is in keeping with Jesus's own words regarding the end times. He affirmed that the first three birth pains of the end times will be false messiahs, war, and famine (Matthew 24:5-7).

The fourth horse, mentioned in Revelation 6:7-8, is pale—"yellowish-green," the color of a corpse. The rider of this horse is appropriately named Death. It appears that the death symbolized here is the natural consequence of the previous judgments of war and famine. The death toll worldwide will be catastrophic—a fourth of earth's population.

At present, there are 7.8 billion people on earth. If the tribulation period starts anytime in the near future, then very close to 2 billion people will die in these initial judgments. It's hard to even grasp such a large number. Perhaps a word picture might help.

Imagine a football stadium that holds 50,000 people. You've seen such stadiums on TV. Now imagine 40,000 such stadiums, each filled with 50,000 people. THAT is how many people will die from the early judgments during the tribulation.

There's a good reason I'm sharing all this with you, and here it is: During the first half of the tribulation the world will experience staggering inflation. Because of this, people will not be able to buy much food. They will get hungry quickly, and famine conditions will escalate.

It is against this backdrop that the false prophet—at the midpoint of the tribulation—will force people to receive the mark of the beast. Only those who receive the mark can buy food. Those without the mark will starve. This is a classic squeeze play, pure and simple.

Do you want to know who will eat well during these years? *Those who have received the mark of the beast and are associated with New Babylon!*

What Is the Mark of the Beast?

During the future seven-year tribulation period, human beings will somehow be branded, just as animals today are branded and as slaves were once branded by their owners. We cannot be certain, however, about how the number 666 relates specifically to the antichrist or his mark.

Through the centuries, Bible interpreters have offered many suggestions as to the meaning of 666. A popular theory is that inasmuch as the number 7 is a number of perfection, and the number 777 is a number reflecting the perfect Trinity, perhaps 666 points to a being who aspires to perfect deity (like the Trinity) but never attains it. (In reality, the antichrist is just a man, though empowered and possibly indwelt by Satan.)

Others have suggested that perhaps the number refers to a specific man—such as the Roman emperor Nero. It is suggested that if Nero's name is translated into the Hebrew language, the numerical value of the letters in his name is 666. Some suggest that the antichrist will be a man like Nero of old. Of course, all this is highly speculative. The truth is, Scripture does not clearly define what is meant by 666. Hence, any attempts to interpret this verse will amount to nothing more than guesswork.

One thing is certain: In some way that is presently unknown to us, this number will be a crucial part of the antichrist's identification. It is sobering to realize that receiving the mark of the beast is apparently an unpardonable sin (Revelation 14:9-10). The decision to receive it is an irreversible decision. Once made, there is no turning back.

Receiving the mark reveals an implicit approval of the antichrist as a leader, and an implicit agreement with his purpose. No one will take this mark by accident. One must volitionally choose to do so, with all the facts on the table. It will be a deliberate choice with eternal consequences. Those who choose to receive the mark will do so with a full awareness of what they have done.

The choice will cause a radical polarization. There will be no middle ground. People will choose either for or against the antichrist. They will choose either for or against God. While people in our present day think they can avoid God and His demands upon their lives by feigning neutrality, no such neutrality will be possible during the tribulation, for every person's very survival will be determined by his or her decision. They must choose to either receive the mark and live (being able to buy and sell food, water, and other items), or reject the mark and face suffering and possible death. They must choose to follow the antichrist and eat well, or reject him and starve.

A Commerce Passport

The mark of the beast will literally serve as a commerce passport during the future tribulation period. Prophecy scholar Arnold Fruchtenbaum suggests that the mark of the beast

> will be given to all who submit themselves to the authority of the antichrist and accept him as god. The mark will serve as a passport for business (v. 17a). They will be able to neither buy nor sell anything unless they have the mark…Only those who have this number will be permitted to work, to buy, to sell, or simply to make a living.[3]

This mark will be required of people during the second half of the tribulation period, during the same time that commercial New Babylon will be in full force. New Babylon is portrayed in Revelation 18:11-13 as a huge buyer of various goods:

> She bought great quantities of gold, silver, jewels, and pearls; fine linen, purple, silk, and scarlet cloth; things made of fragrant thyine wood, ivory goods, and objects made of expensive wood; and bronze, iron, and marble.

She also bought cinnamon, spice, incense, myrrh, frankincense, wine, olive oil, fine flour, wheat, cattle, sheep, horses,
wagons, and bodies—that is, human slaves.

This is likely only a partial list. All who sell their goods to New Babylon—including all kinds of food items—will have already received
the mark of the beast (see Revelation 18:11-15). No sales will be permitted without that mark. Hence, the antichrist will control the
commercial success of New Babylon.

Prophecy scholar Mark Hitchcock suggests that there is ancient
historical precedence for such a mark. He points to Ezekiel 9:4,
where the Lord said, "Walk through the streets of Jerusalem and
put a mark on the foreheads of all who weep and sigh because of the
detestable sins being committed in their city."[4] In this context, the
mark on the forehead was one of preservation, like the blood that
"marked" the doorposts of the Israelite homes in Egypt and spared
the Jewish people from death during the tenth plague inflicted on
the Egyptians (see Exodus 12:21-29).

In ancient times, such a mark was also used in connection with
pagans and false deities. Bible scholar Robert Thomas explains it
this way:

> The mark must be some sort of branding similar to that
> given soldiers, slaves, and temple devotees in John's day.
> In Asia Minor, devotees of pagan religions delighted in
> the display of such a tattoo as an emblem of ownership
> by a certain god. In Egypt, Ptolemy Philopator I branded
> Jews, who submitted to registration, with an ivy leaf in
> recognition of their Dionysian worship (cf. 3 Macc. 2:29).
> This meaning resembles the long-time practice of carrying
> signs to advertise religious loyalties (cf. Isa. 44:5) and fol-
> lows the habit of branding slaves with the name or special
> mark of their owners (cf. Gal. 6:17). *Charagma* ("mark")
> was a [Greek] term for the images or names of emperors

on Roman coins, so it fittingly could apply to the beast's emblem put on people.[5]

John MacArthur likewise notes that

in the Roman Empire, this was a normal identifying symbol, or brand, that slaves and soldiers bore on their bodies. Some of the ancient mystical cults delighted in such tattoos, which identified members with a form of worship. Antichrist will have a similar requirement, one that will need to be visible on the hand or forehead.[6]

The mark of the beast will serve to indicate that one is religiously "orthodox"—that is, orthodox as defined by the antichrist and the false prophet. As David Jeremiah says, "The mark will allow the antichrist's followers to buy and sell because it identifies them as religiously orthodox—submissive followers of the beast and worshipers of his image. Those without the mark are forbidden to buy because they are identified as traitors."[7] So, though receiving the mark is essentially a spiritual decision, this spiritual decision will have life-and-death economic consequences.

The Mark Itself Is Not High Technology

Though I believe that modern technology will make it possible for the antichrist and false prophet to bring about a cashless society and control all commerce on earth through the mark of the beast, we must differentiate between this technology and the mark itself, for the technology itself *is not* the mark. I make this point because there have been a number of prophecy expositors in the past who have claimed that the mark will be something like a high-tech chip inserted under the skin.

This is not the case. The mark itself will identify allegiance to the antichrist, but that is separate and distinct from the technology that enables him to enforce his economic system. My former prophecy mentor John F. Walvoord commented on how technology will make it possible to exercise such economical control, based on whether or not people have received the mark:

> There is no doubt that with today's technology, a world ruler, who is in total control, would have the ability to keep a continually updated census of all living persons and know day-by-day precisely which people had pledged their allegiance to him and received the mark and which had not.

It is highly likely that "chip implants, scan technology, and biometrics will be used as tools to enforce his policy that one cannot buy or sell without the mark."[8]

Notice in the biblical text (Revelation 13:16) that this mark will be *on* people, not *in* them (as would be done with a microcomputer chip). It will be *on* the right hand or *on* the forehead and will be visible to the eye (perhaps like a tattoo), not hidden beneath the skin. It will be universally rejected by believers in God, but universally accepted by those who choose against God.

The Consequences of Receiving the Mark of the Beast

Receiving this mark will have serious consequences. Revelation 14:9-10 says,

> Anyone who worships the beast and his statue or who accepts his mark on the forehead or on the hand must drink the wine of God's anger. It has been poured full strength into God's cup of wrath. And they will be tormented with fire and burning sulfur in the presence of the holy angels and the Lamb.

We are likewise told in Revelation 16:2, "The first angel left the Temple and poured out his bowl on the earth, and horrible, malignant sores broke out on everyone who had the mark of the beast and who worshiped his statue." Such words are sobering. Anyone who expresses loyalty to the antichrist and his cause will suffer the wrath of our holy and just God. How awful it will be for them to experience the full force of God's divine anger and unmitigated vengeance (see Psalm 75:8; Isaiah 51:17; Jeremiah 25:15-16).

This necessarily means that all those who sold their goods to New Babylon during the second half of the tribulation period will be on the receiving end of God's judgment. After all, they cannot sell to New Babylon without having received the mark of the beast. So, not only will New Babylon be judged; all who do business with her will be judged as well!

Revelation 20:4 tells us, by contrast, that believers in the Lord Jesus Christ will refuse the mark of the beast and choose death instead:

> Then I saw thrones, and the people sitting on them had been given the authority to judge. And I saw the souls of those who had been beheaded for their testimony about Jesus and for proclaiming the word of God. They had not worshiped the beast or his statue, nor accepted his mark on their foreheads or their hands. They all came to life again, and they reigned with Christ for a thousand years.

The Coming Cashless World

A modern development that will help facilitate the mark of the beast as well as the commercial success of New Babylon is that we are now rapidly moving toward becoming a cashless society. If the world were still using cash during the tribulation period, it would be very difficult for the antichrist to enforce his rule that no one can buy or sell without receiving his mark. However, in a cashless society—where every seller and every buyer has a distinct account number and dollar bills are no longer in use—it would be easy to enforce the mark of the beast. It seems evident, then, that as we continue to go deeper into the end times, our world will become increasingly cashless.

Our society has already gone "cashless" in a number of areas. For example, if you take a flight on American Airlines, like I do dozens of times each year, the flight attendant will tell you that you can buy sandwiches to eat, but you cannot use cash to purchase them. "American Airlines has gone cashless," travelers are informed. Other airlines have likewise gone cashless—including Southwest, Alaska Airlines, JetBlue, AirTran, Virgin America, and Midwest Airlines.

Meanwhile, as people cruise on toll roads, smart technologies automatically charge their credit cards or bank accounts so that they do not have to slow down and manually give cash at a tollbooth. It all happens behind the scenes, and people are not even cognizant of the instant and seamless financial transaction that takes place as they traverse those toll roads.

Cash has met the beginning of its demise. Economists tell us that the amount of real cash in circulation today is rapidly waning. In fact, the amount of cash being used today is less than half that used in the 1970s. Why so? Because more and more people are using cashless options—such as credit cards, debit cards, Apple Pay, and Android Pay. RFID chips (Radio Frequency Identification chips), which can be implanted underneath the skin and can store financial data, are another possible means of making cashless payments. All of this is the wave of the future. Even the few who choose to pay by check today typically have their checks read by a "check scanner" that instantly transfers money from their bank account to the vendor to whom they wrote the check.

Presently, more than 70 percent of all consumer payments are electronic in nature. More than two billion credit cards are in use in the United States alone. One economist observes, "The long-predicted 'cashless society' has quietly arrived, or nearly so. Electronic money is cheaper than cash or checks...[and] it is more convenient…We have crossed a cultural as well as an economic threshold when plastic and money are synonymous."[9]

Some economists suggest that cash could soon become obsolete. Dollar bills and coins will be relegated to the history books. It is entirely possible that retail establishments will soon begin charging surcharges every time you try to use cash in their establishments.

I often tell people that prophecies sometimes cast their shadows before them. Hence, as Bible expositor David Jeremiah has said, "We are on the cutting edge of having all the technology that the antichrist and false prophet would need to wire this world together for their evil purposes. Right now it is well within the range of possibility for a centralized power to gain worldwide control of all banking and purchasing." Jeremiah further exhorts, "As we see things that are prophesied for the tribulation period beginning to take shape right now, we are made aware of the fact that surely the Lord's return is not far off."[10] All of this is "greasing the skids" for the rise of commercial New Babylon.

Supercomputers and a Cashless World

There is plenty of computer power available in today's technological world to monitor and even control a one-world economy. We do not need to invent anything new to make it all possible. The technology that exists today is more than sufficient for the antichrist's future control of the global economy. The technology that exists today will play a huge role in commercial New Babylon's success.

One example I might cite is IBM's supercomputer called the Sequoia. It is so fast that it can easily do 20,000 trillion calculations per second. How fast is that? Look at it this way: If you had billions of people on earth all using an electronic calculator to work together on one massive calculation—and they were all working 24/7, 365 days a year—it would take them more than 300 years to do what Sequoia can do in a single hour.[11]

The Lure of a Cashless Society

There is a strong movement toward a cashless society today because, in the perception of many, there are numerous benefits to going cashless. Think about it: Technology always makes things easier. Telephones make it easier to communicate than yelling down the street. Cars make it easier to go to the store than walking. Toilets that flush are easier to use than outhouses. Air conditioners are much more comforting and convenient than hand-held fans. Likewise, going cashless is easier and more convenient than carrying around paper bills and coinage.

There are other advantages to going cashless. For example, there are presently very few places where people cannot use a credit card or debit card. The great majority of grocery store purchases in our day are put on cards. Internet purchases are put on cards. Many bills are paid via online banking. Cashless options are already widely available because they are so convenient, and that will only increase in the future.

As well, federal authorities tell us that at present more than $100 million of counterfeit money is removed from circulation each year. Over a ten-year period, that amounts to a billion dollars in counterfeit money.[12] In a cashless society, counterfeit money will become a thing of the past.

In addition, a cashless economy would make it impossible for would-be thieves to rob a store's cash register. There cannot be cash robberies in a cashless world.

Various forms of crime would also decrease. In a recent op-ed in *The Wall Street Journal*, Harvard economics professor Kenneth Rogoff listed various crimes that are presently facilitated by paper money: "Racketeering, extortion, money laundering, drug and human trafficking, corruption of public officials, and terrorism."[13] All of these and more will become far less likely in a cashless world.

Moreover, in a cashless society, no one will become infected with germs that are passed around on dollar bills and coins. I realize that statement might seem slightly germophobic. But *Scientific American* magazine recently ran an article providing scientific proof that dollar bills can be veritable "reservoirs" for flu viruses—and such viruses can survive on a dollar bill for as long as 17 days.[14] So, no kidding—going cashless might help keep you healthier.

Still further, in a cashless society, losing your wallet or purse will be less painful because you won't lose any cash.

There's one more thing: Many workers today are involved in service businesses that take cash payments—and many of those transactions are not reported on tax returns. In a cashless society, tax fraud would become a thing of the past. That alone is especially appealing to the government.

Get Used to the Idea!

Whether you like it or not, we are headed toward becoming a cashless planet. It's on the horizon. A recent article titled "Cash Not Welcome Here" tells us,

> To get a glimpse of the future of commerce in America, look no further than Sweden…The Scandinavian country is largely a cashless society, with consumers relying on mobile phone payments or plastic. While the U.S. is still far from achieving the same level of cash-free existence, increasing numbers of restaurants and retailers are now snubbing the lowly dollar bill.[15]

One reason the United States government may be in favor of going cashless is that at present our country spends $200 billion each year to keep cash in circulation. Going cashless would save us a lot of time and money.

A 2016 Gallup poll reveals that "sixty-two percent of Americans said they believe the country would be a cashless society in their lifetimes. The belief is fueled by the expanded use of credit cards, debit cards, and other electronic payment options. In short, the survey found that more people are becoming comfortable without cash in their pockets." The Gallup poll concluded that "cash is becoming less a part of American's purchasing behavior."[16]

A number of countries have recently been exploring the possibility of developing a digital currency. "The central banks of China, the UK, and Canada, to name just a few, have been investigating the possibility of creating digital currencies." What is the appeal? "Issuing digital currency would be far cheaper than printing and distributing notes and coins…It would also enable nations to more accurately track developments in the economy—including inflation."[17]

My friend, things are in motion. The prophetic stage is now being set for events that will transpire during the future tribulation period. We're going cashless! One day the mark of the beast will be enforced. And those living during the tribulation will witness the incredible rise—*and the catastrophic fall*—of New Babylon. I'll address this in the next chapter.

The Destruction of Commercial New Babylon, Part 1

When it comes to God, many people today focus almost exclusively on His love. While it's true that God is a God of love, we must never forget that He is also a holy and righteous Judge. This has always been true of Him.

Theologian Paul Enns notes that "because God is holy, He must judge all that is unholy or He would no longer be holy. Judgment is a necessary expression of God's own character...All people, without exception, will die and come under the judgment of God (Heb. 9:27)."[1]

Theologian Henry C. Thiessen comments that "the whole philosophy of the future judgments rests upon the sovereign right of God to punish disobedience." He then provides this biblical summary regarding God's prerogative to judge humankind:

> In Genesis, Abraham recognized God as the judge of all the earth (18:25), and Hannah said that "the LORD will judge the ends of the earth" (1 Sam. 2:10). David spoke of the Lord "coming to judge the earth" (1 Chron. 16:33; cf. Ps.

96:13; 98:9) and said that he had "established His throne for judgment" (Ps. 9:7). In Joel, God says, "Let the nations be aroused and come up to the valley of Jehoshaphat, for there I will sit to judge all the surrounding nations" (3:12; cf. Isa. 2:4). In the New Testament this fact is more frequently asserted. Jesus said, "For the Son of Man is going to come in the glory of His Father with His angels; and will then recompense every man according to his deeds" (Matt. 16:27). At Athens Paul declared that God had "fixed a day in which He will judge the world in righteousness through a Man whom He has appointed" (Acts 17:31; cf. Rom. 2:16; 2 Thess. 1:7-9). He further declared that "we must all appear before the judgment seat of Christ, that each one may be recompensed for his deeds in the body, according to what he has done, whether good or bad" (2 Cor. 5:10; cf. Rom. 14:10). The writer to the Hebrews says that after death comes the judgment (9:27). It was John who "saw the dead, the great and the small, standing before the throne" to be judged (Rev. 20:12). God has given assurance of the fact of judgment by raising Christ, the judge, from the dead (Acts 17:31).[2]

There are many examples of such judgment in the pages of Scripture. In his modern classic *Knowing God*, popular writer J.I. Packer provides this summary:

> The reality of divine judgment, as a fact, is set forth on page after page of Bible history. God judged Adam and Eve, expelling them from the Garden and pronouncing curses on their future earthly life (Gen. 3). God judged the corrupt world of Noah's day, sending a flood to destroy mankind (Gen. 6–8). God judged Sodom and Gomorrah, engulfing them in a volcanic catastrophe (Gen. 18–19). God judged Israel's Egyptian taskmasters, just as He foretold He would (see Gen. 15:14), unleashing against them

the terrors of the ten plagues (Ex. 7–12). God judged those who worshipped the golden calf, using the Levites as His executioners (Ex. 32:26-35). God judged Nadab and Abihu for offering Him strange fire (Lev. 10:1ff.), as later He judged Korah, Dathan, and Abiram, who were swallowed up in an earth tremor. God judged Achan for sacrilegious thieving; he and his family were wiped out (Josh. 7). God judged Israel for unfaithfulness to Him after their entry into Canaan, causing them to fall under the dominion of other nations (Judg. 2:11ff., 3:5ff., 4:1ff.).[3]

In the New Testament we find that judgment fell on the Jews for rejecting Jesus Christ (Matthew 21:43), on Ananias and Sapphira for lying to God (Acts 5), on Herod for his self-exalting pride (Acts 12:21), and on Christians in Corinth who were afflicted with illness in response to their irreverence in connection with the Lord's Supper (1 Corinthians 11:29-32). We read about the judgment of the nations (Matthew 25:31-46) as well as the judgment of the Jews (Ezekiel 20:34-38), both following the second coming of Christ. We also read about the judgment seat of Christ, which Christians will one day face (Romans 14:8-10; 1 Corinthians 3:10-15; 9:24-27; 2 Corinthians 5:10), and the great white throne judgment, which unbelievers will face (Revelation 20:11-15).

God truly is a God of judgment. For us to forget or ignore this fact is to do so at our own peril. God will hold all human beings accountable for the things done during their earthly lives. This includes all who are associated with New Babylon in the end times.

How the Proud and Mighty Fall!

Revelation 18 prophesies the catastrophic fall and judgment of commercial New Babylon. This anti-God materialistic city will flourish beyond belief, but then will be brought down calamitously:

After all this I saw another angel come down from heaven with great authority, and the earth grew bright with his splendor. He gave a mighty shout:

> "Babylon is fallen—that great city is fallen!
> She has become a home for demons.
> She is a hideout for every foul spirit,
>> a hideout for every foul vulture
>> and every foul and dreadful animal.
> For all the nations have fallen
>> because of the wine of her passionate immorality.
> The kings of the world
>> have committed adultery with her.
> Because of her desires for extravagant luxury,
>> the merchants of the world have grown rich."
> Then I heard another voice calling from heaven,
> "Come away from her, my people.
> Do not take part in her sins,
>> or you will be punished with her.
> For her sins are piled as high as heaven,
>> and God remembers her evil deeds.
> Do to her as she has done to others.
> Double her penalty for all her evil deeds.
> She brewed a cup of terror for others,
>> so brew twice as much for her.
> She glorified herself and lived in luxury,
>> so match it now with torment and sorrow.
> She boasted in her heart,
> 'I am queen on my throne.
> I am no helpless widow,
>> and I have no reason to mourn.'
> Therefore, these plagues will overtake her in a single day—
>> death and mourning and famine.
> She will be completely consumed by fire,
>> for the Lord God who judges her is mighty"
>> (Revelation 18:1-8).

There is irony in the biblical account of New Babylon's fall. Contextually, the antichrist is busy preparing his forces to attack Israel. This attack occurs early in the campaign of Armageddon. The antichrist thinks he is secure, assumes his great power and wealth are rock solid, and considers himself invulnerable. Suddenly and without warning, God Himself judges and utterly destroys the antichrist's mighty economic headquarters in New Babylon (see Isaiah 13:19; Jeremiah 50:11-27,40). *What an unimaginably devastating blow this is.*

This destruction will come upon Babylon as a direct, decisive judgment from the hand of the Almighty. God will definitively settle the score for Babylon's long history of standing against His people of Israel. Just as Babylon had showed no mercy in its oppression against Israel throughout biblical history and now during the tribulation period, so will God show no mercy to Babylon. This judgment will occur at the very end of the seven-year tribulation.

Revelation 18:1 informs us that John witnessed an angel coming down from heaven with "great authority." The earth "grew bright with his splendor." This does not necessarily mean the angel has intrinsic glory. It is more likely that, having just come out of God's presence in heaven, the angel still shines forth the radiating glory of God. This is similar to what happened to Moses when he received the two stone tablets of the law. On that occasion, "when Moses came down Mount Sinai carrying the two stone tablets inscribed with the terms of the covenant, he wasn't aware that his face had become radiant because he had spoken to the LORD" (Exodus 34:29).

The angel immediately cried out, "Babylon is fallen—that great city is fallen" (Revelation 18:2). The dual occurrence of the word "fallen" indicates both the woeful condition of commercial New Babylon as well as the certainty of its coming judgment (see Isaiah

21:9; Jeremiah 51:8). Things are about to get terribly bad for this sinful city.

Notice that our text says "Babylon *is* fallen," as if its devastation had already occurred. This is a proleptic announcement common to prophetic Scripture, in which a future action is described as if it had already happened. It is a literary device that emphasizes that God's triumph over evil New Babylon is an accomplished fact, though its execution is yet future during the seventh bowl judgment.

Let's pause a moment to make sure there's no confusion on the chronology of New Babylon's fall. The false religion associated with New Babylon will be destroyed at the midpoint of the tribulation by the antichrist and his forces (Revelation 17). By contrast, the destruction of commercial New Babylon will take place at the end of the seven-year tribulation (Revelation 18). Revelation 18:2 describes the city of Babylon as it will be once God finally judges it at the end of the tribulation: "Babylon is fallen—that great city is fallen!" (see also Isaiah 13:21; 34:11,14; 47:7-9; Jeremiah 50–51; Ezekiel 26–28; Nahum 3; Zephaniah 2:15).

So horrific will God's judgment be on commercial New Babylon that the city will become "a home for demons" and "a hideout for every foul spirit, a hideout for every foul vulture and every foul and dreadful animal" (Revelation 18:2). These graphic descriptions point to a devastation and annihilation so complete that only the lowest life forms will be able to inhabit the region.

Ripe for Judgment

The biblical text, speaking of commercial New Babylon, informs us that "all nations have drunk the wine of the passion of her sexual immorality" (Revelation 18:3 ESV). The words of this verse are quite similar to those in Revelation 17:2, which refers to the false religious system associated with New Babylon, "with whom the kings of the earth have committed sexual immorality" (ESV). Just as the false religion of Babylon will entice the people of the world to commit spiritual fornication (Revelation 17:2,4), so commercial New Babylon will entice the unbelieving world into anti-God, humanistic materialism. In both cases, people will be drawn into unfaithfulness toward God.

The anti-God political, economic, and commercial system of New Babylon will influence everyone on earth—"all the nations" and "the kings of the world" (Revelation 18:3). New Babylon's influence will be universal. It will have an octopus-like reach around the globe. And because of the commercial success of this city, merchants and political leaders around the world will become very wealthy. Anti-God materialism will have run rampant. The city and all that it represents will therefore be ripe for judgment, and people worldwide will mourn when it happens.

God's People Called to Separate

John then heard another voice: "Come away from her, my people. Do not take part in her sins, or you will be punished with her" (Revelation 18:4). This may be an angel speaking forth a warning from God Himself, urging those who are faithful to God—faithful Jews, in particular—to dissociate from commercial New Babylon. Otherwise, they may end up being on the receiving end of the plagues that will shortly fall upon New Babylon (see Isaiah 52:11; 2 Corinthians 6:14-17; 1 John 2:15-17).

The implication is that if these people separate, they will come under God's protection (see Revelation 12:14; Matthew 24:16). One might recall that in Old Testament times, both Isaiah and Jeremiah called the people of God to leave Babylon (see Isaiah 48:20; Jeremiah 50:8; 51:6-9,45).

Prophecy scholars Thomas Ice and Timothy Demy provide these helpful words regarding how many Jews will be able to make it out of New Babylon before judgment falls on the city:

> When Babylon is destroyed, the Antichrist will not be pres-
> ent in the city. He will be told of its destruction by messen-
> gers (Jeremiah 50:43; 51:31,32)...The attack will be swift,
> but there will be some warning or opportunity for Jews
> who are living in Babylon to flee from the city (Jeremiah
> 50:6-8,28; 51:5,6). Even in these last days, God will pre-
> serve a remnant of His people. These refugees are to go to
> Jerusalem and tell them of the city's destruction and their
> escape (Jeremiah 51:10,45,50; Revelation 18:4,5).[4]

Why will the Jews need to exit Babylon with a sense of great immediacy? Because "her sins are piled as high as heaven, and God remembers her evil deeds" (Revelation 18:5). Babylon's sins will be almost immeasurable. God will remember them all. His patience will eventually be exhausted. Judgment will be inevitable and inescapable. A righteous and holy God *must of necessity* render judgment upon unrepentant evil.

There is an interesting observation we can make here. While God will not forget the sins of the unrepentant Babylonians, God purposefully chooses to forget the sins of His own children: "I will forgive their wickedness, and I will never again remember their sins" (Jeremiah 31:34; Hebrews 8:12). This is in keeping with Psalm 103:12, which tells us that God "has removed our sins as far from us as the east is from the west." This is entirely because of what Jesus has done for us at the cross.

Yet another interesting point is this: Just as God will call the Jews to separate themselves from Babylon as soon as possible, so does God call Christians—you and me—to separate ourselves from all that is ungodly. First Timothy 5:22 urges Christians not to "share in the sins of others." Ephesians 5:11 urges us, "Take no part in the worthless deeds of evil and darkness; instead, expose them." Second Corinthians 6:14-15 instructs, "Don't team up with those who are unbelievers. How can righteousness be a partner with wickedness? How can light live with darkness? What harmony can there be between Christ and the devil? How can a believer be a partner with an unbeliever?"

Those who become believers during the tribulation period will be expected to avoid loving the worldly and luxurious things of New Babylon. This brings to mind 1 John 2:15-17, which applies to each of us:

> Do not love this world nor the things it offers you, for when you love the world, you do not have the love of the Father in you. For the world offers only a craving for physical pleasure, a craving for everything we see, and pride in our achievements and possessions. These are not from the Father, but are from this world. And this world is fading away, along with everything that people crave. But anyone who does what pleases God will live forever.

Bible expositor Warren Wiersbe thus warns:

> How easy it is to become fascinated by the things the world has to offer. Like a person taking a sip of wine, we can soon find ourselves drinking deeply and then wanting more. The world system that opposes Christ has always been with us, and we must beware of its subtle influence.
>
> The world system satisfies the desires of the earth-dwellers who follow "the beast" and reject the Lamb. But worldly things never permanently satisfy or last. The love of pleasures and possessions is but an insidious form of idolatry, demonic in its origin and destructive in its outcome.[5]

The instruction for the Jews to make a rapid escape out of commercial New Babylon is thus prudent advice. We can observe that New Babylon is about to be on the receiving end of what we might call the *double-boomerang effect*: "Do to her as she has done to others. Double her penalty for all her evil deeds. She brewed a cup of terror for others, so brew twice as much for her" (Revelation 18:6).

Here we find an echo of the *lex talionis*, the law of retaliation. As Matthew 7:2 says, "For with the judgment you pronounce you will be judged, and with the measure you use it will be measured to you" (ESV). Galatians 6:7 assures us, "Whatever one sows, that will he also reap" (ESV). In Babylon's case, the city will receive a *double dose* of *lex talionis*. To pay back double was a common judicial requirement in Old Testament law:

- "If someone steals an ox or a donkey or a sheep and it is found in the thief's possession, then the thief must pay double the value of the stolen animal" (Exodus 22:4).

- "Suppose someone leaves money or goods with a neighbor for safekeeping, and they are stolen from the neighbor's house. If the thief is caught, the compensation is double the value of what was stolen" (Exodus 22:7).

- "Suppose there is a dispute between two people who both claim to own a particular ox, donkey, sheep, article of clothing, or any lost property. Both parties must come before God, and the person whom God declares guilty must pay double compensation to the other" (Exodus 22:9).

- "Speak tenderly to Jerusalem. Tell her that her sad days are gone and her sins are pardoned. Yes, the LORD has punished her twice over for all her sins" (Isaiah 40:2).

- "I will double their punishment for all their sins, because they have defiled my land with lifeless images of their detestable gods and have filled my territory with their evil deeds" (Jeremiah 16:18).

- "Bring a day of terror on them. Yes, bring double destruction upon them" (Jeremiah 17:18).

In keeping with God's longstanding policy, Babylon's judgment will be thorough—that is, *double*! New Babylon will not survive this judgment.

Granted, such judgment might seem harsh. We must keep in mind, however, that all the people associated with commercial New Babylon will engage in deep wickedness with no repentance in view. They will be beyond the point of no return in their moral degradation. They will be irrevocably committed to the person and program of the antichrist. They will permanently cross the line when they declare allegiance to the antichrist and against God. *Therefore, judgment will be unavoidable.*

A Touch of Irony

There is a touch of irony in Revelation 18:7: "She glorified herself and lived in luxury, so match it now with torment and sorrow. She boasted in her heart, 'I am queen on my throne. I am no helpless widow, and I have no reason to mourn.'" Though Babylon will be proud, she will go on to be humbled. Though Babylon will enjoy great glory and luxury, she will be brought exceedingly low in torment and mourning. Though Babylon will feign queenship, she will be brought low by the royal King of kings. While Babylon will seem superior in every way, her moral inferiority will be judged.

We cannot help but notice that the description of New Babylon in this verse bears at least some resemblance to the character of the Laodicean church. Christ said to this church, "You say, 'I am rich. I have everything I want. I don't need a thing!' And you don't realize that you are wretched and miserable and poor and blind and naked" (Revelation 3:17). *Self-delusion is a wretched state.*

We may be inclined to think that the destruction of such a powerful city with global influence would take a substantial amount of time to accomplish. However, Revelation 18:8 tells us, "These plagues will overtake her *in a single day*—death and mourning and famine. She will be completely consumed by fire, for the Lord God who judges her is mighty" (emphasis added). This is why God will urge His people to make great haste in getting out of New Babylon, for New Babylon's annihilation at God's hand will come *in a single day*, and the Jews will need to get out before that day arrives.

In the next chapter, I'll narrow my attention to how New Babylon's destruction is a part of the campaign of Armageddon. I'll also address prophecies about the permanence of New Babylon's destruction.

10

The Destruction of Commercial New Babylon, Part 2

I n the previous chapter we firmly established that our God is a God of judgment, and that all human beings will one day give an account for how they lived during their earthly lives. We then zeroed in on how the high and mighty New Babylon will be judged and brought low by God Almighty. In this chapter, we will continue our look at New Babylon's judgment. Let's start by reading Revelation 18:9-20:

> The kings of the world who committed adultery with her and enjoyed her great luxury will mourn for her as they see the smoke rising from her charred remains. They will stand at a distance, terrified by her great torment. They will cry out,
>
>> How terrible, how terrible for you,
>>> O Babylon, you great city!
>> In a single moment
>>> God's judgment came on you.

The merchants of the world will weep and mourn for her, for there is no one left to buy their goods. She bought great quantities of gold, silver, jewels, and pearls; fine linen, purple, silk, and scarlet cloth; things made of fragrant thyine wood, ivory goods, and objects made of expensive wood; and bronze, iron, and marble. She also bought cinnamon, spice, incense, myrrh, frankincense, wine, olive oil, fine flour, wheat, cattle, sheep, horses, wagons, and bodies—that is, human slaves.

> "The fancy things you loved so much
>   are gone," they cry.
> "All your luxuries and splendor
>   are gone forever,
>   never to be yours again."

The merchants who became wealthy by selling her these things will stand at a distance, terrified by her great torment. They will weep and cry out,

> "How terrible, how terrible for that great city!
>   She was clothed in finest purple and scarlet linens,
>   decked out with gold and precious stones and pearls!
>   In a single moment
>   all the wealth of the city is gone!"

And all the captains of the merchant ships and their passengers and sailors and crews will stand at a distance. They will cry out as they watch the smoke ascend, and they will say, "Where is there another city as great as this?" And they will weep and throw dust on their heads to show their grief. And they will cry out,

> "How terrible, how terrible for that great city!
>   The shipowners became wealthy
>   by transporting her great wealth on the seas.
>   In a single moment it is all gone."

> Rejoice over her fate, O heaven
>   and people of God and apostles and prophets!
> For at last God has judged her
>   for your sakes.

I cannot think of a more horrific description of judgment in the Bible than God's judgment of New Babylon. In this passage, we witness the rulers of the earth grieving and wailing—literally, *loudly lamenting*—when they witness the collapse of the economic system that enabled them to live so luxuriously (Revelation 18:9). The destruction of New Babylon will indicate to the world's rulers that the luxurious empire of the antichrist is utterly doomed. This is devastating news for them, for the antichrist and New Babylon are their source of power and wealth.

As I've noted previously, the "sexual immorality" of these leaders is not to be taken literally, but is rather a graphic metaphor indicating that these leaders have been intimately connected—metaphorically, *prostituting themselves*—with the anti-God Babylonian economic system (see Ezekiel 26:16; 27:30-35). They will all witness the smoke of New Babylon rising, perhaps indicating that the primary instrument of judgment against New Babylon will be fire—maybe even nuclear fire.

New Babylon will fall rapidly, "in a single moment" (Revelation 18:10). This means that the world leaders, watching from a distance—perhaps by live television and Internet feeds—will have insufficient time to prepare for the calamity. They will be surprised—*even stunned*—at this sudden turn of events.

For destruction to fall suddenly upon the wicked is a common occurrence in the Bible. Proverbs 6:15 warns, "They will be destroyed suddenly, broken in an instant beyond all hope of healing." Proverbs 24:22 warns that "disaster will hit them suddenly." Isaiah 47:11 warns that "a catastrophe will strike you suddenly, one for which you are not prepared." God affirms in Jeremiah 15:8, "I will cause anguish and terror to come upon them suddenly." In 1 Thessalonians 5:3, the apostle Paul warns, "When people are saying, 'Everything is peaceful and secure,' then disaster will fall on them as suddenly as a pregnant woman's labor pains begin. And there will be no escape."

New Babylon will be a mighty city. But more mighty than this city will be the divine Judge—*God Almighty*—who brings New Babylon to utter ruin. No wonder the world leaders will cower in fear.

Revelation 18:11 prophesies, "The merchants of the world will weep and mourn for her, for there is no one left to buy their goods." Clearly, it is not only the world's rulers who will lament over the fall of New Babylon. The world's merchants—business men and women all over the globe—will lament over Babylon's fall. Gone forever is their source of easy income.

We recall from Revelation 13 that no one on earth will be able to buy or sell without having received the mark of the beast. In the chapters that follow, it becomes increasingly clear that commercial Babylon—a global economic system—will be the heart and center of economic operations for the antichrist. When this commercial Babylon collapses, the merchants of the earth will no longer be able to buy or sell their goods. Economic ruin will come quickly. And, of course, having taken the mark of the beast, those who are part of this system will also face the wrath of God. All temporal *and* eternal hope will be gone forever.

Notice the irony here. This economic system set up by the antichrist will prohibit people from buying or selling if they haven't received the mark of the beast. But when the economic system itself collapses, all those who have the mark of the beast and are affiliated with this system will no longer be able to buy or sell.

This reminds me of how wicked people are often on the receiving end of "the boomerang effect"—that is, they often receive what they've dished out to others. Proverbs 26:27 tells us, "Whoever digs a pit will fall into it, and a stone will come back on him who starts it rolling" (ESV). Psalm 7:15-16 says, "He makes a pit, digging it out, and falls into the hole that he has made. His mischief returns upon his own head, and on his own skull his violence descends." Psalm 9:15 says, "The nations have sunk in the pit that they made; in the net that they hid, their own foot has been caught." Psalm 35:8 says, "Let the net that he hid ensnare him; let him fall into it—to his destruction!"

In Revelation 18:12-13 we read a list of all the commercial products traded in New Babylon. This indicates that prior to the city's fall, the amount of global imports into the city will be extensive. These products include precious metals and gems, clothing, furnishings, spices, food, animals, and even people.

It appears that there will be some form of slavery in New Babylon during the end times (Revelation 18:13). Tragically, slavery exists in our own day as well. Across the globe, for example, young girls and boys are abducted and forced into sexual servitude. This is an awful reality that will one day be judged by God.

Revelation 18:14 reveals that these trade merchants will lose all the luxurious possessions that their eyes of avarice had longed for. Gone forever will be their culinary delicacies. Gone forever will be their splendorous clothing. These items will be "gone forever, never to be yours again." The phrasing of this verse in the original Greek text—involving two double negatives—indicates the absolute certainty and finality of the loss of these items of wealth.

These who take part in all this commerce will be stunned in disbelief at what has happened to New Babylon (Revelation 18:15).

They will be mentally and emotionally unprepared for this cata-strophic turn of events, for it will happen so very quickly.

Notice how New Babylon, as an economic system, is described in a way quite similar to New Babylon as a religious system (Revelation 18:16). The false religious system is presented as a prostitute: "The woman wore purple and scarlet clothing and beautiful jewelry made of gold and precious gems and pearls" (Revelation 17:4). These words point to the "prostitute" dressing in such a luxurious and splendorous way as to entice people to join with her. Commercial New Babylon will likewise entice people to join with her in all of her great splendor. But when Babylon falls—"how terrible, how terrible"—the splendor will be gone, and the economy will collapse.

Revelation 18:17 reiterates how "in a single moment all the wealth of the city is gone!" The devastation will occur quickly. It will be far worse than the collapse of the stock market in 1929. This event will catastrophically and permanently devastate the global economy and world trade.

Three categories of sea people will be affected by this dire turn of events: captains, sailors, and their crews (Revelation 18:17). They will mourn over what has happened to New Babylon because their commercial transport business will have collapsed. With New Babylon and all its commercial products going up in flames, their business prospects go up in flames as well.

Scripture reveals that "they will weep and throw dust on their heads to show their grief" (Revelation 18:19). In Old Testament times, putting dust on one's head was a common means of expressing great grief. For example, when Job's friends beheld Job's suffering, they put dust on their heads (see Job 2:12). Joshua and the elders, in fear of being destroyed by the Amorites, "threw dust on their heads" (Joshua 7:6). When the Israelites were defeated in battle by the Philistines, a man "put dust on his head to show his grief," made his way to Shiloh, and informed the high priest Eli that his two sons had been killed (1 Samuel 4:12; see also 2 Samuel 1:2; 13:19; 15:32; Job 2:12; Lamentations 2:10). Likewise, those who make their living via the sea will be filled with grief over the sudden, fatal demise of New Babylon. Indeed, New Babylon will be flattened—*laid waste*—"in a single moment." Therefore they will "throw dust on their heads."

In Revelation 18:20 we witness a change of scenery—from earth's perspective to heaven's. In contrast to the grief-ridden earth-dwellers, God's people in heaven will respond with exuberant joy when commercial New Babylon collapses. Heaven always rejoices when sin is overthrown and God's righteousness and justice prevail.

Notice in our passage that there are three categories of the redeemed in heaven—the people of God, the apostles, and the prophets. The phrase "people of God" comes from a Greek word, *agios*, literally meaning "saints." All who become born again are "saints" (see Philippians 1:1 ESV). God's apostles and prophets are in a special category of saints, for they were the instruments of God's revelation to humankind. All these believers will collectively rejoice at the collapse of commercial New Babylon. God had earlier pronounced His verdict, and here we see His verdict executed.

Never Again

As if to drive a final nail into New Babylon's coffin, our passage continues with verses 21-24:

> Then a mighty angel picked up a boulder the size of a huge millstone. He threw it into the ocean and shouted,
>
> "Just like this, the great city Babylon
>   will be thrown down with violence
>   and will never be found again.
> The sound of harps, singers, flutes, and trumpets
>   will never be heard in you again.

No craftsmen and no trades
    will ever be found in you again.
The sound of the mill
    will never be heard in you again.
The light of a lamp
    will never shine in you again.
The happy voices of brides and grooms
    will never be heard in you again.
For your merchants were the greatest in the world,
    and you deceived the nations with your sorceries.
In your streets flowed the blood of the prophets and of God's
        holy people
    and the blood of people slaughtered all over the world."

What a vivid word picture! "A mighty angel picked up a boulder the size of a huge millstone. He threw it into the ocean" (Revelation 18:21). The imagery of one of God's angels throwing a boulder into the sea symbolizes, in a graphic way, the demise of New Babylon in judgment (see Jeremiah 51:63-64; Matthew 18:6). In Bible times, millstones were huge stones weighing thousands of pounds. They were used to grind grain. When such large and weighty stones are thrown into the sea, they will never rise again. All they can do is sink.

The same is true for New Babylon. Once this city falls and sinks in judgment, it will never rise again (see Exodus 15:5; Nehemiah 9:11). New Babylon's destruction will be a permanent reality.

Our text indicates that when New Babylon ends, many other things will end with it. There will be no more musicians playing, no more craftsmen working, no more lamps shining, and no more married couples talking to each other in the city. What had once been a vibrant and busy place—alive and bustling with activity—will be permeated by a deathly silence.

This severe judgment against New Babylon will be justified, for all the nations of the earth will have been seduced by its economic system. This seduction will be rooted in anti-God materialism, the philosophy that says that an accumulation of wealth and living in luxury are what give people meaning in life. In such a worldview, God is left entirely out of the picture. Scripture tells us that the city that embodies humanistic materialism will be materially destroyed, and all humans within it will die.

Revelation 18:24 then indicts Babylon: "In your streets flowed the blood of the prophets and of God's holy people and the blood of people slaughtered all over the world." The passage thus closes with a reminder that an underlying reason for God's judgment and destruction is that this city was responsible for slaying God's prophets and His saints. God's people had been martyred because of their testimonies for Jesus. Those associated with New Babylon shed the blood of God's "testifiers," and now, in response, their own blood was shed. God always brings about His justice. Vengeance is His (Romans 12:19-21). Economic Babylon will fall. And at this juncture, the second coming of Jesus Christ is imminent. It won't be long now.

We learn a very important lesson from our passage: *Great wealth is fleeting.* Scripture affirms that "riches don't last forever" (Proverbs 27:24). All people die, and at death they leave "all their wealth behind" (Psalm 49:10). King Solomon lamented, "I came to hate all my hard work here on earth, for I must leave to others everything I have earned" (Ecclesiastes 2:18). The apostle Paul affirmed that "we brought nothing with us when we came into the world, and we can't take anything with us when we leave it" (1 Timothy 6:7). Such truths help us to keep wealth and luxury in proper perspective.

Another lesson we learn here is that our true citizenship is not this temporal earth, which is passing away, but rather heaven above, which will last forever. The earth-dwellers who are alive during the tribulation period will be "citizens of Babylon"—even though they may not live in Babylon itself along the Euphrates River. They will be citizens of it because they live according to its values—that is, anti-God and materialistic values. You and I, even though we live in different cities on earth, are ultimately citizens of above. The apostle Paul said, "We are citizens of heaven, where the Lord Jesus Christ lives" (Philippians 3:20). Paul also said, "You are citizens along with all of God's holy people. You are members of God's family" (Ephesians 2:19). We are pilgrims passing through on earth, on our way to another country, another land, another city (Hebrews 11:16). And we are to behave here *below* as citizens of that city *above*.

Babylon's Destruction: Stage Two of Armageddon

New Babylon's destruction will take place during Armageddon, that final campaign of battles that will occur just prior to Jesus's second coming. It's important to understand, however, that the destruction of New Babylon is only one small part of a much bigger puzzle in prophetic Scripture.

The book of Revelation tells us that those who dwell on earth during the tribulation will suffer through the seal judgments, the trumpet judgments, and the bowl judgments. Worse comes to worse, however, when these already-traumatized human beings find themselves engaged in a catastrophic war campaign called Armageddon (see Daniel 11:40-45; Joel 3:9-17; Zechariah 14:1-3; Revelation 16:14-16). Virtually millions of people will perish in the worst conflict ever to hit planet Earth.

The word *Armageddon* means "Mount of Megiddo." It refers to a location some 60 miles north of Jerusalem. This is a famous site— it is the location of Barak's battle with the Canaanites (Judges 4) as well as Gideon's battle with the Midianites (Judges 7). Napoleon is reported to have once commented that this site is perhaps the greatest battlefield he had ever set his eyes on. It is here that the final horrific battles of humankind will unfold immediately prior to the second coming of Christ (Revelation 16:16). The carnage will be so horrible that not a single person would survive if it were not for Christ coming again (Matthew 24:22).

In chapter 1 of this book, I noted that there will be eight stages to the campaign of Armageddon. Here, I will expand upon these stages a bit so that you can see how New Babylon's destruction fits into the overall scheme of what will take place during Armageddon.

Stage 1 of Armageddon: The allied armies of the antichrist will gather for the final destruction of the Jews (Revelation 16:12-16). This attack will be demon-inspired. Also at this time, the Euphrates River will be dried up, thereby making it easier for the armies of the East (Asian armies) to assemble. Things are about to get really bad!

Stage 2 of Armageddon: Commercial New Babylon is destroyed. This destruction is predicted by several Old Testament prophets. In Jeremiah 50:13-14, we read that because of God's wrath, Babylon will become "a deserted wasteland. All who pass by will be horrified and will gasp at the destruction they see there. Yes, prepare to attack Babylon, all you surrounding nations. Let your archers shoot at her; spare no arrows. For she has sinned against the LORD." We then read, "Babylon, the mightiest hammer in all the earth, lies broken and shattered. Babylon is desolate among the nations! Listen, Babylon, for I have set a trap for you. You are caught, for you have fought against the LORD. The LORD has opened his armory and brought out weapons to vent his fury" (verses 23-25).

Isaiah 13:19 then tells us that Babylon "will be devastated like Sodom and Gomorrah when God destroyed them." God affirms in no uncertain terms, "I will destroy it as I destroyed Sodom and Gomorrah and their neighboring towns...No one will live there; no one will inhabit it" (Jeremiah 50:40). God's destruction of New Babylon will be so thorough that nothing will be recoverable.

Stage 3 of Armageddon: Despite the fact that the antichrist's commercial capital has just been destroyed, he is not distracted away from his primary goal of destroying the Jewish people. He therefore instructs his military forces to attack Jerusalem. We read about the city's destruction in Zechariah 14:1-2:

> Watch, for the day of the LORD is coming when your possessions will be plundered right in front of you! I will gather all the nations to fight against Jerusalem. The city will be taken, the houses looted, and the women raped. Half the population will be taken into captivity, and the rest will be left among the ruins of the city.

Notice that *all the nations* of the world gather against Jerusalem. This apparently means that the United States will be part of that group. Of course, following the rapture of the church, there will be no more Israel-loving Christians in the United States. It seems likely that after the rapture, the United States will become an ally of the revived Roman Empire—the United States of Europe, headed up by the antichrist.

Stage 4 of Armageddon: The antichrist then moves south against the Jewish remnant. Prophetic Scripture reveals that not all the Jews will be in Jerusalem when the forces of the antichrist attack. Recall that at the midpoint of the tribulation, the antichrist will break his covenant with Israel, exalt himself as deity, and set up an image of himself in the Jewish temple. Christ, in His Olivet Discourse, warned of how quickly the Jews must flee for their lives (Matthew 24:16-31). Many of the Jews will immediately flee to the deserts and mountains (24:16), perhaps in the area of Bozrah/Petra, about 80 miles south of Jerusalem.

This escape from Jerusalem is described for us in Revelation 12:6: "The woman [a metaphor for Israel] fled into the wilderness, where God had prepared a place to care for her for 1,260 days [three-and-a-half years]" (inserts added for clarity). Indeed, the woman "was given two wings like those of a great eagle so she could fly to the place prepared for her in the wilderness. There she would be cared for and protected from the dragon for a time, times, and half a time" (verse 14). "A time, times, and half a time" refers to a year, two years, and half a year, which, added up, refers to the last three-and-a-half years of the tribulation period. During this time God will watch over the Jewish remnant.

It is this remnant of Jews that the antichrist now targets. The Jews sense that doom is about to come upon them as the forces of the antichrist gather in the rugged wilderness, poised to attack and annihilate them. They are helpless, and, from an earthly perspective, utterly defenseless.

Stage 5 of Armageddon: Israel—now endangered by the forces of the antichrist—then experiences national regeneration by turning to their Messiah, Jesus Christ. Hosea 6:1-3 indicates that the Jewish leaders will call for the people of the nation to repent—and their collective repentance will take two days:

> Come, let us return to the LORD. He has torn us to pieces; now he will heal us. He has injured us; now he will bandage our wounds. In just a short time he will restore us, so that we may live in his presence. Oh, that we might know the LORD! Let us press on to know him. He will respond to us as surely as the arrival of dawn or the coming of rains in early spring.

Just as it was the Jewish leaders who led the Jewish people to reject Jesus as their Messiah in the first century, so now—at the end of the tribulation period—the Jewish leaders urge repentance and instruct all to turn to Jesus as their Messiah. This the remnant will do, and they will be saved (see Joel 2:28-29; Zechariah 12:2–13:1).

Stage 6 of Armageddon: The second coming of Jesus Christ occurs. The prayers of the Jewish remnant are answered! Jesus the divine Messiah returns personally to rescue His people from danger. He will come again physically and visibly, and every eye will see Him (see Acts 1:9; 1 Timothy 6:14; Titus 2:13; 1 Peter 4:13).

The second coming will be a universal experience in the sense that every eye on earth will witness the event. Revelation 1:7 says, "Look! He comes with the clouds of heaven. And everyone will see him—even those who pierced him. And all the nations of the world will mourn for him." Jesus Himself affirmed: "The sign that the Son of Man is coming will appear in the heavens, and there will be deep mourning among all the peoples of the earth. And they will see the Son of Man coming on the clouds of heaven with power and great glory" (Matthew 24:30).

When Jesus returns, there will be magnificent signs in the heavens (Matthew 24:29-30). Christ will come as the King of kings and Lord of lords, and there will be many crowns on His head—crowns that represent absolute sovereignty (Revelation 19:11-16).

Old Testament prophetic scriptures reveal that Jesus will return first to the mountain wilderness of Bozrah, where the Jewish remnant is endangered (Isaiah 34:1-7; 63:1-6; Habakkuk 3:3; Micah 2:12-13). They will not be in peril for long!

Stage 7 of Armageddon: Jesus confronts the antichrist and his military forces and slays them with the sword of His mouth. The book of Revelation describes the second coming of Jesus this way:

> I saw heaven opened, and a white horse was standing there. Its rider was named Faithful and True, for he judges fairly and wages a righteous war. His eyes were like flames of fire, and on his head were many crowns. A name was written on him that no one understood except himself. He wore a robe dipped in blood, and his title was the Word of God. The armies of heaven, dressed in the finest of pure white linen, followed him on white horses. From his mouth came a sharp sword to strike down the nations. He will

rule them with an iron rod. He will release the fierce wrath of God, the Almighty, like juice flowing from a winepress. On his robe at his thigh was written this title: King of all kings and Lord of all lords (Revelation 19:11-16).

Revelation 19:19-21 then describes Christ's utter defeat of the antichrist, the false prophet, and the military forces under the antichrist's command:

> Then I saw the beast and the kings of the world and their armies gathered together to fight against the one sitting on the horse and his army. And the beast was captured, and with him the false prophet who did mighty miracles on behalf of the beast—miracles that deceived all who had accepted the mark of the beast and who worshiped his statue. Both the beast and his false prophet were thrown alive into the fiery lake of burning sulfur. Their entire army was killed by the sharp sword that came from the mouth of the one riding the white horse. And the vultures all gorged themselves on the dead bodies.

Stage 8 of Armageddon: At this point Jesus Christ victoriously ascends the Mount of Olives. Zechariah 14:3-4 describes the scene:

> Then the Lord will go out to fight against those nations, as he has fought in times past. On that day his feet will stand on the Mount of Olives, east of Jerusalem. And the Mount of Olives will split apart, making a wide valley running from east to west. Half the mountain will move toward the north and half toward the south.

Following the second coming of Christ, Jesus will personally set up His kingdom on earth. In theological circles, this is known as the millennial kingdom (Revelation 20:2-7; see also Isaiah 65:18-23; Jeremiah 31:12-14,31-37; Ezekiel 34:25-29; 37:1-13; 40–48). Christ will physically rule on earth from the throne of David (2 Samuel

7:12-14). It is during this time that God finally and definitively fulfills all His covenant promises to Israel. God never goes back on His promises!

It is fascinating to ponder the reality that there are many prophetic signs of the times which indicate not only that the tribulation period may be drawing near, but that the rapture of the church is all the nearer. I'll address this in the next chapter. These are exciting times in which to live!

Near-Term Prophetic Expectations, Part 1

I n anticipation of the rise of New Babylon—both the religious and commercial aspects—we would expect to see a continued rise in false apostles, false prophets, and false teachers; a continued rise in false religions and cults; a continued escalation of apostasy and a turning away from biblical Christianity; an increase in tolerance for all religious belief systems, truth claims, moral convictions, and lifestyle choices; a steady decrease in religious freedom around the world, particularly as related to Bible-believing Christians; a continued rise in anti-Semitism, accompanied by a parallel rise in the number of Jews returning to the Holy Land from countries around the world; a continued escalation of the Middle East conflict with Israel at the epicenter; continuing efforts toward the rebuilding of the Jewish temple, accompanied by Muslim resentment toward those efforts; a continued escalation in terrorist acts around the world; the stage continuing to be set for the eventual Russia-Muslim invasion into Israel; an increase in the persecution—*even martyrdom*—of Christians; an increasingly cashless society in preparation for the antichrist's eventual control of the world economy; a continued interest in globalist solutions to global problems; a continued increase in "connecting" through the Internet and cyberspace; the increasing use of biometric technologies with a parallel decrease in personal privacy around the world; and a growing nuclear and electromagnetic pulse threat. In what follows I will briefly address each of these as related to the rise of New Babylon, both religious and commercial.

In the study of Bible prophecy, these trends and events are known as "signs of the times." This phrase describes specific characteristics or conditions that will exist in the end times. When these signs are witnessed by people on earth, they can rightly deduce they are living in the last days. Such signs may be considered God's "intel in advance." (*Intel* is short for "intelligence report.") By these signs, God gives us intel regarding what the world will look like as we enter the end times.

Prophecy scholars emphasize that many of the signs of the times recorded in Scripture relate specifically to the tribulation period. In Matthew 24:3, the disciples asked Jesus, "Tell us, when will all this happen? What sign will signal your return and the end of the world?" In verses 4 and following, Jesus spoke of a number of signs of the times that will emerge during the years prior to the second coming— years that unfold during the tribulation period.

You may be wondering if the tribulation-era signs of the times are relevant for us today, especially since the rapture of the church will precede the tribulation. My answer is that we are currently witnessing many events in the world that are quite obviously setting the stage for the fulfillment of many of these prophecies pertaining to the tribulation period. Of course, any stage-setting that indicates the tribulation period may be drawing near is also evidence that the rapture of the church is all the nearer.

The late Dr. John F. Walvoord gave an illustration that helps us to put all this into perspective. He compared the rapture to Thanksgiving and the second coming to Christmas. There are all kinds of "signs"—media ads, manger scenes, lights and decorations—indicating that Christmas is drawing near. The signs are everywhere. But Thanksgiving can sneak up on us. We don't see very many obvious signs that Thanksgiving is approaching. But one fact is certain: If Thanksgiving has not yet taken place, and yet we're seeing clear "signs" for the soon arrival of Christmas, we automatically know that Thanksgiving is all the nearer. By analogy, as we witness the stage being set today for events that will transpire during the tribulation, we can know that the rapture is indeed drawing all the nearer.

Just as tremors (or foreshocks) often occur before major earthquakes, so preliminary manifestations of some of these signs will emerge prior to the tribulation period. Someone said that prophecies cast their shadows before them. I believe this is true. Prophecies that relate specifically to the tribulation period are presently casting their shadows before them. The stage is now being set for their fulfillment.

In the pages that follow, allow me to be your tour guide through some of these signs of the times, and we'll consider how they may relate to the rise of New Babylon during the tribulation.

False Christs, False Prophets, and False Apostles

Jesus, in His Olivet Discourse, taught His followers about the end times. He emphasized that His followers would witness an escalation of false Christs:

> False messiahs and false prophets will rise up and perform great signs and wonders so as to deceive, if possible, even God's chosen ones. See, I have warned you about this ahead of time. So if someone tells you, "Look, the Messiah

is out in the desert," don't bother to go and look. Or, "Look, he is hiding here," don't believe it! (Matthew 24:24-26).

The apostle Paul—Jesus's "chosen instrument" to take His message "to the Gentiles and to kings, as well as to the people of Israel" (Acts 9:15)—also warned of those who believed in a different Jesus (2 Corinthians 11:4).

The danger, of course, is that a counterfeit Jesus who preaches a counterfeit gospel yields a counterfeit salvation (see Galatians 1:8). There are no exceptions to this maxim.

Even in our own day, we witness an unprecedented rise in false Christs and self-constituted messiahs affiliated with the kingdom of the cults and the occult. The late Reverend Moon, of the Unification Church, taught his followers that he was the "Lord of the Second Advent." David Koresh, of the Branch Davidians, claimed to be the final prophet and "the Son of God, the Lamb." Jim Jones, founder of the Peoples' Temple, claimed to be the reincarnation of Jesus. New Ager David Spangler taught that all people may become the Christ, just as Jesus became the Christ. There are countless other examples. This will no doubt continue as we move further into the end times.

Scripture also contains many warnings against false prophets for the simple reason that God's own people can be deceived. Ezekiel 34:1-7, for example, indicates that God's sheep can be abused and led astray by wicked shepherds. Jesus Himself warned, "Beware of false prophets who come disguised as harmless sheep but are really vicious wolves" (Matthew 7:15). The apostle Paul warned Christians about the possibility of deception (Acts 20:28-30; 2 Corinthians 11:2-3). First John 4:1-3 thus exhorts believers to test those who claim to be prophets:

> Dear friends, do not believe everyone who claims to speak
> by the Spirit. You must test them to see if the spirit they

have comes from God. For there are many false prophets in the world. This is how we know if they have the Spirit of God: If a person claiming to be a prophet acknowledges that Jesus Christ came in a real body, that person has the Spirit of God. But if someone claims to be a prophet and does not acknowledge the truth about Jesus, that person is not from God. Such a person has the spirit of the Antichrist, which you heard is coming into the world and indeed is already here.

There are a number of Bible verses that warn us what to watch for in false prophets. Among other things, false prophets may...

- offer prophecies that do not come true (Deuteronomy 18:21-22)
- cause people to follow false gods or idols (Exodus 20:3-4; Deuteronomy 13:1-3)
- deny the deity of Jesus Christ (Colossians 2:8-9)
- deny the humanity of Jesus Christ (1 John 4:1-2)
- promote immorality (Jude 4-7)
- encourage legalistic self-denial (Colossians 2:16-23)

A basic rule of thumb is that if a so-called prophet says anything that clearly contradicts any part of God's Word, his teachings should be rejected (1 Thessalonians 5:21). God's Word is our barometer of truth.

Scripture further warns about false apostles who "are deceitful workers who disguise themselves as apostles of Christ" (2 Corinthians 11:13). The two key characteristics we see here are that these individuals deceive people doctrinally and that they pretend to be true apostles of Jesus Christ.

Christ commends those who take a stand against false apostles. Recall what He said to the church of Ephesus: "I know all the things you do. I have seen your hard work and your patient endurance. I know you don't tolerate evil people. You have examined the claims of those who say they are apostles but are not. You have discovered they are liars" (Revelation 2:2).

How can we test the claims of apostles? Like the ancient Bereans, all Christians should make a regular habit of testing all things against Scripture (Acts 17:11). No true apostle will ever say anything that contradicts the Word of God (see Galatians 1:8).

Here is something to think about: As we continue to move deeper into the end times, it is logical to assume that the continued rise in false Christs, false prophets, and false apostles will set the stage for the eventual emergence of the ultimate false prophet and false religion that will emanate from New Babylon.

False Religions and Cults

In keeping with the rise in false Christs, false prophets, and false apostles, we can expect the continued growth in false religions and cults. World religions include Islam, Hinduism, Buddhism, Zoroastrianism, Jainism, Sikhism, Taoism, Confucianism, and Shintoism. Each of these religions sets forth false ideas about God, how to be saved, and other important matters.

Cults are generally smaller. Theologically, a cult is a religious group that emerges out of a parent religion (such as Christianity, Islam, or Hinduism), but departs from that parent religion by denying—explicitly or implicitly—one or more of the essential doctrines of that religion. Cults include such groups as Jehovah's Witnesses, the Mormons, the Unification Church, the Mind Sciences, Satanism, Spiritism, Baha'ism, the Way International, Wiccans, and the Unitarian Universalists.

Among the cults and false religions, one typically finds an emphasis on new revelation from God, a denial of the sole authority of the Bible, a distorted view of God and Jesus, a distorted view of

Christ's work at the cross, a distorted view of the Holy Spirit, and a denial of salvation by grace through faith. The deceptions are many, and they are growing rapidly.

Who do you think is ultimately behind all the false teachings in false religions and cults? I believe it is Satan. Jesus said in John 8:44, "He has always hated the truth, because there is no truth in him. When he lies, it is consistent with his character; for he is a liar and the father of lies." In keeping with his role as the father of lies, Satan is also continuously involved in blinding people from the truth: "Satan, who is the god of this world, has blinded the minds of those who don't believe. They are unable to see the glorious light of the Good News" (2 Corinthians 4:4).

It is my belief that Satan has become a master niche marketer of false ideas in these last days. There's virtually something for everyone in the kingdom of the cults as well as the various false religions. Satan provides a variety of deceptive options to satisfy peoples' desires. Those who find appeal in being their own gods might look to the New Age movement or Mormonism. If personal empowerment and creating your own reality appeals to you, then (again) the New Age movement might be for you. If you like health and wealth, then the Word-Faith movement is what you want. If you don't like the ideas of pain, suffering, and death, then maybe Christian Science is your ticket (since pain, suffering, and death are denied in this cult). If you're more interested in contacting dead loved ones, then perhaps Spiritism is your choice. Do you like the idea of living many lives through reincarnation? Then maybe Hinduism is for you.

As I said, Satan is a master niche marketer of false ideas. With each cultic group and false religion, he seeks to keep people away from the true God, the true Jesus, and the true gospel. It is no wonder that Scripture exhorts Christians to beware of Satan's "evil schemes" (2 Corinthians 2:11).

I find all this quite relevant to this book: As we continue to move deeper into the end times, it is logical to assume that the continued rise in false religions and cults will set the stage for the eventual emergence of the ultimate false religion that will emanate from New Babylon.

Apostasy and the Turning Away from Biblical Christianity

Apostasy comes from a similar-sounding Greek word, *apostasia*, which means "falling away." The word pictures a determined, willful "defection from the faith" or an "abandonment of the faith."

There are a variety of ways that people can apostatize or "fall away" from the truth. These include a denial of God (2 Timothy 3:4-5), a denial of Christ (1 John 2:18-23), a denial of Christ's return (2 Peter 3:3-4), a denial of "the faith" (1 Timothy 4:1-2), a denial of sound doctrine (2 Timothy 4:3-4), a denial of morals (2 Timothy 3:1-8), and a denial of authority (2 Peter 2:10).

Scripture soberly warns that there will be a notable increase of apostasy in the end times. In 1 Timothy 4:1, Paul lamented, "The Holy Spirit tells us clearly that in the last times some will turn away from the true faith; they will follow deceptive spirits and teachings that come from demons."

Paul continued his warning about end-times apostasy in 2 Timothy 4:3-4: "A time is coming when people will no longer listen to sound and wholesome teaching. They will follow their own desires and will look for teachers who will tell them whatever their itching ears want to hear. They will reject the truth and chase after myths."

Paul gets even more explicit in 2 Timothy 3:1-5:

> In the last days there will be very difficult times. For people will love only themselves and their money. They will be boastful and proud, scoffing at God, disobedient to their parents, and ungrateful. They will consider nothing sacred. They will be unloving and unforgiving; they will slander

others and have no self-control. They will be cruel and hate
what is good. They will betray their friends, be reckless, be
puffed up with pride, and love pleasure rather than God.
They will act religious, but they will reject the power that
could make them godly.

Notice that in the last days there will be *lovers of self* (we might
call this humanism), *lovers of money* (materialism), and *lovers of pleasure* (hedonism). Humanism, materialism, and hedonism are three
of the most prominent philosophies in our world today, and they
often go together in a complementary fashion. These philosophies
grow more popular with each passing day.

Of course, as we continue to move deeper into the end times, the
rise in apostasy will be like a fertile soil for the easy blossoming of
the false religion associated with New Babylon. We can also expect
the philosophies of humanism, materialism, and hedonism to permeate New Babylon.

Increase in Tolerance on Religious and Moral Issues

We are now living in an age of radical "tolerance." One risks
being accused of intolerance if one criticizes someone's beliefs or
actions. One even risks being accused of intolerance if one simply
tells a person about what he or she believes to be true. The apostle
Paul asked, "Have I now become your enemy because I am telling
you the truth?" (Galatians 4:16). Speaking the truth these days can
get you into big trouble!

I've always loved the golden rule: "Do to others whatever you
would like them to do to you" (Matthew 7:12). Our present day
has witnessed the emergence of a different—or *perverted*—version of the golden rule: "Be tolerant of others [their beliefs, actions,
and lifestyle] as you would have them to be tolerant of you [your

beliefs, actions, and lifestyle]—for all beliefs, actions, and lifestyles are equally valid."

Today, the "tolerant" person is expected to be wholly accepting of other belief systems, truth claims, moral convictions, and lifestyle choices. He or she typically believes that "whatever works for me is my truth" just as "whatever works for you is your truth." We should all just live and let live. Being tolerant today means more than merely recognizing another person's right to hold to beliefs different from our own; it insists that we agree that all views are *equally valid* and all lifestyles are *equally appropriate*.

Such tolerance is rooted in relativism—the idea that anything can be true for the individual, but nothing can be true for everyone. It is considered presumptuous for anyone to think he or she knows the truth for all people. We are told that the truly loving thing to do is to unquestioningly allow everyone to hold their own truth without challenge. That's how tolerance has been defined!

The "tolerant" mindset of today views members of all religions—Buddhists, Hindus, Muslims, Jains, Sikhs, Confucians, Taoists, Zoroastrians, Baha'is, Theosophists, Rastafarians, witches, goddess worshippers, and whoever else—as being on equally valid paths to God, with no one path higher or more virtuous than another. Another supposedly equally valid path is not believing in any deity at all. According to this line of thinking, we ought never to evangelize those outside our personal faith.

It is a given that the deeper we go into the end times, this tolerance for all beliefs will make it easy for the false religion associated with New Babylon to rise unchallenged. Following the rapture of Bible-believing and "narrow minded" Christians, all who remain behind will be tolerant and open to anything that comes down the path.

Continued Rise in Anti-Semitism

Anti-Semitism may be defined as hostility toward or discrimi-nation against Jews as a religious or racial group. It is sobering that anti-Semitism seems to be escalating everywhere around the world. A European study surveyed some 6,000 self-identified Jews, and the findings were alarming:

- Two-thirds of the respondents affirmed that anti-Semitism was a serious problem in their country.

- Three out of four respondents felt that anti-Semitism had worsened in the past five years.

- Close to a quarter said they sometimes refrained from visiting Jewish events or sites out of safety concerns.

- Nearly two out of five said they usually avoided public dis-plays of Jewish identity such as wearing a Star of David.

- Almost one in three had considered emigrating because they did not feel safe as Jews.[1]

The April 2015 issue of *U.S. News & World Report* tells us that "seventy years after the Holocaust, anti-Semitism is again growing more virulent in Europe. From Toulouse to Paris, London to Ber-lin, Brussels to Copenhagen, Jews are being harassed, assaulted, and even killed."[2]

Newsweek magazine published an article titled "Exodus: Why Europe's Jews Are Fleeing Once Again." In the article we read of some recent events:

> France has suffered the worst violence, but anti-Semitism is spiking across Europe…In Britain there were around 100 anti-Semitic incidents…In Berlin a crowd of anti-Israel protesters had to be prevented from attacking a synagogue. In Liege, Belgium, a café owner put up a sign saying dogs

were welcome, but Jews were not allowed...Yet for many French and European Jews, the violence comes as no surprise. Seventy years after the Holocaust, from Amiens to Athens, the world's oldest hatred flourishes anew.[3]

A recent report issued by the Pew Research Center indicates that Jews are being persecuted in 34 out of 45 European countries, and anti-Semitic harassment worldwide has reached a seven-year high. A Lamb and Lion Ministries report tells us:

> All over Europe, and particularly in Greece, France, and Belgium, Jews are seeing their religious freedoms violated, their cemeteries vandalized, and their synagogues desecrated. They are also experiencing increasing personal attacks that often result in death. In France, the annual number of anti-Semitic incidents is currently seven times as high as in the 1990s. In 2014, they doubled.[4]

Are you thinking what I'm thinking? Today's anti-Semitism is preparing the ground for the catastrophic anti-Semitism that will emerge during the tribulation period. We know from prophetic Scripture that the antichrist will engage in a campaign to annihilate the Jews (see Daniel 7:21,25; Matthew 24:15-22; 2 Thessalonians 2:4). New Babylon, too, will be a vile persecutor of the Jews (Revelation 18:24). This widespread campaign against the Jews will be motivated by Satan (Revelation 2:10; 12:12-13; see also John 8:44).

There are yet more signs of the times we need to touch on. Let's continue in the next chapter.

12

Near-Term Prophetic Expectations, Part 2

In the previous chapter, I addressed some of the key signs of the times—*God's "intel in advance"*—relating to the rise of New Babylon, both religious and commercial. Let's now continue our discussion, beginning with the Middle East conflict.

Continued Escalation of the Middle East Conflict

Jerusalem literally means "city of peace." However, peace seems elusive in Jerusalem nowadays. In fact, there is little peace in all of Israel—due to external threats. The truth is, the entire Middle East has been an arena of conflict for the past 70 years. Wars in the region include the War of Independence (which brought Israel's statehood—1947–1948), the Suez War/Sinai Campaign (1956), the Six-Day War (1967), the War of Attrition (1968–1970), the Yom Kippur/October War (1973), the Lebanese Civil War (1975–1976), the Iran-Iraq War (1980–1988), the Lebanon War (1982–1985), the Persian Gulf War (1991), the War on Terror (2001 to present), and the War with Iraq (1991–2003).

At the heart of the conflict is the fact that Jerusalem is the holiest of cities for the Jews. At the same time, it is the third holiest city for Muslims, behind Mecca and Medina. Jews believe Jerusalem belongs to them alone by divine right. Muslims, too, believe Jerusalem belongs to them alone by divine right. Because neither side will budge, conflict is inevitable.

In 1948, in fulfillment of the prophecy in Ezekiel 37, Israel became a living, breathing nation, brought back from the dead, as it were. Since then, Islamists have viewed Israel's existence as an aggression. The initial settlement of Jews in the land was illegitimate to start with, they say, for the Jews had no right to "return" or "come back" to a land under Islamic authority. Following the Islamic logic of the Fatah and of jihad, any territory that was at some time "opened" by a legitimate Islamic authority cannot revert to a non-Islamic authority. This means Israel cannot reemerge on Muslim land; this constitutes a grievous offense to Allah.

During the nineteenth and twentieth centuries, three significant ideologies emerged in the Middle East related to the current Middle East conflict: Zionism, Arab nationalism, and Islamic fundamentalism. Zionism is a type of Jewish nationalism that has the goal of reestablishing the Jewish ancestral homeland. It involves not just the idea that the Jews have returned to the land but also the return of Jewish sovereignty to the ancestral homeland. Zionism, then, is essentially a national liberation movement of the Jewish people.

Arab nationalism emerged as a movement that seeks to unify Arabs as one people by appealing to a sense of their common history, culture, and language. This movement is secular and seeks to gain and maintain Arab power in the Arab lands of the Middle East. Arab nationalists seek to end—or at least minimize—direct Western influence in the Arab world. As well, Israel is viewed as a cancerous tumor that must be removed.

Islamic fundamentalism is a religious philosophy that seeks to establish Islamic dominance in the Middle East and eventually the rest of the world. Israel, a symbol of Jewish power, is viewed as a grievous insult to Allah and cannot be allowed to exist in the Islamic world. Israel must therefore be pushed into the sea.

Many believe that the current existence of these three ideologies constitutes a powder-keg formula:

Zionism

+

Arab nationalism

+

Islamic fundamentalism

=

MIDDLE EAST CONFLICT

To make matters worse, an apocalyptic strain of Muslim theology has emerged that has made the world a much more dangerous place to live. Mainstream Shiites have long believed in the eventual return of the Twelfth Imam, believed to be a direct bloodline descendant of Muhammad's son-in-law, Ali (whose family, it is believed, constitutes the only legitimate successors to Muhammad). The Twelfth Imam—who allegedly disappeared as a child in AD 941—will allegedly return in the future as the Mahdi ("the rightly guided One"), who will bring about a messianic-like era of global order and justice for Shiites in which Islam will be victorious and reign supreme.

It is believed that the time of the appearance of the Twelfth Imam can be hastened through apocalyptic chaos and violence—that is, by unleashing an apocalyptic holy war against Christians and Jews (the United States and Israel). Hence, the destruction of Israel and the United States is one of the key global developments that allegedly will trigger the appearance of the Mahdi.

All this is no surprise to those familiar with biblical prophecy. Prophetic Scripture tells us that Israel will increasingly be a sore spot in the world during the end times. In Zechariah 12:2 we read, "Behold, I am about to make Jerusalem a cup of staggering to all the surrounding peoples" (ESV). This can also be translated, "I am going to make Jerusalem a cup that sends all the surrounding peoples reeling" (NIV). If there's one thing this verse tells us, it's that even though Israel is small, the end-times turmoil generated by this nation will affect many large countries. Notice that the nations that surround Israel are Islamic. And they are brutally anti-Semitic.

My friend, we may expect "reeling" in the Middle East to steadily increase in the years to come. Eventually, however, the antichrist will solve the Middle East problem and sign a covenant with Israel (Daniel 9:27). During the second half of the tribulation period he will apparently assume control of the entire Middle East with his headquarters established at New Babylon. I fully expect the antichrist to seize all the oil fields in the Middle East and put them under New Babylon's control.

The Coming Ezekiel Invasion into Israel

Some 2,600 years ago, the ancient prophet Ezekiel prophesied that the Jews would be regathered from "many nations" to the land of Israel in the end times (Ezekiel 36–37). This is the reason 1948 is such a significant year. Ezekiel then prophesied that, sometime later, there would be an all-out invasion into Israel by a massive northern assault force, with Russia heading up a coalition of Muslim nations.

Ezekiel 38:1-6 mentions the specific nations that will make up this invading force:

- Rosh[1] is modern-day Russia.
- Magog is the geographical area in the southern portion of

the former Soviet Union, including Kazakhstan, Kyrgyzstan, Uzbekistan, Turkmenistan, Tajikistan, and probably parts of modern Afghanistan.

- Meshech and Tubal, Gomer, and Beth-togarmah all refer to modern Turkey.
- Persia is modern Iran.
- Cush is the Sudan.
- Put is modern-day Libya.

The primary unifying factor among these nations is that they are all Islamic, with the exception of Russia—whose population is more than 20 percent Islamic.

Ezekiel prophesied that this invasion would take place "in the latter years" (Ezekiel 38:8 ESV) and "in the latter days" (38:16 ESV) from the standpoint of his day. Such phrases point to the end times.

It is possible that this invasion may take place prior to the tribulation period. My book *Northern Storm Rising* provides many details as to why this scenario makes good sense.

Ezekiel reveals that God will utterly annihilate the Muslim invaders. They will no doubt scream "Allahu akbar!" as they invade, which means "Allah is the greatest." But Yahweh—the one true God—will effortlessly obliterate the Allah-worshipping invaders. As Moses often said, there is none like Yahweh in all the universe.

Now, if God destroys these invaders prior to the tribulation period, this will make it easier for other prophecies to quickly fall into place:

- The antichrist will be able to rise more easily to world domination during the tribulation, with Muslims who seek a world caliphate now out of the picture.
- The Jews will have a much easier time rebuilding the temple

on the Temple Mount, with Muslim resistance now greatly reduced.

• The false religions associated with New Babylon will be able to rise to prominence more quickly. After all, not only will Muslims be out of the picture, Christians will have been raptured prior to the tribulation. This means that the two religious groups most likely to resist the false religion of New Babylon—Muslims and biblical Christians—will no longer be around to resist.

Rebuilding the Jewish Temple

Prophetic Scripture reveals that a Jewish temple will exist during the future seven-year tribulation period. Of course, there can be no rebuilt Jewish temple unless there is first a Jewish land—a reborn Israel—in which to rebuild the temple. This makes Israel's rebirth as a nation in 1948 highly significant. Ever since then, the Jews have been streaming back to the Holy Land from all over the world in fulfillment of biblical prophecy (see Ezekiel 36–37). Now that the Jews are back in their own land, it makes sense that they would eventually want to rebuild the temple (see Matthew 24:15-16).

Even today we hear reports that various Jewish individuals and groups—such as the Temple Institute—have been working behind the scenes to prepare various materials for the future temple, including priestly robes, temple tapestries, and worship utensils. These items are being prefabricated so that when the temple is finally rebuilt, everything will be ready for it.[2]

Meanwhile, three times a day, many Jews pray at the Western Wall in Jerusalem, crying out, "May our temple be rebuilt in this day here in the holy city."[3] Many Jews see a connection between the building of this temple and the soon return of their Messiah.

There are other recent developments that portend the rebuilding of the Jewish temple. For example, the Sanhedrin—after 1,600 years of absence—has been reestablished. In Bible times, the Sanhedrin was the supreme court and legislative body of the Jews, made up of 71 rabbis. Prophecy scholar Thomas Ice notes, "The reinstitution of the Sanhedrin is seen as a harbinger for the rebuilding of the Temple and the coming of Messiah. Orthodox Jews believe that a body like the Sanhedrin is needed today to oversee the rebuilding of the Temple and to identify Messiah should he appear on the scene."[4]

One reason for the necessity of a new Sanhedrin with regard to the temple is that only the Sanhedrin can select the man who will serve as the high priest of the temple.[5] Now that the Sanhedrin is in place, the selection of the high priest will be an easier task to accomplish, once it becomes necessary.

Of course, there can't be a rebuilding of the temple unless architectural plans are first drawn up. Toward this end, the new Sanhedrin has issued a call for such plans. They are also calling for donations from Jews to acquire the materials necessary for the building of the temple.[6]

The relevance of all this to the present book is obvious. At the midpoint of the tribulation, the antichrist will claim to be god and set up an image of himself in the Jewish temple. Soon after, he and his forces will destroy the false religion associated with New Babylon. From that point forward, he intends to be the sole object of worship on earth. He will then move his headquarters to commercial New Babylon, along the Euphrates River.

Persecution and Martyrdom of Christians

The persecution of Christians is now taking place on a global basis. Current estimates are that 80 percent of all acts of religious persecution around the world today are directed specifically against Christians.[7] That is staggering!

The prophetic scriptures indicate that the persecution and martyrdom of believers will increase greatly during the future seven-year tribulation. To clarify, Christians on earth will be raptured prior to the tribulation period (1 Thessalonians 1:10; 4:13-17; 5:9; Revelation 3:10). But many people will become believers after the rapture, during the tribulation (Matthew 25:31-46; Revelation 7:9-10). It is they who will become targets for persecution and martyrdom during the tribulation. Not all will be martyred, for many of them will still be alive at the time of the second coming of Christ (Matthew 25:31-46). But there will be many casualties during this seven-year period.

Revelation 13:7 reveals that the antichrist, who will be energized by Satan, will be the primary instigator of persecution against God's people during the tribulation: The antichrist "was allowed to make war on the saints and to conquer them. And authority was given it over every tribe and people and language and nation." A parallel passage is Daniel 7:21, which tells us that the antichrist "made war with the saints and prevailed over them" (ESV). Just as Revelation tells us that the antichrist will *conquer* them, so Daniel tells us that he will *prevail over* them. Apparently there will be many martyrs during the tribulation.

Not only will the antichrist persecute believers; New Babylon will do the same. The false religion associated with New Babylon will be "drunk with the blood of the saints, the blood of the martyrs of Jesus" (Revelation 17:6). In commercial New Babylon will be found "the blood of prophets and of saints, and of all who have been slain on earth" (Revelation 18:24 ESV).

It is sobering to realize that even though these prophecies of persecution and martyrdom describe what will happen during the tribulation, even now we are witnessing all this around the world. Just as foreshocks often occur before major earthquakes, so preliminary manifestations of some of the prophecies will emerge prior to the tribulation itself. Prophecies that relate specifically to the tribulation—such as the persecution of God's people—are presently casting their shadows before them.

Movement Toward a Cashless Society

I noted in chapter 8 that certain aspects of our society are already cashless. This includes buying food on airlines, toll roads auto-debiting your bank account as you drive along, receiving your paycheck by auto-deposit, buying products online, and much more.

The amount of cash being used today is less than half that used in the 1970s. More and more people are using cashless options, such as credit cards, debit cards, Apple Pay, and other smartphone options. That is the wave of the future.

A cashless system will clearly be the means the antichrist uses to control who can buy or sell on earth (Revelation 13:16-17). After all, if the world economy were still cash-based, people who possessed cash could still buy and sell. It would not be possible for the antichrist to control all trade in a cash-based society. Only in a cashless world—with a centralized electronic transaction system—would such control be possible.

I believe Thomas Ice and Timothy Demy are right when they say,

> It is becoming increasingly apparent that today's developing cashless system will become the instrument through which the antichrist will seek to control all who buy or sell, based upon whether they are a follower of Jesus Christ or a follower of the European ruler, and thus, Satan. It is obvious that any leader wanting to control the world's economy

would avail themselves of the power that an electronic cash-less system holds as a tool for implementing total control.[8]

It is my firm belief that this cashless world—in conjunction with the mark of the beast in Revelation 13:16-17—will play a significant role in the success of commercial New Babylon as described in Revelation 18. *The whole world will be wired for commercialism.*

Globalist Solutions to Global Problems

Prophetic scriptures reveal that the antichrist will rule the entire world. Globalism is clearly indicated in Revelation 13. We are told that "the whole world...gave allegiance to the beast" (verse 3). The antichrist "was given authority to rule over every tribe and people and language and nation. And all the people who belong to this world worshiped the beast" (verses 7-8). We are also told that the false prophet "required all the earth and its people to worship the first beast" (verse 12). This is where the infamous mark of the beast comes into play. Revelation 13:16-17 tells us that the false prophet "required everyone—small and great, rich and poor, free and slave—to be given a mark on the right hand or on the forehead. And no one could buy or sell anything without that mark, which was either the name of the beast or the number representing his name." Ultimately, there will be a globalized political union, religious union, and economic union.

Even today, we see globalist policies emerging in economics, banking, commerce and trade, business, management, manufacturing, environmentalism, population control, education, religion, agriculture, information technologies, the entertainment industry, the publishing industry, science and medicine, and even government. We are headed toward a global union—an anti-God union (see Revelation 13:3-18).

Current world conditions are ripe for globalist solutions. When one considers the multiple cascading problems now facing humanity—including the Middle East conflict, terrorism, overpopulation, pollution, famine, national and international crime, cyberwarfare, and economic instability—it is entirely feasible that increasing numbers of people will come to believe that such problems can be solved only on a global level. They may think that the only hope for human survival is a strong and effective world government.

As conditions worsen, people worldwide will yearn for a leader who can take control and fix everything, who can chart a clear global course toward stability. Such a leader is coming, and he may already be alive in the world. Scripture identifies him as the antichrist.

As we have seen, the technology that would make a world government possible—including instant global media via television and radio, cyberspace, and supercomputers—is now in place. Technology has "greased the skids" for the emergence of globalism in our day.

Economics is an especially important factor with regard to the globalism predicted in biblical prophecy. Especially in today's age of cyberspace, the respective economies of different nations are more deeply interconnected and intertwined than ever before. Each of our economies is built on global trade, global capital markets, and global communication. As a result, our respective economies rise or fall together. What is good for one is good for all. What is bad for one is bad for all.

Eventually the whole world will be politically and commercially connected to New Babylon. The political leaders of the world will be so closely connected to New Babylon that they will live in indescribable luxury as a result (verses 3,9). Likewise, the merchants of the world—through their connection to New Babylon—will grow incredibly rich (verse 3). Economically, commercial New Babylon will thrive during the second half of the tribulation.

The Growing Nuclear Threat

There are no direct references in prophetic scriptures to nuclear bombs. But there are a number of prophecies that may well portray the use of nuclear weaponry.

We are told that during the future seven-year tribulation, "one-third of the earth [will be] set on fire, one-third of the trees [will be] burned, and all the green grass [will be] burned" (Revelation 8:7). A large portion of the earth will be incinerated in a very short time. One wonders how this could happen so quickly without the use of nuclear bombs.

Soon after, Revelation 16:2 informs us that "malignant sores" will break out on everyone. Is it possible that these sores might be the result of radiation poisoning following the detonation of nuclear weapons?

Some have suggested that Jesus may have been alluding to nuclear detonations in Luke 21:26 when He prophesied of the end times that "people will be terrified at what they see coming upon the earth, for the powers in the heavens will be shaken."

It may also be that nuclear weapons will be used in the annihilation of New Babylon. We read of commercial New Babylon that "she will be completely consumed by fire" (Revelation 18:8). People will witness "the smoke rising from her charred remains" (18:9). Many "will cry out as they watch the smoke ascend" (18:18). We are told that "in a single moment it is all gone" (18:19). What kind of power could completely consume a city in a single moment? Some believe this may be describing a nuclear detonation.

How Should This Affect the Way We Live?

In chapter 1 of this book, I said I wanted to show you how various prophetic events mentioned in the Bible relate to the emergence of New Babylon. In reviewing all that is to come, we can more easily grasp how all the prophetic pieces of the puzzle fit together. As we now approach the end of this book, I hope and pray that this goal has been accomplished.

In the next chapter, I want to offer some closing insights on how we ought to live as end-time Christians. We should all be *rapture-ready*!

13

Tying It All Together: An Overview

In this book we've covered many details about Bible prophecy and have considered many subtopics related to New Babylon. It can be a bit dizzying to ponder all of what the future holds. As part of my overall goal to take complicated subjects and make them simpler to understand, I'm going to use this chapter to provide you with a summary as a means of tying together everything we've learned about New Babylon. These are the "big ideas"—the main things I want to pass on to you about this fascinating prophetic topic. Please take your time as you peruse these summary points:

Babylon Plays a Big Role in the Bible. While Jerusalem is the most oft-mentioned city in the Bible, Babylon is the second. A whopping 11 percent of the book of Revelation deals with Babylon. That means it is a very important city for us to know about.

Jerusalem and Babylon Are Opposites in Notable Ways. While Jerusalem means "city of peace," Babylon means "city of confusion and war." While Jerusalem is portrayed as God's city (Revelation 21:2-3), Babylon is portrayed as a demonic city (18:2). While the future New Jerusalem is portrayed as a chaste bride (21:9-10), Babylon is portrayed as a great prostitute (17:1,3).

Some Prophecy Students Believe We Must Interpret Babylon in Revelation 17–18 Allegorically. These students look at the KJV rendering of Revelation 17:5 and assume that the term "mystery" belongs with "Babylon" (unlike modern Bible translations). They then ponder what might be meant by the term "mystery Babylon." It is typically assumed that here, the word "mystery" must mean "mystical, symbolical, or allegorical."

Some Believe Allegorical Babylon Is Rome. Proponents say this view fits the description of Babylon in Revelation 17–18. After all, Rome was engulfed in paganism, full of rampant idolatry, relentlessly persecuted the early believers, and was a "great city." Against this view, however, is the reality that Rome did not fall suddenly, dramatically, completely, or permanently, as is true of the Babylon in Revelation 18. Moreover, Rome is not located in a desert or a wilderness, nor is it a seaport city, as is true of the Babylon in Revelation 17–18.

Others Believe Allegorical Babylon Is the Roman Catholic Church. Proponents of this view point to the prostitute metaphor, which indicates unfaithfulness to Christ. It is also suggested that the majestic adornment of the prostitute seems similar to the clothing of popes and cardinals. Moreover, being "drunk from the blood of the saints" may point to Roman Catholicism's persecution and martyrdom of Protestants throughout church history.

Against this view, critics argue that the Roman Catholic Church—though wealthy—is not the global commercial powerhouse described in Revelation 18. Nor has it ever ruled over the political leaders and peoples of the world. Nor does it engage in slave trade, as will New Babylon.

You already know from reading this book that I hold to a literal (not allegorical) interpretation of Babylon. I believe there is one literal city of Babylon with two aspects—a religious aspect and a commercial one. So, I believe it is entirely possible that Roman Catholicism may be *a part* of the religious aspect of New Babylon (Revelation 17). (More on all this shortly.)

Some Believe Allegorical Babylon Is Apostate Christianity. Proponents of this view say apostate Christianity fits the prostitute metaphor quite well. Against this interpretation, critics say New Babylon is described as being an actual city, in the desert or wilderness, as having a seaport, as being involved in slave trade, as ruling over the political leaders and peoples of the world, and as being a commercial powerhouse (Revelation 17–18). These things simply do not relate to apostate Christianity. (Again, though, in the literal interpretation, it's entirely possible that apostate Christianity may be *a part* of the religious system associated with New Babylon. More on this shortly.)

Others Believe Allegorical Babylon Is the Evil World System. The main argument for this view is that the evil world system perpetually stands against God just as Babylon stands against God. Against this view is that Babylon is said to be an actual city in the wilderness with a seaport (Revelation 17:18), is a global political power (17:15,18), and is a bastion of global commerce (18:9-19).

Others Believe Allegorical Babylon Is New York City. Proponents reason that both Babylon and New York City are excessively rich and dominant economic powers (Revelation 18:11-20), both are a source of global immorality (18:2-9), and both have sins "piled up as high as heaven" (18:5). Moreover, New York is a "great city" with a seaport.

Against this view, it can hardly be said of New York City—as it can be said of New Babylon—that "in your streets flowed the blood of the prophets and of God's holy people" (Revelation 18:24).

Moreover, New York City does not represent a global religion, nor has it ruled over the political leaders and peoples of the world, nor is it located in a desert or wilderness (17:1-6).

Others Believe Allegorical Babylon Is Jerusalem. Proponents of this view say that because of Israel's covenant unfaithfulness, she was often viewed as a prostitute in Old Testament times (Isaiah 1:21; Jeremiah 2:20-24). Moreover, Jerusalem was responsible for killing Old Testament prophets and New Testament apostles (Matthew 23:35; Luke 1:50-51; Acts 7:52). Jerusalem ("Babylon") was then destroyed by God using the whipping rod of the Roman Empire ("the beast") in the first century. This view is popular among preterists.

Against this view is the historical fact that the book of Revelation was written in the AD 90s, far after Rome destroyed Jerusalem in AD 70. Revelation was therefore prophesying something *yet future* from the vantage point of AD 90. Moreover, Jerusalem never ruled over many nations of the world, never became a global commercial powerhouse, and did not control the antichrist and his forces for a time. Further, Revelation 18:21-23 says New Babylon will be so completely destroyed that it will never rise again. Jerusalem *did* rise again, and in the future will be prominent in Christ's millennial kingdom.

Still Others Believe Allegorical Babylon Is Mecca. Proponents say Mecca is a real city, fits the requirement of being in a desert terrain, and is a "great city" because more than a billion Muslims pray daily in the direction of Mecca. This view also suggests that the antichrist will be a Muslim, and that Islam will be the persecutor of Jews and Christians in the end times.

Against this view is the fact that the Ezekiel invasion—involving a massive offensive strike into Israel by Russia, Iran, Sudan, Turkey, Libya, and other Islamic nations—will take place either prior to the tribulation period, or at the very beginning of it. Ezekiel 38:19-22 reveals that God will utterly annihilate—*completely destroy*—the Muslim forces. God will also rain down fire "on Magog and on all your allies who live safely on the coasts" (Ezekiel 39:6). The blow to Islamic nations will be catastrophic. One must therefore wonder how it will be possible for a Muslim antichrist and a Muslim Babylon (Mecca) to rise from the widespread ashes in the aftermath of the Ezekiel invasion and God's utter annihilation of the invaders. It's also problematic that Mecca does not have a seaport, as does New Babylon.

There are also many problems with the idea of a Muslim antichrist. No Muslim leader would want to sign a covenant that protects Israel. Israel certainly wouldn't entrust its very survival to a covenant signed by a Muslim leader. And it's impossible to believe that a Muslim would ever claim to be God (an action that trashes the Muslim creed). Besides, Daniel 9:26 indicates that the antichrist will be a Roman.

References to Babylon in Revelation Should Be Taken Not Allegorically, But Rather as a Literal Revived City of Babylon. This is my personal position. Notice that all the other towns and cities listed in the book of Revelation are literal locations—such as Ephesus, Smyrna, Pergamum, Thyatira, Sardis, Philadelphia, and Laodicea. Babylon, too, should be taken as a literal location.

It is a fact that in the Old Testament the term *Babylon* always refers to a literal city. Because the book of Revelation draws heavily from the Old Testament, it stands to reason that the term *Babylon* is used in the New Testament in the same sense as the Old. Further, because Babylon is mentioned in the context of the Euphrates River in the book of Revelation, a literal city must be in view.

Relevant to this discussion is the fact that Jeremiah 50–51 provides prophecies about the literal city of Babylon that have not yet been fulfilled. John draws quite heavily from Jeremiah. Since Jeremiah 50–51 refers to a literal city of Babylon, Revelation 17–18 must also be seen as referring to the same city.

Ancient Babylon Had Religious and Commercial Aspects, Just as New Babylon Will Have in the Book of Revelation. Ancient Babylon was a pagan culture that espoused false religion. Moreover, because of its ideal location, the city became an important commercial and trade center in the ancient world. New Babylon will likewise be a single city that promotes false religion during the first half of the tribulation period and will become a global commercial and trade center during the second half.

Revelation 17 and 18 Provide Detailed Characteristics of the False Religion that Emanates from New Babylon, as well as Commercial New Babylon. The false religious system of the end times is likened to a "great prostitute," symbolizing unfaithfulness to God. This great prostitute will likely be some form of apostate and paganized Christendom, embracing all those who were left behind following the rapture. All the streams of apostate Christianity—Roman Catholicism, Eastern Orthodoxy, and liberal Protestantism—will converge into ecclesiastical Babylon (Revelation 17).

This false religious system will be numerically immense and will exercise control over peoples, multitudes, nations, and languages around the world during the first half of the tribulation. It will also apparently open the door for people to engage in any kind of immoral lifestyle they want.

This false religious system will control the antichrist and his forces for a time. Moreover, it will be responsible for widespread Christian martyrdom.

Revelation 17 reveals that initially, the antichrist will utilize this false religious system to bring unity to the peoples of the world. Once he has accomplished this purpose, he will no longer need the false religious system. He will hate it and dispose of it with the help of his ten sub-commanders.

While Revelation 17 speaks of the false religious system associated with New Babylon, Revelation 18 provides us with important facts about the commercial aspect of the city. This passage reveals that the political leaders of the world will play a key role in the global influence and affluence of commercial New Babylon. Moreover, business people from around the world will grow rich because of their connection to this prosperous city. Our text tells us that the city will purchase a wide array of commercial products from all over the world, many of which will be transported via merchant ships on the ocean. New Babylon will be headed up by an economic genius—*the Satan-inspired antichrist.*

We Gain Key Historical Insights on Babylon from Genesis 10–11. Nimrod founded Babel, which is an early name for Babylon. He also headed up the effort to build the tower of Babel.

Nimrod is a "type" of antichrist. That is, he *prefigures* the antichrist in notable ways. Nimrod, for example, was the political head of Babylon, just as the antichrist will be the political head of New Babylon. He was a promoter of false religion, just as the antichrist will promote a false religion that forces people to worship him. His name means "rebel" and foreshadows the antichrist as a rebel against God. He was a hunter of human beings, much like the antichrist will hunt down Christians and Jews during the tribulation. He was an enemy of Israel, just as the antichrist will be.

Nimrod's ultimate goal in building the city and tower of Babel was to attain overarching unity, or oneness, of the populace. The people of that day wanted to build a city so that they could have political unity as well as religious, which was symbolized by the tower or the ziggurat.

There are obvious parallels to New Babylon in Revelation 17 and

18. Religious unity will come upon the world through the religious system associated with New Babylon during the first half of the tribulation. Political and commercial unity will arise in the literal city of New Babylon and have worldwide influence during the second half of the tribulation.

Babel was humanity's first united attempt to short-circuit God's purpose. Babylon, the city of humankind trying to rise to heaven, was built in direct opposition to God's plan. New Babylon, too, will function in direct opposition to God.

The Book of Daniel Reveals Many Specific Parallels Between Ancient Babylon and New Babylon, Between Nebuchadnezzar and the Antichrist. Just as Nebuchadnezzar and ancient Babylon were dominant over the Jewish people and their temple, so the antichrist and New Babylon in the end times will be dominant over the Jews. Just as the ancient Jewish temple was defiled by Nebuchadnezzar, who plundered its sacred objects, so the antichrist will defile the tribulation-era Jewish temple by sitting within it and setting up an image of himself in it.

Just as idolatry was rampant in ancient Babylon, so idolatry will be rampant in New Babylon. Just as Nebuchadnezzar had religious assistants (astrologers and other occultists), so the antichrist will have a religious assistant called the false prophet.

Just as an image was erected in Babylon representing the authority and divine status of Nebuchadnezzar, so the antichrist will place an image of himself in the Jewish temple representing his godhood and authority. Just as Nebuchadnezzar with his image called for both religious and political submission, so the antichrist and New Babylon will call for religious and political submission.

Just as forced submission to a false religion took place in ancient Babylon (with Daniel's friends being commanded to bow down to

Nebuchadnezzar's golden image), so forced submission to a false religion—worship of the antichrist, enforced by the mark of the beast—will take place during the tribulation period. Just as a death penalty awaited those who refused to bow to Nebuchadnezzar's image, so will many of those who reject the antichrist during the end times face martyrdom. Just as Nebuchadnezzar considered himself as god above all other deities, so the antichrist will "exalt himself and defy everything that people call god and every object of worship" (2 Thessalonians 2:4).

There Is a Close Connection Between the Antichrist, Satan, and New Babylon. Satan is pictured in Scripture as being extremely powerful and influential. He is called the "ruler of this world" (John 12:31) and "the god of this world" (2 Corinthians 4:4). He is called "the commander of the powers in the unseen world" (Ephesians 2:2). He is also said to deceive everyone globally (Revelation 12:9; 20:3). He is portrayed as having power in the governmental realm (Matthew 4:8-9; 2 Corinthians 4:4), the physical realm (Luke 13:11,16; Acts 10:38), the angelic realm (Jude 9; Ephesians 6:11-12), and the ecclesiastical (church) realm (Revelation 2:9; 3:9).

Of great significance is the fact that this powerful spiritual being will empower and control the antichrist. In 2 Thessalonians 2:9 we are told, "The coming of the lawless one is *by the activity of Satan* with all power and false signs and wonders" (esv, emphasis added). Revelation 13:2 likewise tells us, "The dragon [Satan] gave the beast [the antichrist] his own power and throne and great authority" (inserts added for clarification).

It is thus understandable that the antichrist will manifest Satan's character. For example, the antichrist will be prideful and self-exalting (2 Thessalonians 2:4) just as Satan is (Isaiah 14:12-17; Ezekiel 28:11-19). It is noteworthy that the same pride and self-exaltation evident in Satan and the antichrist will also be evident in New Babylon, who "boasted in her heart, 'I am queen on my throne'" (Revelation 18:7).

In addition, the antichrist will engage in deception just as Satan does (John 8:44; Revelation 12:9). Because Satan is the "father of lies" and "deceiver of the whole world," it makes sense that the one whom he energizes—the antichrist—will also be characterized by lies and deception (2 Thessalonians 2:9-10). The deception evident in Satan and the antichrist will also be evident in New Babylon, who is said to have "deceived the nations" (Revelation 18:23).

Finally, the antichrist will persecute God's people (Revelation 13:7; Daniel 7:21), just like Satan does (Revelation 12:12-17). The same persecution evident in Satan and the antichrist will also be evident in New Babylon. Indeed, in New Babylon's streets will flow "the blood of the prophets and of God's holy people and the blood of people slaughtered all over the world" (Revelation 18:24; see also 17:6).

Here's something to think about: We know that Satan's character will be reflected in the antichrist. We also know, though, that wicked spirits will be hard at work in New Babylon. After all, we are told that New Babylon will be "a home for demons," and "a hideout for every foul spirit" (Revelation 18:2). It is therefore understandable why Satan, the antichrist, and New Babylon have such similar characteristics.

There Is a Close Connection Between the Mark of the Beast, a Cashless World, and the Commercial Success of New Babylon. Revelation 13:16-18 reveals that the diabolical beastly duo—the antichrist and the false prophet—will economically subjugate the entire world so that no one who does not first receive the mark of the beast can buy or sell anything. We can infer that every seller on earth will have a distinct account number, as will every buyer. Only those buyers who have the mark will be permitted to make purchases from sellers who have the mark. The mark of the beast will literally serve as a commerce passport during the future tribulation period.

This is particularly relevant with regard to the necessities of life—such as food and water. Only those with the mark of the beast will be able to buy such items during this time of worldwide famine (Revelation 6:5-6).

Receiving the mark reveals an implicit approval of the antichrist as a leader. It also reveals an implicit agreement with his purposes (including those related to New Babylon).

We can surmise that all who sell their goods to New Babylon—including all kinds of food items—will have received the mark of the beast (see Revelation 18:11-15). No sales will be permitted to New Babylon without that mark. Hence, through the mark, the antichrist will control the commercial success of New Babylon.

Of course, the only way the mark can be enforced globally is if the entire world has gone cashless. In such a world—where every seller and every buyer has a distinct account number and dollar bills are no longer in use—it would be easy to enforce the mark of the beast. As we continue to go deeper into the end times, our world will become increasingly cashless.

Commercial New Babylon Will Suffer Complete Destruction at the Very End of the Tribulation. Revelation 18 prophesies the catastrophic fall and judgment of commercial New Babylon. This high and mighty city will be brought low and take a calamitous hit.

Contextually, the antichrist will be busy preparing his forces to attack Israel. This invasion will occur early in the campaign of Armageddon. The antichrist will think he is secure, assume that his great power and wealth are rock solid, and consider himself invulnerable. Then suddenly and without warning, God Himself will judge and utterly destroy the antichrist's mighty economic headquarters in New Babylon along the Euphrates River (see Isaiah 13:19; Jeremiah 50:11-27,40).

This destruction will come upon Babylon as a direct, decisive judgment from the hand of the Almighty. He will finally and definitively settle the score for Babylon's long history of standing against His people of Israel. Just as Babylon showed no mercy in its oppression against Israel throughout biblical history and again during the tribulation period, so God will show no mercy to Babylon. This judgment will occur at the very end of the seven-year tribulation.

We read that an angel will cry out, "Babylon is fallen—that great city is fallen" (Revelation 18:2). The dual occurrence of the word "fallen" indicates both the woeful condition of commercial New Babylon as well as the certainty of its coming judgment (see Isaiah 21:9; Jeremiah 51:8).

Notice that our text says that "Babylon *is* fallen," as if it has already occurred. This is a proleptic announcement common to prophetic Scripture, in which a future action is described as if it had already occurred. It is a literary device that emphasizes that God's triumph over evil New Babylon is an accomplished fact, though its execution is still future.

Signs of the Times Reveal that the Stage Is Being Set for the Rise of New Babylon. In anticipation of the rise of New Babylon—both the religious and commercial aspects—we would expect to see the following prophetic signs of the times in the coming years:

- a continued rise in false apostles, false prophets, and false teachers
- a continued rise in false religions and cults
- a continued escalation of apostasy and a turning away from biblical Christianity

- an increase in tolerance of false religious ideas and moral compromises
- a steady decrease in religious freedom around the world, particularly as related to Bible-believing Christians
- a continued rise in anti-Semitism, accompanied by a parallel rise in the number of Jews returning to the Holy Land from countries around the world
- a continued escalation of the Middle East conflict with Israel at the epicenter
- continuing efforts toward the rebuilding of the Jewish temple, accompanied by Muslim resentment in response
- a continued escalation in terrorist acts around the world
- the stage continuing to be set for the eventual Russian-Muslim invasion into Israel
- an increase in the persecution—even martyrdom—of Christians
- an increasingly cashless society in preparation for the antichrist's eventual control of the world economy
- a continued interest in globalist solutions to global problems
- a continued increase in connecting through the Internet and cyberspace
- the increasing use of biometric technologies with a parallel decrease in personal privacy around the world
- a growing nuclear and electromagnetic pulse threat

At this point, you may be thinking that all this talk about wicked New Babylon, the antichrist, Satan, judgment, and destruction is downright depressing. I want to assure you, however, that God does not give us prophecy to depress us but rather to show us that He's in control of the world. Let us not forget, as theologian Robert

Lightner reminds us, that "what has happened in the past, what is happening now, and what will happen in the future is all evidence of the unfolding of the purposeful plan devised by the personal God of the Bible. All the circumstances of life—past, present, and future—fit into the sovereign plan like pieces of a puzzle."[1]

In the next and final chapter, I want to provide some encouraging words to you regarding how we should live as end-time Christians.

14

Living as an End-Times Christian

We have finished our journey. We've taken a fascinating look at the rise of New Babylon in the end times—both the religious and commercial aspects. We've also considered how a variety of biblical prophecies relate to this infamous city.

While various Bible interpreters might have different views on New Babylon's identity and role in the end times, there's one fact that everyone agrees on: Our Lord Jesus Christ, who is the King of kings and the Lord of lords, is coming again, and He will render judgment upon the wicked and reign supreme forever and ever.

My friend, I'm convinced we are living in the last days. I say this because we are witnessing the convergence of many ancient prophecies coming to pass in our own day, or, in some cases, we are witnessing the stage being set for the fulfillment of prophecies that have to do with the future tribulation period.

Today we are witnessing...

- a massive falling away from the truth
- a widespread embracing of doctrinal error

- a profound moral decline
- a growing tolerance for all things evil
- a widespread outbreak of a variety of sexual sins and perversions, with no repentance in sight
- the steady diminishing of religious freedom
- the ever-increasing global persecution of God's people
- Israel being a relentless sore spot in the world
- ever-escalating conflict in the Middle East
- efforts being made toward the rebuilding of the Jewish temple
- the stage being set for a massive invasion of Israel by Russia and Muslim nations
- the steady rise and influence of globalism
- political and economic steps toward the establishment of a revived Roman Empire—a United States of Europe
- the emergence of a cashless world in preparation for the antichrist's control of the global economy during the tribulation
- and much more

It is sobering—even a bit frightening—to recognize that all these things are taking place in our present day. They are setting the stage for the rise of New Babylon during the tribulation period.

All this moves me to ask: Should we be discouraged about world events? Should we be worried about the future? Should we change the way we live? What should be our attitude as we face the end times?

The Bible provides us with helpful answers, and I want to camp here for a while because I have a strong suspicion that it might be hard for some Christians to live confidently in these end times without wavering a bit in their faith and commitment. I want this closing chapter to be an encouragement to you.

Avoid Making Unhealthy Choices

Some people have taken unhealthy paths as a result of their understanding of Bible prophecy. I know of one person who—because he believed the Lord was coming shortly—put off going to college. I know of another who stopped saving money for the future because he believed the Lord's return was imminent. I read about another person who chose not to go to the doctor to address some rather serious symptoms because he believed the rapture would take place soon.

To avoid such unhealthy life choices, I have always advised people to follow one simple principle:

> *Live your life as if the rapture could happen today, but plan your life as if you will be here for your entire lifetime expectancy. That way you are prepared for both time and eternity.*

Pray Always, Love Always

One of my favorite passages that instructs us on how to live as end-time Christians is 1 Peter 4:7-10. Consider these words:

> The end of the world is coming soon. Therefore, be earnest and disciplined in your prayers. Most important of all, continue to show deep love for each other, for love covers a multitude of sins. Cheerfully share your home with those who need a meal or a place to stay. God has given each of you a gift from his great variety of spiritual gifts. Use them well to serve one another.

Far too many people tend to become sensationalistic and alarmist about end-time prophecies. They get so focused on the finer points of prophecy that they tend to forget or ignore God's instruction to pray for people and love them. Don't let that happen to you.

Pray always.

Love always.

Don't Be Troubled in Your Heart

Jesus spoke often to His followers about the end times. On one such occasion, He offered these words of great comfort:

> Don't let your hearts be troubled. Trust in God, and trust also in me. There is more than enough room in my Father's home. If this were not so, would I have told you that I am going to prepare a place for you? When everything is ready, I will come and get you, so that you will always be with me where I am (John 14:1-3).

Dr. John F. Walvoord has a great insight on this passage:

> These verses are the Bible's first revelation of the rapture, in which Christ will come back to take His own to heaven. He exhorted the disciples not to be troubled. Since they trusted the Father, they also should trust Christ, whose power was demonstrated in His many miracles...They need not be anxious about His leaving because later He would return for them.[1]

My friend, no matter what happens in this world, no matter what punches life throws at us, no matter what scary developments emerge in different parts of the world, *we need not be troubled. We need not fear.* Jesus is currently preparing our eternal homes, and He's coming for us soon (John 14:1-3). The assurance of that future reality can give us the strength we need to make it through any present difficulties.

Seek to Please the Lord by How You Live

Through biblical prophecy, God has revealed many future events to us. When God reveals what lies ahead, He does not do so merely to show off. Nor does He give us prophecies so we can have mere head knowledge about the end times.

Of great significance is the fact that many verses in the Bible that deal with prophecy are followed by an exhortation to personal purity in the way we live our lives. This means that as we study biblical prophecy, it ought to change the way we live. It ought to have an effect on our behavior.

Allow me to give you a few examples from prophetic scriptures. The apostle Paul provides this exhortation in Romans 13:11-14, which appears in the context of biblical prophecy:

> This is all the more urgent, for you know how late it is; time is running out. Wake up, for our salvation is nearer now than when we first believed. The night is almost gone; the day of salvation will soon be here. So remove your dark deeds like dirty clothes, and put on the shining armor of right living. Because we belong to the day, we must live decent lives for all to see. Don't participate in the darkness of wild parties and drunkenness, or in sexual promiscuity and immoral living, or in quarreling and jealousy. Instead, clothe yourself with the presence of the Lord Jesus Christ. And don't let yourself think about ways to indulge your evil desires.

The connection between biblical prophecy and purity is also evident in 2 Peter 3:10-14:

> The day of the Lord will come as unexpectedly as a thief. Then the heavens will pass away with a terrible noise, and the very elements themselves will disappear in fire, and the earth and everything on it will be found to deserve judgment. Since everything around us is going to be destroyed like this, what holy and godly lives you should live, looking forward to the day of God and hurrying it along. On that day, he will set the heavens on fire, and the elements will melt away in the flames. But we are looking forward to the new heavens and new earth he has promised, a world filled

with God's righteousness. And so, dear friends, while you are waiting for these things to happen, make every effort to be found living peaceful lives that are pure and blameless in his sight.

We see something similar in 1 John 3:2-3:

Dear friends, we are already God's children, but he has not yet shown us what we will be like when Christ appears. But we do know that we will be like him, for we will see him as he really is. And all who have this eager expectation will keep themselves pure, just as he is pure.

The appearance John speaks of is the future rapture. What a glorious day that will be! One prophecy expert affirms that "the hope of the rapture, when we will meet the Savior, should be a sanctifying force in our lives. We will be made completely like Him then; so we should endeavor with His help to serve Him faithfully now and to lead lives of purity."[2]

With regard to the rapture, we find a great analogy in ancient Jewish marriage customs. In biblical times, following the marriage betrothal, the groom would go to his father's house to prepare a place for the couple to stay. Meanwhile, the betrothed woman would eagerly await the coming of her groom to take her away to his father's house in marriage celebration. During this time of anticipation, the bride's loyalty to her groom was tested. In similar manner, as the bride of Christ (the church) awaits the coming of the messianic Groom (Jesus), the church is motivated to live in purity and godliness until He arrives at the rapture (see John 14:1-3).

My friend, *let us daily choose purity.*

Resist the Temptation to Set Dates

God controls the timing of all last-days events, and He hasn't given you and me the specific details. In Acts 1:7 we read Jesus's words to the disciples before He ascended into heaven: "The Father alone has the authority to set those dates and times, and they are not for you to know."

We are encouraged by Jesus to be accurate observers of the signs of the times (Matthew 24:32-33; Luke 21:25-28), but we are not given the details on the precise timing of when the rapture will take place. This means we must resolve to trust God with that information.

In my long career in Christian ministry, I've noticed that Christians who get caught up in date-setting (such as setting a date for the rapture) can do great damage to the cause of Christ. Humanists enjoy scorning Christians who have put stock in end-time predictions—especially when specific dates have been attached to last-days events. Why give "ammo" to the enemies of Christianity? We can be excited about events that appear to be setting the stage for the eventual fulfillment of prophecy without engaging in such sensationalism (see Mark 13:32-37).

Allow Prophecy to Exalt God in Your Heart

Biblical prophecy points to the awesome greatness of God. One cannot study prophecy for long without becoming aware of the greatness of God. Consider Isaiah 44:6-8:

> This is what the LORD says—Israel's King and Redeemer, the LORD of Heaven's Armies: "I am the First and the Last; there is no other God. Who is like me? Let him step forward and prove to you his power. Let him do as I have done since ancient times when I established a people and explained its future. Do not tremble; do not be afraid. Did I not proclaim my purposes for you long ago? You are my witnesses—is there any other God? No! There is no other Rock—not one!"

The book of Daniel points to God's greatness in His control of all that takes place:

> Praise the name of God forever and ever, for he has all wisdom and power. He controls the course of world events; he removes kings and sets up other kings. He gives wisdom to the wise and knowledge to the scholars. He reveals deep and mysterious things and knows what lies hidden in darkness, though he is surrounded by light (Daniel 2:20-22).

An exercise I sometimes engage in during my personal devotional times is to ponder God's greatness—that is, meditate upon His wondrous attributes—as they relate to the unfolding of God's prophetic plan on earth. Here are some of the kinds of things I reflect upon:

God Is Eternal. One theologian describes God as "the eternal without beginning, He who is above the whole course of time, He who in harmony beyond explanation possesses unity and life, the Father, the Son, and the Holy Spirit, the basis of eternity, the Living One, the only God."[3] My friend, God transcends time altogether. He is above the space-time universe. As an eternal being, He has always existed. He is the eternal King (1 Timothy 1:17), who alone is immortal (6:16). He is "the Alpha and the Omega" (Revelation 1:8) and "the First and the Last" (Isaiah 44:6; 48:12). He exists "from beginning to end" (Psalm 90:2). He lives forever from eternal ages past (Psalm 41:13; 102:12,27; Isaiah 57:15). While events transpire on a daily basis here on planet Earth and while prophecies are fulfilled temporally, God Himself is beyond time altogether.

One comfort we can experience in relation to God's eternal nature is the absolute confidence that God will never cease to exist. He will always be present for us. His continued providential control of our lives is thereby assured. Human leaders come and go. Cities—such as New Babylon—come and go as well. But God is eternal and is always there! The prophetic future is in His hands. *Praise His name!*

God Is Everywhere-Present. That God is everywhere-present does not mean that He is diffused—stretched thin—throughout space as if part of Him is here and part of Him is there. Rather, God, in His whole being, is in every place. There is nowhere we can go where God is not present (Psalm 139:7-8; Jeremiah 23:23-24; Hebrews 1:3; Acts 17:27-28). Hence, whether we are in the United States, Iran, Russia, Sudan, Libya, New Babylon, or anywhere else in the entire universe, God is there.

While the world in these last days often seems to be spinning out of control, we can take comfort in knowing that no matter where we go, we will never escape the presence of our beloved God. Because He is everywhere-present, we can be confident of His real presence at all times. We will always know the blessing of walking with Him in every trial and circumstance of life. *Praise His name!*

God Is All-Knowing. I noted earlier in the book that because God transcends time—because He is above it—He can see the past, present, and future all at once. God sees everything from the vantage point of eternity, so that the past (Isaiah 41:22), present (Hebrews 4:13), and future (Isaiah 46:10) are all known to Him in fullness. Psalm 147:5 affirms that "His understanding is beyond comprehension" (see also Psalms 33:13-15; 139:11-12; 147:5; Proverbs 15:3; Isaiah 40:14; 46:10; Acts 15:18; Hebrews 4:13; 1 John 3:20). This is why we can trust God when He communicates prophecies about the future to us. God knows all. *Praise His name!*

God Is All-Powerful. Scripture portrays God as being all-powerful (Jeremiah 32:17). He can do all that He desires and wills. We are told some 56 times that God is almighty (for example, Revelation 19:6). He is abundant in strength (Psalm 147:5) and has incomparably great power (2 Chronicles 20:6; Ephesians 1:19-21). No one can hold back His hand (Daniel 4:35), reverse Him (Isaiah 43:13), or thwart Him (Isaiah 14:27). Nothing is impossible with Him (Matthew 19:26; Mark 10:27; Luke 1:37), and nothing is too difficult for Him (Genesis 18:14; Jeremiah 32:17,27). The Almighty reigns (Revelation 19:6). This means that none of the cities and nations of the world—including New Babylon—are beyond God's control. No matter what threat one nation might make against another, we must remember that our God, who is all-powerful, is in control. His prophetic plan will unfold just as He decreed. *Praise His name!*

God Is Sovereign. Scripture portrays God as being absolutely sovereign. He rules the universe, controls all things, and is Lord over all (see Ephesians 1). There is nothing that can happen in this universe that is beyond the reach of His control. All forms of existence are within the scope of His absolute dominion. Psalm 66:7 affirms that "by his great power he rules forever." We are assured in Psalm 93:1 that "the LORD is king." God asserts, "Everything I plan will come to pass, for I do whatever I wish" (Isaiah 46:10). God assures us, "It will all happen as I have planned. It will be as I have decided" (Isaiah 14:24). Proverbs 16:9 tells us, "We can make our plans, but the LORD determines our steps." Proverbs 19:21 says, "You can make many plans, but the LORD's purpose will prevail."

I'm convinced that experiencing complete peace in our hearts is the natural result of trusting that God is sovereignly overseeing all that comes into our lives. No matter what we may encounter— no matter how much we may fail to understand why certain things happen in life and how horrible the news headlines are—the knowledge that our sovereign God is in control is like a firm anchor in the midst of life's storms. This means we can be at peace no matter what the prophetic future may hold. *Praise His name!*

God Is Holy. God's holiness means not only that He is entirely separate from all evil but also that He is absolutely righteous (Leviticus 19:2). He is pure in every way.

Scripture places great emphasis upon this attribute of God:

- "Who is like you…glorious in holiness?" (Exodus 15:11)
- "No one is holy like the LORD!" (1 Samuel 2:2)
- "The LORD our God is holy" (Psalm 99:9)
- "What a holy, awe-inspiring name he has" (Psalm 111:9)
- "Holy, holy, holy is the LORD of Heaven's Armies" (Isaiah 6:3)
- "You alone are holy" (Revelation 15:4)

One important ramification of God's holiness is that He will not allow persons or nations to get away with sinful actions. This means that both the antichrist and New Babylon will one day face God in judgment at the end of the tribulation. *Praise His name!*

God Is Just. That God is just means He carries out His righteous standards justly and with equity. There is never any partiality or unfairness in God's dealings with people (Genesis 18:25; Psalm 11:7; Zephaniah 3:5; John 17:25; Romans 3:26; Hebrews 6:10). The fact that God is just is both a comfort and a warning. For those who have been wronged in life, it is a comfort. They can rest assured that God will right all wrongs in the end. For those who think they have been getting away with evil, it is a warning. Justice will prevail in the end. God's end-time judgments will see to that. *Praise His name!*

Most Important: Maintain an Eternal Perspective

As we study biblical prophecy—particularly dark subjects like New Babylon and the antichrist—one of the wisest things we can do is to perpetually maintain an eternal perspective. I never tire of saying that a daily pondering of the incredible glory of the afterlife is one of the surest ways to stay motivated to live faithfully during our relatively short time on earth. We are but pilgrims on our way to another land—to the final frontier of heaven, where God Himself dwells (see Hebrews 11:16).

Back when I was in grad school, I had the opportunity with about half a dozen other doctoral students to sit in a classroom with J.I. Packer, one of my favorite Christian authors. I'll never forget how that class motivated me to read a book of his that, up till then, I'd not yet read. In this book, Packer affirmed that the "lack of long, strong thinking about our promised hope of glory is a major cause of our plodding, lackluster lifestyle." He pointed to the Puritans as a much-needed example for us. They believed that "it is the heavenly Christian that is the lively Christian." Indeed, the Puritans understood that we "run so slowly, and strive so lazily, because we so little mind the prize...So let Christians animate themselves daily to run the race set before them by practicing heavenly meditation."[4]

Packer spoke a lot about Puritan Richard Baxter. He said Baxter's recommended daily habit was to "dwell on the glory of the heavenly life to which one was going." Baxter daily practiced "holding heaven at the forefront of his thoughts and desires." The hope of heaven brought him joy, and that joy, in turn, brought him strength. He once said, "A heavenly mind is a joyful mind; this is the nearest and truest way to live a life of comfort...A heart in heaven will be a most excellent preservative against temptations, a powerful means to kill thy corruptions."[5]

I believe that such comments reflect the thinking of the apostle Paul in Colossians 3:1-2, one of my all-time favorite Bible passages: "Since you have been raised to new life with Christ, set your sights on the realities of heaven, where Christ sits in the place of honor at God's right hand. Think about the things of heaven, not the things of earth." The original Greek text of this verse is intense, communicating the idea, "Diligently, actively, single-mindedly think on the things of heaven." Moreover, the present tense in the original Greek text communicates, "Perpetually keep on thinking on the things of heaven…Make it an ongoing process 24/7." This ought to be our attitude every single day.

Part of maintaining an eternal perspective is being cognizant of our mortality. We ought to pray with the psalmist, "Teach us to realize the brevity of life, so that we may grow in wisdom" (Psalm 90:12). And, "Lord, remind me how brief my time on earth will be. Remind me that my days are numbered—how fleeting my life is" (Psalm 39:4). Christians who wisely ponder their mortality are most often the ones who maintain the eternal perspective described in Colossians 3:1-2.

It makes good sense that all human beings be concerned about eternal matters. After all, Ecclesiastes 3:11 affirms that God "has planted eternity in the human heart." Though we live in a world of time, we have intimations of eternity within our hearts. We instinctively think of *forever*. We seem to intrinsically realize that beyond this life lies the possibility of a shoreless ocean of time. It is wondrous to even think about this. We are heaven-bent; our hearts have an inner tilt upward.

I've been studying Scripture for a very long time. And from the first book in the Bible to the last, we read of great men and women of God who gave evidence that eternity permeated their hearts. We read of people like Abel, Enoch, Noah, Abraham, and David—each yearning to live with God in eternity (see Hebrews 11).

The psalmist put it this way: "As the deer longs for streams of water, so I long for you, O God. I thirst for God, the living God. When can I go and stand before him?" (Psalm 42:1-2). David exulted, "I will live in the house of the Lord forever" (Psalm 23:6).

Moses is another great example:

It was by faith that Moses, when he grew up, refused to be

called the son of Pharaoh's daughter. He chose to share the
oppression of God's people instead of enjoying the fleeting
pleasures of sin. He thought it was better to suffer for the
sake of Christ than to own the treasures of Egypt, for he
was looking ahead to his great reward. It was by faith that
Moses left the land of Egypt, not fearing the king's anger.
He kept right on going because he kept his eyes on the one
who is invisible (Hebrews 11:24-27).

It is interesting that the writer of Hebrews said Moses "thought it
was better to suffer for the sake of Christ than to own the treasures
of Egypt," because Moses lived at least 1,500 years before Christ. It
is difficult to ascertain how much Moses knew about Jesus, but our
text clearly indicates that Moses had a personal faith in Christ on
the basis of which he forsook Egypt. God had apparently revealed
to him things invisible to the natural eye. Moses became aware of
another King, another kingdom, and a *better reward.*

Our text indicates that Moses carefully thought through his
decision, weighing the pros and cons. He weighed what Egypt had
to offer against the promises of God for the prophetic future. He
concluded that what God offered in eternity was far superior to anything Egypt could offer on temporal earth. Moses lived with eternity
in view. He made his decisions based on how they would impact his
existence in the afterlife.

If we were to try to reconstruct Moses's reasoning, we might
come up with something like this:

God has revealed future things to me—invisible things,
but things of glory, heavenly things. I believe what He says.
At the same time, He has made known to me that I am
His chosen instrument to deliver His people from bondage, my fellow Hebrews according to the flesh. But I am
the adopted son of Pharaoh's daughter. To me the throne

of Egypt has been promised as heir through her. If I follow God's program for me, I must suffer reproach. If, on
the other hand, I remain in the royal court, all the wealth
of Egypt is mine—and how great is that wealth! If I take
the course God has laid out for me, I must suffer affliction
with my fellow Hebrews, and I have seen how heavy their
burdens are. Whereas if I am ready to be called Pharaoh's
grandson, the pleasures of all that Egypt has to offer, the
pleasures of sin, may be enjoyed. Each of these things—the
affliction of the people of God and the pleasures of sin—
is temporal.

It is wiser to look to life after death. In the afterlife, he
who has suffered within the will of God will be rewarded,
but he who has followed the way of the flesh will be judged.
What God has spoken is surely true, and on that basis I
make my choice. I refuse to be called the son of Pharaoh's
daughter and I prefer, by choice, to suffer affliction with
God's people than to enjoy the temporary pleasures of sin.
I count the reproach of the divine Messiah, with its present
satisfaction and eventual reward, to be greater riches by far
than the treasures of Egypt.

As He did with Moses, God has also revealed future things to
you and me—from the pages of Scripture. And like Moses, we have
a choice to make. We can either live for the fleeting pleasures this
world has to offer, or we can live in light of eternity, choosing purposefully to live God's way as we sojourn through earthly life toward
the heavenly country (Hebrews 11:16). We can live *now* in light of
then.

Moses surely would have agreed with what the apostle Paul
wrote to the Corinthian church:

> Our present troubles are small and won't last very long. Yet
> they produce for us a glory that vastly outweighs them and

> will last forever! So we don't look at the troubles we can see now; rather, we fix our gaze on things that cannot be seen. For the things we see now will soon be gone, but the things we cannot see will last forever (2 Corinthians 4:17-18).

That's an eternal perspective.

Moses gave up temporal pleasure for the sake of his Savior, Jesus Christ. His priorities were as they should have been. And what joy Moses's commitment must have brought to the heart of God!

Do you not sense within your heart a calling to follow Moses's lead?

I close with the recognition that the great revivalist preacher, philosopher, and theologian Jonathan Edwards mirrored Moses's commitment. Edwards, who lived from 1703 to 1758, was in the Puritan habit of framing spiritual resolutions to discipline himself. In a number of these resolutions he reminded himself, as he had been taught since childhood, to think of his own dying—or to live as though he had only an hour left before he passed through death's door. In his thinking, his life was a step-by-step journey toward heaven—a journey so important that he ought to subordinate all other concerns of life to it. This heavenly mindset led him to make the following resolutions[*]:

- "Resolved, to endeavor to obtain for myself as much happiness, in the other world, as I possibly can."

- "Resolved, that I will live so as I shall wish I had done when I come to die."

- "Resolved, to endeavor to my utmost to act as I can think I should do, if I had already seen the happiness of heaven and hell's torments."

May the prophetic truths in this book motivate you to make Edwards's resolutions your own.

---

[*] For more on such resolutions, see George W. Marsden, *Jonathan Edwards: A Life* (New Haven, CT: Yale University Press, 2003), chapter 3, "The Pilgrim's Progress."

And now, as we come to a close in our journey, I can think of no better words than those of my prophecy colleague Mark Hitchcock:

> In Revelation 21–22, God introduces the heavenly city, the New Jerusalem. The contrast is clear. Man's city, Babylon, is a corrupt harlot; God's city, the New Jerusalem, is a clean bride. Man's city is eliminated; God's city is enshrined. Man's city is removed from the earth; God's heavenly city will come to the earth. The call for God's people is to live for that which is above, that which will last, as we await our Lord's coming.[6]

Amen!

Appendix A:
If You're Not a Christian

E ntering a personal relationship with Jesus is the most important decision you could ever make in your life. It is unlike any other relationship. If you go into eternity without this, you will spend eternity apart from Him.

If you will allow me, I would like to tell you how you can come into a personal relationship with Jesus.

First you need to recognize that...

God Desires a Personal Relationship with You

God created you (Genesis 1:27). And He did not make you to exist all alone and apart from Him. He created you with a view to coming into a personal relationship with Him.

God has fellowshipped with His people throughout Bible times (for example, Genesis 3:8-19). Just as God fellowshipped with them, so He desires to fellowship with you (1 John 1:5-7). God loves you (John 3:16). Never forget that fact.

The problem is...

Humanity Has a Sin Problem that Blocks a Relationship with God

When Adam and Eve chose to sin against God in the Garden of

Eden, they catapulted the entire human race—to which they gave birth—into sin. Since that time, every human being has been born into the world with a propensity to sin.

The apostle Paul affirmed that "when Adam sinned, sin entered the world. Adam's sin brought death, so death spread to everyone" (Romans 5:12). We are told that "because one person disobeyed God, many became sinners" (Romans 5:19). Ultimately this means that "death came into the world through a man" (Adam), and "everyone dies because we all belong to Adam" (1 Corinthians 15:21-22).

Jesus often spoke of sin in metaphors that illustrate the havoc it can wreak in one's life. He described sin as blindness (Matthew 23:16-26), sickness (Matthew 9:12), being enslaved in bondage (John 8:34), and living in darkness (John 8:12; 12:35-46). Moreover, Jesus taught that this is a universal condition and that all people are guilty before God (Luke 7:37-48).

Jesus also taught that both inner thoughts and external acts render a person guilty (Matthew 5:28). He taught that from within the human heart come evil thoughts, sexual immorality, theft, murder, adultery, greed, malice, deceit, envy, slander, arrogance, and folly (Mark 7:21-23). Moreover, He affirmed that God is fully aware of every person's sins, both external acts and inner thoughts; nothing escapes His notice (Matthew 22:18; Luke 6:8; John 4:17-19).

Of course, some people are more morally upright than others. However, we all fall short of God's infinite standards (Romans 3:23). In a contest to see who can throw a rock to the moon, I am sure a muscular athlete would be able to throw it much further than I could. But all human beings will fall short of the mark. No one can throw a rock that far. Similarly, all of us fall short of measuring up to God's perfect, holy standards.

Though the sin problem is a serious one, God has graciously provided a solution:

Jesus Died for Our Sins and Made Salvation Possible

God's absolute holiness demands that sin be punished. The good news of the gospel, however, is that Jesus has taken this punishment on Himself. God loves us so much that He sent Jesus to bear the penalty for our sins!

Jesus affirmed that it was for the very purpose of dying that He came into the world (John 12:27). Moreover, He perceived His death as being a sacrificial offering for the sins of humanity (Matthew 26:26-28). Jesus took His mission with utmost seriousness, for He knew that without Him, humanity would certainly perish (Matthew 16:25; John 3:16) and spend eternity apart from God in a place of great suffering (Matthew 10:28; 11:23; 23:33; 25:41; Luke 16:22-28).

Jesus therefore described His mission this way: "The Son of Man came not to be served but to serve others and to give his life as a ransom for many" (Matthew 20:28). "The Son of Man came to seek and save those who are lost" (Luke 19:10). "God sent his Son into the world not to judge the world, but to save the world through him" (John 3:17).

Please beware that the benefits of Christ's death on the cross are not automatically applied to your life. *To receive the gift of salvation, you must...*

Believe in Jesus Christ the Savior

By His sacrificial death on the cross, Jesus took the sins of the entire world on Himself and made salvation available for everyone (1 John 2:2). But this salvation is not automatic. Only those who personally choose to believe in Christ are saved. This is the consistent testimony of Jesus. Listen to His words:

- "This is how God loved the world: He gave his one and only Son, so that everyone who believes in him will not perish but have eternal life" (John 3:16).

- "It is my Father's will that all who see his Son and believe in him should have eternal life. I will raise them up at the last day" (John 6:40).

- "I am the resurrection and the life. Anyone who believes in me will live, even after dying" (John 11:25).

Choosing *not* to believe in Jesus, by contrast, leads to eternal condemnation: "There is no judgment against anyone who believes in him. But anyone who does not believe in him has already been judged for not believing in God's one and only Son" (John 3:18).

Free at Last: Forgiven of All Sins

When you believe in Christ the Savior, a wonderful thing happens. God forgives you of all your sins. *All of them!* He puts them completely out of His sight. Ponder for a few minutes the following verses, which speak of the forgiveness of those who have believed in Christ:

- "He is so rich in kindness and grace that he purchased our freedom with the blood of his Son and forgave our sins" (Ephesians 1:7).

- God said, "I will never again remember their sins and lawless deeds" (Hebrews 10:17).

- "Oh, what joy for those whose disobedience is forgiven, whose sin is put out of sight! Yes, what joy for those whose record the Lord has cleared of guilt, whose lives are lived in complete honesty!" (Psalm 32:1-2).

- "His unfailing love toward those who fear him is as great as the height of the heavens above the earth. He has removed our sins as far from us as the east is from the west" (Psalm 103:11-12).

Such forgiveness is wonderful indeed, for none of us can possibly work our way into heaven or be good enough to warrant God's good favor. Because of what Jesus has done for us, we can freely receive the gift of salvation. It is a gift provided solely through the grace of God (Ephesians 2:8-9). And it becomes ours by placing our faith in Jesus.

Don't Put It Off

It is a dangerous thing to put off turning to Christ for salvation, for you do not know the day of your death. What if it happens this evening? "Everyone dies—so the living should take this to heart" (Ecclesiastes 7:2).

If God is speaking to your heart now, then now is your door of opportunity to believe. "Seek the LORD while you can find him. Call on him now while he is near" (Isaiah 55:6).

Follow Me in Prayer

Would you like to place your faith in Jesus for the forgiveness of sins, thereby guaranteeing your eternal place in heaven by His side? If so, pray the following prayer with me.

Keep in mind that it is not the prayer itself that saves you. It is the faith in your heart that saves you. Let the following prayer be a simple expression of the faith that is in your heart:

> *Dear Jesus:*
> *I want to have a relationship with You.*
> *I know I cannot save myself because I know I am a sinner.*
> *Thank You for dying on the cross on my behalf.*
> *I believe you died for me and resurrected from the dead.*
> *I accept Your free gift of salvation.*
> *Thank You, Jesus.*
> *Amen.*

250 NEW BABYLON RISING

Welcome to God's Forever Family

On the authority of the Word of God, I can now assure you that you are a part of God's forever family. If you prayed the above prayer with a heart of faith, you will spend all eternity by the side of Jesus in heaven. Welcome to God's family! I will one day see you in heaven.

What to Do Next

1. Purchase a Bible and read from it daily. Read at least one chapter a day, followed by a time of prayer. If you've not read the Bible before, I recommend that you obtain an easy-to-understand translation—such as the New Living Translation (NLT). I also recommend starting with the Gospel of Luke.

2. Join a Bible-believing church immediately. Get involved in it. Join a Bible study group at the church so you will have regular fellowship with other Christians. This will bring great blessing to your spiritual life.

3. Send me an email at ronrhodes@earthlink.net. I would love to hear from you if you have made a decision for Christ.

Appendix B:
Why a Literal Approach Is Best

The literal approach to interpreting Scripture embraces the normal, common understanding of the terms. Words are given the meaning that they normally have in everyday communication. Following are characteristics of the literal approach to interpreting Scripture:

Literal. The word *literal,* as used in hermeneutics—the science of interpretation—comes from the Latin *sensus literalis,* meaning the literal sense of the text as opposed to a nonliteral or allegorical sense of it. It refers to the understanding of a text that any person of normal intelligence would get without using any special keys or codes.

Normal. Another way to describe the literal meaning of Scripture is that it embraces the normal, everyday understanding of the terms. Words are given the meaning that they normally have in common communication. It is the basic or plain way of interpreting a passage.

Historical. The word *historical* means that the sentences should be understood in their historical setting. They should not be taken out of the space-time cultural context in which they were uttered. The interpreter ought to seek to transfer himself mentally into the historical context in which the author uttered the words. This guards against the interpretive error of making the reader's contemporary cultural context the norm for understanding the text.

Grammatical. This term indicates that the proper meaning of a sentence is rooted in its grammar. The sense of the passage emerges from the grammatical structure wherein all parts of speech—including nouns, verbs, adjectives, adverbs, articles, prepositions, and the like—are placed in a proper form from which only a certain meaning can be derived. This method involves giving each word the same exact basic meaning it would have in the normal, ordinary, customary usage of its day.

Contextual. Every sentence in Scripture should be understood in the context of its paragraph, and the paragraph in the context of the whole book. And in the case of Bible books, the given book should be understood in the context of the whole Bible. In all these ways, meaning is discovered by context—both the *immediate* context and the *broader.*

Authorial. Finally, the historical-grammatical meaning is *the author's* expressed meaning. It is the author who gives the meaning to the text, not the reader. It is the reader's obligation to discover the meaning intended by the author. To put it another way, only a *meaner* can give *meaning* to a text. Hence, what is *meant* in the text is what the *meaner meant* by it, not what the reader desires it to mean.

A literal approach—as described above—is the only sane and safe check on the subjectively prone imagination of human beings. Further, it is the only approach in line with the nature of the inspiration of Scripture—the idea that the very words of Scripture are "God-breathed" (2 Timothy 3:16-17 NIV).

God's Purpose for Language

God gave Adam the gift of intelligible speech. This enabled him to communicate with his Maker and with other humans (Genesis

1:26; 11:1,7). God sovereignly chose to use human language as His means of communicating revelation to people, often through the "Thus saith the LORD" pronouncements of the prophets (see Isaiah 7:7; 10:24; 22:15; 28:16; 30:15; 49:22; 51:22; 52:4 KJV).

Keep in mind that if God created language so He could give revelations to humans, and so humans could communicate with each other, He would no doubt predominantly use language—and expect humans to use it—in its normal and plain sense. This view of language is a prerequisite to understanding not only God's spoken word but His written Word (Scripture) as well.

When the plain, literal sense of Scripture makes good sense, seek no other sense. For example, when God says in His Word that human beings are fallen in sin, we need to accept that harsh reality (Isaiah 53:6). When God says that He loves us so much that He sent His Son to die for us (Romans 5:8), let's accept that literally and give thanks to God for it. When God says that His gift of salvation comes only by faith in Christ (Acts 16:31), let's receive that literally and respond accordingly. When God says that those who reject this gift will spend eternity in hell (Matthew 25:41), we need to accept that literally as well without trying to spin biblical Christianity into a "kinder and gentler" religion.

Literal Interpretations Illustrated in the Biblical Text

The literal method of interpreting Scripture is illustrated in the biblical text itself. I say this because later biblical texts often take earlier texts as literal. A good example is how Exodus 20:10-11 (a later text) interprets the earlier creation events in Genesis 1–2 as literal. This is likewise the case regarding the creation of Adam and Eve (Matthew 19:6; 1 Timothy 2:13), the fall of Adam and his resulting death (Romans 5:12,14), Noah's flood (Matthew 24:38), and the accounts of Jonah (Matthew 12:40-42), Moses (1 Corinthians

10:2-4,11), and numerous other historical figures. This means that even within the text of Scripture itself, we find that the normal means of interpreting God's Word was a literal approach.

A Brief Case Study: Messianic Prophecies

More than 100 predictions about the Messiah were fulfilled literally during Jesus's first coming, including that He would be (1) from the seed of a woman (Genesis 3:15); (2) from the line of Seth (Genesis 4:25); (3) a descendent of Shem (Genesis 9:26); (4) an offspring of Abraham (Genesis 12:3); (5) from the tribe of Judah (Genesis 49:10); (6) a son of David (Jeremiah 23:5-6); (7) conceived of a virgin (Isaiah 7:14); (8) born in Bethlehem (Micah 5:2); (9) be the heralded Messiah (Isaiah 40:3); (10) the coming King (Zechariah 9:9); (11) the sacrificial offering for our sins (Isaiah 53); (12) the One pierced in His side at the cross (Zechariah 12:10); (13) predicted to be "cut off" or die about AD 33 (Daniel 9:24-25); and (14) the One who would resurrect from the dead (Psalms 2; 16).

All these prophecies were *literally* fulfilled in Jesus Christ. This sets a strong precedent for how we are to interpret prophecies relating to the second coming of Christ and all the events that lead up to it. Here is a wise policy: *If you want to understand how God will fulfill prophecy in the future, examine how He has fulfilled it in the past.*

The Literal Method Allows for Symbols in Prophetic Books

There are many symbols found in prophetic scriptures. It is important to note, however, that each symbol is emblematic of something literal. For example, the book of Revelation contains many symbols that represent literal things. John said the "seven stars" in Christ's right hand were "the angels [or messengers] of the seven churches" (Revelation 1:20). Likewise, He said "the seven lampstands" were "the seven churches" (1:20); the "bowls filled with incense" were "the prayers of God's people" (5:8); and "the waters" were "masses of people of every nation and language" (17:15). Clearly, then, each symbol represents something literal.

There are often textual clues that point us to the literal truth found in a symbol—either in the immediate context or in the broader context of Scripture as a whole. In the book of Revelation many of the symbols are defined within the text of Revelation itself (for example, Revelation 1:20; 5:8; 17:15). Others are found in the Old Testament. One of my former professors at Dallas Theological Seminary—Dr. J. Dwight Pentecost, author of the prophecy textbook *Things to Come*—once said that if you have six months to study the book of Revelation, you should spend the first few months studying the Old Testament, for many of the symbols in the book of Revelation are found in the Old Testament.

The basic rule of thumb is that when you encounter a symbol you are unsure about, consult other Scripture verses that relate to that symbol. For example, if you want more information about Jesus being called "Lamb" in Revelation 5:6, look up verses relating to sacrificial lambs (for example, Exodus 12:11-13; 29:38-42; Isaiah 53:7,10; Jeremiah 11:19). That way, you can discover the intended literal meaning of the symbol (in this case, that Jesus was a substitutionary sacrifice for our sins).

The Literal Method Allows for Figures of Speech

When the Bible speaks of the eyes, arms, or wings of God (Psalms 34:15; 91:4; Isaiah 51:9), these should not be taken as literally true. God does not have these physical features because He is pure spirit (John 4:24). Likewise, He cannot literally be a rock (Psalm 42:9), which is material. But we would not know what is *not* literally true of God unless we first know what *is* literally true.

For example, if it were not literally true that God is pure spirit and infinite, then we would not be able to say that certain things attributed to God elsewhere in the Bible are not literally true—such as having material body parts. When Jesus said, "I am the vine" (John 15:1), the literal method of interpretation does not take this as physically true. Rather, we understand this as a figure of speech that communicates that believers derive their spiritual life from Christ, who is the spiritual vine. It is important to understand all this because prophetic apocalyptic literature—such as the books of Daniel and Revelation—makes heavy use of figures of speech.

I grant that sometimes it may be difficult to ascertain when a passage should not be taken literally. But certain guidelines are helpful in making this determination. Briefly put, a text should be taken figuratively...

- when it is obviously figurative, as when Jesus said He was a door (John 10:9);

- when the text itself authorizes the figurative sense, as when Paul said he was speaking "allegorically" (Galatians 4:24 ESV); and

- when a literal interpretation would contradict other truths inside or outside the Bible, as when the Bible speaks of the "four corners of the earth" (Revelation 7:1).

In short, as the famous dictum puts it, "When the literal sense makes good sense, seek no other sense, lest it result in nonsense."

The Literal Method Allows for Types

A type may be defined as "an Old Testament institution, event, person, object, or ceremony which has reality and purpose in biblical history, but which also by divine design foreshadows something yet to be revealed."[1] The New Testament clearly affirms that Christ is the fulfillment of many Old Testament types that prefigured Him. These include the Passover lamb (1 Corinthians 5:7) and the Levitical sacrificial system (Hebrews 10:12-14). These Old Testament types point to Christ, the antitype (Colossians 2:17). In this book, I have addressed types of both the antichrist and New Babylon.

The Literal Method Allows for Parables and Allegories

Jesus often used parables that are not to be taken literally. Yet there is always a literal point that each parable conveys. That Jesus wanted His parables to be clear to those who were receptive is evident in the fact that He carefully interpreted two of them for the disciples—the parables of the sower (Matthew 13:3-9) and the tares (13:24-30). He did this not only so there would be no uncertainty as to their meaning, but to guide believers as to the proper method to use in interpreting the other parables. The fact that Christ did not interpret His subsequent parables indicates that He fully expected believers to understand the literal truths He intended to communicate by following the methodology He illustrated for them.

Allegorical language also appears in Scripture. Paul, for example, used an allegory and labeled it as such (Galatians 4:24). Comparing different Bible translations of this verse shows Paul's meaning: "This may be interpreted *allegorically*" (ESV); or: "These things may be taken *figuratively*" (NIV); or: These "things are *symbolic*" (NKJV). But even such allegorical statements communicate a literal truth that can be understood.

Taking Biblical Genres into Account

Let us also keep in mind that the historical-grammatical method of Bible interpretation recognizes that there are different genres of literature in the Bible, each of which have certain peculiar characteristics that must be recognized to interpret the text properly. Biblical genres include the historical (for example, Acts), the dramatic epic (Job), poetry (Psalms), wise sayings (Proverbs), and apocalyptic writings (Revelation). Obviously, an incorrect genre judgment will lead one far astray in interpreting Scripture. A parable should not be treated as history, nor should poetry or apocalyptic literature (both of which contain many symbols) be treated as straightforward narrative.

Babylon in Revelation 17–18

Taking all these interpretive points into consideration, I believe it is best for us to interpret the Babylon of Revelation 17 and 18 as a literal city that sits along the Euphrates River. I say this because...

- other geographical locations in the book of Revelation are obviously intended to be taken literally. Babylon should be too.

- other references to Babylon throughout the rest of the Bible always point to the literal city of Babylon.

- a key geographical marker is mentioned in Revelation in association with Babylon—the Euphrates River. This indicates Babylon should be understood as the literal city of Babylon.

- Revelation 17–18 draws heavily from Jeremiah 50–51 and Isaiah 13:19-22. These passages speak of the prophetic future of the literal city of Babylon. That being so, Revelation 17–18 should also be taken as referring to the literal city of Babylon, which sits alongside the Euphrates River.

Bibliography

Ankerberg, John, and Dillon Burroughs. *Middle East Meltdown*. Eugene, OR: Harvest House, 2007.

Ansari, Ali. *Confronting Iran: The Failure of American Foreign Policy and the Next Great Conflict in the Middle East*. New York: Basic Books, 2006.

Barnhouse, Donald Grey. *Revelation: An Expository Commentary*. Grand Rapids, MI: Zondervan, 1971.

Berman, Ilan. *Tehran Rising: Iran's Challenge to the United States*. New York: Rowman & Littlefield, 2005.

Bernis, Jonathan. *A Rabbi Looks at the Last Days*. Minneapolis, MN: Chosen, 2013.

Block, Daniel. *The Book of Ezekiel: Chapters 25–48*. Grand Rapids, MI: Eerdmans, 1998.

Charles River Editors. *The Greatest Cities of Ancient Mesopotamia: The History of Babylon, Nineveh, Ur, Uruk, Persepolis, Hattusa, and Assur*. CreateSpace, 2016.

Corsi, Jerome. *Atomic Iran: How the Terrorist Regime Bought the Bomb and American Politicians*. Nashville, TN: WND Books, 2005.

Dyer, Charles. *The Rise of Babylon: Sign of the End Times*. Chicago, IL: Moody, 2003.

Feinberg, Charles. *A Commentary on Revelation*. Winona Lake, IN: BMH Books, 1985.

Feinberg, Charles. *The Prophecy of Ezekiel*. Eugene, OR: Wipf & Stock, 2003.

Fruchtenbaum, Arnold. *The Footsteps of the Messiah*. Tustin, CA: Ariel, 2004.

Gaffney, Frank. *War Footing: Ten Steps America Must Take to Prevail in the War for the Free World*. Annapolis, MD: Naval Institute Press, 2006.

Geisler, Norman. *Systematic Theology: Church/Last Things*, vol. 4. St. Paul, MN: Bethany House, 2005.

Gold, Dore. *The Fight for Jerusalem: Radical Islam, the West, and the Future of the Holy City*. Washington, DC: Regnery, 2007.

Goodspeed, George Stephen. *A History of the Babylonians and Assyrians*. CreateSpace, 2013.

Hays, J. Daniel, J. Scott Duvall, and C. Marvin Pate. *Dictionary of Biblical Prophecy and End Times*. Grand Rapids, MI: Zondervan, 2007.

Heitzig, Skip. *You Can Understand the Book of Revelation*. Eugene, OR: Harvest House, 2011.

Helyer, Larry, and Richard Wagner. *The Book of Revelation for Dummies*. Hoboken, NJ: Wylie, 2008.

Hindson, Ed. *Revelation: Unlocking the Future*. Chattanooga, TN: AMG, 2002.

Hitchcock, Mark. *Bible Prophecy*. Wheaton, IL: Tyndale House, 1999.

Hitchcock, Mark. *Iran: The Coming Crisis*. Sisters, OR: Multnomah, 2006.

Hitchcock, Mark. *Is America in Bible Prophecy?* Sisters, OR: Multnomah, 2002.

Hitchcock, Mark. *The Coming Islamic Invasion of Israel*. Sisters, OR: Multnomah, 2002.

Hitchcock, Mark. *The Late Great United States*. Colorado Springs, CO: Multnomah, 2009.

Hitchcock, Mark. *The Second Coming of Babylon*. Sisters, OR: Multnomah, 2003.

Hoyt, Herman. *The End Times*. Chicago, IL: Moody, 1969.

Ice, Thomas, and Randall Price. *Ready to Rebuild: The Imminent Plan to Rebuild the Last Days Temple*. Eugene, OR: Harvest House, 1992.

Ice, Thomas, and Timothy Demy. *Prophecy Watch*. Eugene, OR: Harvest House, 1998.

Ice, Thomas, and Timothy Demy. *When the Trumpet Sounds*. Eugene, OR: Harvest House, 1995.

Ironside, H.A. *Revelation*. Grand Rapids, MI: Kregel, 1978.

Jeffress, Robert. *Countdown to the Apocalypse*. New York: Faith Words, 2015.

Jeremiah, David. *Agents of Babylon: What the Prophecies of Daniel Tell Us About the End of Days*. Carol Stream, IL: Tyndale House, 2015.

Jeremiah, David. *Agents of the Apocalypse*. Carol Stream, IL: Tyndale House, 2014.

Jeremiah, David. *Escape the Coming Night: An Electrifying Tour of the World as It Races Toward Its Final Days*. Dallas, TX: Word, 1990.

Kriwaczek, Paul. *Babylon: Mesopotamia and the Birth of Civilization*. New York: Thomas Dunne Books, 2012.

LaHaye, Tim, and Jerry Jenkins. *Are We Living in the End Times?* Wheaton, IL: Tyndale House, 1999.

LaHaye, Tim, and Thomas Ice. *Charting the End Times*. Eugene, OR: Harvest House, 2001.

LaHaye, Tim. *The Beginning of the End*. Wheaton, IL: Tyndale House, 1991.

LaHaye, Tim. *The Coming Peace in the Middle East*. Grand Rapids, MI: Zondervan, 1984.

Lindsey, Hal. *There's a New World Coming: A Prophetic Odyssey*. Santa Ana, CA: Vision House, 1973.

Newell, William. *Revelation Chapter-by-Chapter*. Grand Rapids, MI: Kregel, 1994.

Pentecost, J. Dwight. *Prophecy for Today*. Grand Rapids, MI: Discovery House, 1989.

Pentecost, J. Dwight. *The Words and Works of Jesus Christ*. Grand Rapids, MI: Zondervan, 1978.

Pentecost, J. Dwight. *Things to Come*. Grand Rapids, MI: Zondervan, 1964.

Phares, Walid. *Future Jihad: Terrorist Strategies Against the West*. New York: Palgrave MacMillan, 2005.

Pink, Arthur W. *The Antichrist: A Study of Satan's Christ*. Blacksburg, VA: Wilder, 2008.

Pollack, Kenneth. *The Persian Puzzle: The Conflict Between Iran and America*. New York: Random House, 2005.

Price, Randall. *Fast Facts on the Middle East Conflict*. Eugene, OR: Harvest House, 2003.

Price, Randall. *Jerusalem in Prophecy*. Eugene, OR: Harvest House, 1998.

Price, Randall. *Unholy War*. Eugene, OR: Harvest House, 2001.

Price, Walter K. *The Coming Antichrist*. Neptune, NJ: Loizeaux Brothers, 1985.

Prophecy Study Bible, ed. Tim LaHaye. Chattanooga, TN: AMG, 2001.

Reid, T.R. *The United States of Europe: The New Superpower and the End of American Supremacy*. New York: Penguin Books, 2004.

Rhodes, Ron. *40 Days Through Revelation: Uncovering the Mystery of the End Times*. Eugene, OR: Harvest House, 2013.

Rhodes, Ron. *40 Days Through Daniel: Revealing God's Plan for the Future*. Eugene, OR: Harvest House, 2013.

Rhodes, Ron. *Northern Storm Rising: Russia, Iran, and the Emerging End-Times Military Coalition Against Israel*. Eugene, OR: Harvest House, 2008.

Rhodes, Ron. *The Middle East Conflict: What You Need to Know*. Eugene, OR: Harvest House, 2009.

Rhodes, Ron. *The Popular Dictionary of Bible Prophecy*. Eugene, OR: Harvest House, 2010.

Rhodes, Ron. *The Topical Guide of Bible Prophecy*. Eugene, OR: Harvest House, 2010.

Richardson, Joel. *Mystery Babylon: Unlocking the Bible's Greatest Prophetic Mystery*. Washington, DC: WND Books, 2016.

Richardson, Joel. *The Islamic Antichrist*. Washington, DC: WND Books, 2009.

Richardson, Joel. *When a Jew Rules the World*. Washington, DC: WND Books, 2015.

Rosenberg, Joel. *Epicenter: Why Current Rumblings in the Middle East Will Change Your Future.* Carol Stream, IL: Tyndale House, 2006.

Rosenberg, Joel. *Israel at War.* Carol Stream, IL: Tyndale House, 2012.

Ruthven, Jon Mark. *The Prophecy that Is Shaping History: New Research on Ezekiel's Vision of the End.* Fairfax, VA: Xulon, 2003.

Rydelnik, Michael. *The Messianic Hope: Is the Hebrew Bible Really Messianic?* Nashville, TN: B&H Publishing Group, 2010.

Ryrie, Charles. *Basic Theology.* Wheaton, IL: Victor, 1986.

Ryrie, Charles. *Dispensationalism Today.* Chicago, IL: Moody, 1965.

Seymour, Michael. *Babylon: Legend, History and the Ancient City.* London: I.B. Tauris, 2014.

Showers, Renald. *Maranatha: Our Lord Come!* Bellmawr, NJ: The Friends of Israel Gospel Ministry, 1995.

Stedman, Ray. *God's Final Word: Understanding Revelation.* Grand Rapids, MI: Discovery House, 1991.

Swindoll, Charles. *Insights on Revelation.* Grand Rapids, MI: Zondervan, 2011.

The MacArthur Study Bible, ed. John MacArthur. Nashville, TN: Thomas Nelson, 2003.

The Popular Bible Prophecy Commentary, eds. Tim LaHaye and Ed Hindson. Eugene, OR: Harvest House, 2006.

The Popular Encyclopedia of Bible Prophecy, eds. Tim LaHaye and Ed Hindson. Eugene, OR: Harvest House, 2004.

The Ryrie Study Bible, ed. Charles Ryrie. Chicago, IL: Moody Press, 2011.

Timmerman, Kenneth. *Countdown to Crisis: The Coming Nuclear Showdown with Iran.* New York: Three Rivers Press, 2006.

Toussaint, Stanley. *Behold the King: A Study of Matthew.* Grand Rapids, MI: Kregel, 2005.

Unger, Merrill F. *Beyond the Crystal Ball.* Chicago, IL: Moody, 1978.

Venter, Al. *Iran's Nuclear Option: Tehran's Quest for the Atomic Bomb.* Philadelphia, PA: Casemate, 2005.

Walvoord, John F., and John E. Walvoord. *Armageddon, Oil, and the Middle East Crisis*. Grand Rapids, MI: Zondervan, 1975.

Walvoord, John F., and Mark Hitchcock. *Armageddon, Oil, and Terror*. Carol Stream, IL: Tyndale House, 2007.

Walvoord, John F. *End Times*. Nashville, TN: Word, 1998.

Walvoord, John F. *Israel in Prophecy*. Grand Rapids, MI: Zondervan, 1970.

Walvoord, John F. *The Millennial Kingdom*. Grand Rapids, MI: Zondervan, 1975.

Walvoord, John F. *The Prophecy Knowledge Handbook*. Wheaton, IL: Victor, 1990.

Walvoord, John F. *The Return of the Lord*. Grand Rapids, MI: Zondervan, 1979.

Wood, Leon J. *The Bible and Future Events: An Introductory Summary of Last-Day Events*. Grand Rapids, MI: Zondervan, 1973.

Wiersbe, Warren. *Be Victorious*. Colorado Springs, CO: David C. Cook, 1985.

Yamauchi, Edwin. *Foes from the Northern Frontier: Invading Hordes from the Russian Steppes*. Eugene, OR: Wipf & Stock, 1982.

Endnotes

Introduction—New Babylon Rising

1. Mark Hitchcock, *101 Answers to Questions About the Book of Revelation* (Eugene, OR: Harvest House, 2012), iBooks edition.
2. Mark Hitchcock, *The Second Coming of Babylon* (Sisters, OR: Multnomah, 2003), iBooks edition.
3. David Jeremiah, *Agents of Babylon: What the Prophecies of Daniel Tell Us About the End of Days* (Carol Stream, IL: Tyndale House, 2015), Kindle edition.
4. Charles H. Dyer, *The Rise of Babylon: Sign of the End Times* (Carol Stream, IL: Tyndale House, 1991), p. 47.
5. Charles R. Swindoll, *Insights on Revelation* (Carol Stream, IL: Tyndale House, 2014), iBooks edition.
6. Gary DeMar, *Last Days Madness* (Brentwood, TN: Wolgemuth & Hyatt, 1999), p. 210; cited in Thomas Ice, "Babylon in Bible Prophecy," posted at the Pre-Trib Research Center website, https://www.pre-trib.org.
7. Arnold Fruchtenbaum, *The Footsteps of the Messiah* (Tustin, CA: Ariel Publishers, 2004), p. 108.
8. Ice, "Babylon in Bible Prophecy."

Chapter 2—A Sampling of Interpretations

1. See Charles H. Dyer, "The Identity of Babylon in Revelation 17–18," Part 2, *Bibliotheca Sacra*, October-December 1987, p. 435.
2. Andy Woods, "What Is the Identity of Babylon in Revelation 17–18?," article posted at http://www.spiritandtruth.org.
3. See, for example, *Adam Clarke's Commentary on the Bible* (Grand Rapids, MI: Baker Books, 1983).
4. J. Massyngberde Ford, *Revelation*, vol. 38 of *The Anchor Bible*, eds. William Foxwell Albright and David Noel Freedman (Garden City, NJ: Doubleday, 1975), pp. 54-56, 93, 259-307.
5. Andrew M. Woods, "Have the Prophecies in Revelation 17–18 About Babylon Been Fulfilled? Part 1," *Bibliotheca Sacra*, January-March 2012, pp. 79-80.
6. Woods, "Have the Prophecies in Revelation 17–18 About Babylon Been Fulfilled? Part 1," pp. 79-80.
7. Thomas Ice, "Babylon in Bible Prophecy," posted at The Pretrib Research Center website: https://www.pre-trib.org/.

Chapter 3—New Babylon: A Literal City

1. Andrew M. Woods, "Have the Prophecies in Revelation 17–18 About Babylon Been Fulfilled? Part 2," *Bibliotheca Sacra*, April-June 2012, p. 228.
2. Woods, "Have the Prophecies in Revelation 17–18 About Babylon Been Fulfilled?," p. 228.
3. Thomas Ice, "Babylon in Bible Prophecy," posted at The Pretrib Research Center website: https://www.pre-trib.org/.
4. I am here indebted to Charles H. Dyer, "The Identity of Babylon in Revelation 17–18, Part 2," *Bibliotheca Sacra*, October-December 1987, pp. 440-41.
5. Dyer, "The Identity of Babylon," p. 444.
6. Dyer, "The Identity of Babylon," p. 445.
7. John F. Walvoord, *The Nations in Prophecy* (Grand Rapids, MI: Zondervan, 1967), pp. 63-64.
8. Ice, "Babylon in Bible Prophecy."
9. *The Bible Knowledge Commentary: Old Testament*, eds. John F. Walvoord and Roy B. Zuck (Wheaton, IL: Victor, 1998), in The Bible Study App, Olive Tree.
10. *The Expositors Bible Commentary*, in Accordance, Oaktree Software.
11. *NKJV Study Bible*, in Accordance, Oaktree Software.
12. Dyer, "The Identity of Babylon," p. 313.
13. Andy Woods, "What is the Identity of Babylon in Revelation 17–18?," posted at http://www.spiritandtruth.org.

Chapter 4—*Religious* and *Commercial* New Babylon

1. Charles C. Ryrie, *Revelation* (Chicago, IL: Moody), in The Bible Study App, Olive Tree.
2. Thomas Ice, "Babylon in Bible Prophecy," posted at The Pretrib Research Center website: https://www.pre-trib.org/.
3. Mark Hitchcock, *101 Answers to Questions About the Book of Revelation* (Eugene, OR: Harvest House, 2012), iBooks edition.
4. Ryrie, *Revelation*.
5. *The Ryrie Study Bible*, ed. Charles C. Ryrie (Chicago, IL: Moody), in The Bible Study App, Olive Tree.
6. Walter K. Price, *The Coming Antichrist* (Neptune, NJ: Loizeaux Brothers, 1985), p. 145.
7. Price, *The Coming Antichrist*, pp. 146-47.
8. Mark Hitchcock, *The Complete Book of Bible Prophecy* (Wheaton, IL: Tyndale House, 1999), pp. 199-200.
9. Warren Wiersbe, *Be Victorious* (Colorado Springs, CO: David C. Cook, 1985), in The Bible Study App, Olive Tree.
10. Mark Hitchcock, *The Second Coming of Babylon* (Sisters, OR: Multnomah, 2003), pp. 147-50.
11. Nathan Jones, "Antichrist Will Be Headquartered in Rome," Lamb and Lion Ministries website, posted June 29, 2009.

Chapter 5—Historical Insights from Genesis 10–11

1. Warren Wiersbe, *Wiersbe's Expository Outlines on the Old Testament* (Colorado Springs, CO: David C. Cook, 1993), in The Bible Study App, Olive Tree Publishers.

2. *Webster's New International Dictionary of the English Language*, 2d ed.; cited in John F. Walvoord, *Jesus Christ Our Lord* (Chicago, IL: Moody, 1980), p. 62.

3. Donald K. Campbell, "The Interpretation of Types," *Bibliotheca Sacra*, July, 1955, p. 250.

4. Paul Lee Tan, *The Interpretation of Prophecy* (Rockville, MD: Assurance Publishers, 1974), p. 168.

5. See, for example, Bernard Ramm, *Protestant Biblical Interpretation* (Grand Rapids, MI: Baker, 1978), pp. 215-40; A. Berkeley Mickelsen, *Interpreting the Bible* (Grand Rapids, MI: Eerdmans, 1977), pp. 236-64.

6. Mickelsen, *Interpreting the Bible*, p. 237.

7. *IVP Old Testament Background Commentary*, in Accordance, Oaktree Software.

8. Warren Wiersbe, *Be Series*, in Accordance, Oaktree Software.

9. *Zondervan Illustrated Bible Backgrounds Commentary: Old Testament*, in Accordance, Oaktree Software.

10. Thomas Constable, *Dr. Constable's Expository Notes*, 2010 Edition, in The Bible Study App, Olive Tree Software.

11. Nahum M. Sarna, *The JPS Torah Commentary: Genesis* (Philadelphia, PA: The Jewish Publication Society, 1989), p. 82.

12. *John Phillips Commentary*, in The Bible Study App, Olive Tree Software.

13. Charles H. Dyer, *The Rise of Babylon: Is Iraq at the Center of the Final Drama?*, rev. ed. (Chicago, IL: Moody, 2003), p. 47.

14. Wiersbe, *Be Series*.

15. Kent Hughes, *Genesis*, in The Bible Study App, Olive Tree Software.

16. Hughes, *Genesis*.

17. Jerome, *Ancient Commentary on Scripture*, The Bible Study App, Olive Tree Software.

18. Augustine, *Ancient Commentary on Scripture*, in The Bible Study App, Olive Tree Software.

19. Mark Hitchcock, *The Second Coming of Babylon* (Sisters, OR: Multnomah Books, 2010), iBooks edition.

20. John F. Walvoord, "Revelation" in *Bible Knowledge Commentary*, eds. John F. Walvoord and Roy B. Zuck (Wheaton, IL: Victor, 1993), 2:970-71.

Chapter 6—Historical Insights from Daniel

1. Donald K. Campbell, "The Interpretation of Types," *Bibliotheca Sacra*, July, 1955, p. 250.

Chapter 8—The Mark of the Beast and the Coming Cashless Society

1. Ed Hindson, "False Prophet," in *The Popular Encyclopedia of Bible Prophecy*, eds. Tim LaHaye and Ed Hindson (Eugene, OR: Harvest House, 2004), p. 103.

2. John F. Walvoord, "The Beginning of the Great Day of God's Wrath," article posted at Bible.org.

3. Arnold Fruchtenbaum, *Footsteps of the Messiah* (Tustin, CA: Ariel Ministries, 2004), p. 255.

4. Mark Hitchcock, *The Complete Book of Bible Prophecy* (Wheaton, IL: Tyndale House, 1999), pp. 163-64.

5. Robert Thomas, cited in Thomas Ice and Timothy Demy, *Fast Facts on Bible Prophecy from A to Z* (Eugene, OR: Harvest House, 2004), p. 129.

6. John MacArthur, *The MacArthur Study Bible* (Nashville, TN: Thomas Nelson, 2003), in The Bible Study App, Olive Tree Software.

7. David Jeremiah, *The Coming Economic Armageddon: What Bible Prophecy Warns About the New Global Economy* (Brentwood, TN: FaithWords, 2010), p. 146.

8. John F. Walvoord, *The Prophecy Knowledge Handbook* (Wheaton, IL: Victor, 1990), cited in Thomas Ice and Timothy Demy, *The Coming Cashless Society* (Eugene, OR: Harvest House, 1996), p. 132.

9. Robert Samuelson, cited in Jeremiah, *The Coming Economic Armageddon*, pp. 162-64.

10. Jeremiah, *The Coming Economic Armageddon*, pp. 162-64.

11. Mark Hitchcock, *Cashless: Bible Prophecy, Economic Chaos, and the Future Financial Order* (Eugene, OR: Harvest House, 2010), pp. 75-76.

12. Jeremiah, *The Coming Economic Armageddon*, pp. 162-64.

13. Kenneth Rogoff, cited in "Will the U.S. Become a Cashless Society?" *Chicago Tribune*, September 9, 2016, online edition.

14. Cited in Jeremiah, *The Coming Economic Armageddon*, pp. 162-64.

15. Aimee Picchi, "Cash Not Welcome Here," *Moneywatch*, August 12, 2016, online edition.

16. "Cash Is Losing Its Luster Among Consumers," *BJBiz*, July 18, 2016, online edition.

17. Fernando Florez, "Cashless Society: The Shape of Things to Come," *Accounting and Business*, July/August 2016, online edition.

Chapter 9—The Destruction of Commercial New Babylon, Part 1

1. Paul Enns, *The Moody Handbook of Theology*, Kindle edition.

2. Henry C. Thiessen, *Lectures in Systematic Theology*, Kindle edition.

3. J.I. Packer, *Knowing God* (Downers Grove, IL: InterVarsity Press, 1983), p. 126.

4. Thomas Ice and Timothy Demy, *Prophecy Watch* (Eugene, OR: Harvest House, 1998), p. 191.

5. Warren Wiersbe, *Be Victorious* (Colorado Springs, CO: David C. Cook, 1985), in The Bible Study App, Olive Tree.

Chapter 11—Near-Term Prophetic Expectations, Part 1

1. Tim LaHaye and Ed Hindson, *Target Israel* (Eugene, OR: Harvest House, 2015), iBooks edition.

2. *U.S. News & World Report;* cited in David Reagan, "The World's Hatred of Israel: Prophecy Fulfilled," Lamb & Lion Ministries.

3. Adam Lebor, "Exodus: Why Europe's Jews Are Fleeing Once Again," *Newsweek*, July 29, 2014, http://www.newsweek.com.

4. Reagan, "The World's Hatred of Israel."

Chapter 12—Near Term Prophetic Expectations, Part 2

1. Some may wonder why the term "Rosh" does not appear in the ESV, NIV, NET, HCSB, and NLT translations except as a marginal reading. The Hebrew word in this verse can be taken as either a proper noun (a geographical place called Rosh) or as an adjective (meaning "chief"). If it's an adjective, it qualifies the meaning of the word prince, so that it is translated "chief prince." Hebrew scholars debate the correct translation. I believe Hebrew scholars C.F. Keil and Wilhelm Gesenius are correct in saying Rosh refers to a geographical place. The evidence suggests that the errant translation of Rosh as an adjective ("chief prince") can be traced originally to an early Jewish translator, and later popularized in the Latin Vulgate, translated by Jerome—who himself admitted that he did not base his translation on grammatical considerations. Jerome resisted translating Rosh as a proper noun primarily because he could not find it mentioned as a geographical place anywhere else in Scripture. Hebrew Scholar Clyde Billington observes: "Jerome's incorrect translation of Rosh as an adjective has been followed by many of today's popular translations of the Bible. It is clear that this translation originated with the Jewish translator Aquila [and] was adopted by Jerome in the Vulgate." (See "Clyde Billington, "The Rosh People in History and Prophecy," part 1, *Michigan Theological Journal*, 3:1, Spring 1992, 65.) Taking Rosh as a geographical place is the most natural rendering of the original Hebrew (as reflected in the ASV and NASB translations). I see no legitimate linguistic reason for taking it as an adjective.

2. Arnold Fruchtenbaum, *Ariel Ministries Newsletter*, Fall 2004/Winter 2005, p. 4.

3. John Ankerberg, Dillon Burroughs, and Jimmy DeYoung, *Israel Under Fire: The Prophetic Chain of Events That Threatens the Middle East* (Eugene, OR: Harvest House, 2009), Kindle edition.

4. Thomas Ice, "Is It Time for the Temple?," article posted at www.pre-trib.org.

5. Ankerberg, Burroughs, and DeYoung, *Israel Under Fire.*

6. "New 'Sanhedrin' Plans Rebuilding of Temple: Israeli Rabbinical Body Calls for Architectural Blueprint," *WorldNetDaily*, June 8, 2005, posted at WDN website.

7. Robert J. Morgan, "The World's War on Christianity," *The Huffington Post*, March 16, 2014, online edition.

8. Thomas Ice and Timothy Demy, *The Coming Cashless Society*, pp. 85-86.

Chapter 13—Tying It All Together: An Overview

1. Robert P. Lightner, *Evangelical Theology* (Grand Rapids, MI: Baker Books, 1986), p. 57.

Chapter 14—Living as an End-Times Christian

1. John F. Walvoord, *End Times* (Nashville, TN: Word, 1998), p. 218.

2. Walvoord, *End Times*, p. 219.

3. Erich Sauer, *From Eternity to Eternity* (Grand Rapids, MI: Eerdmans, 1979), p. 13.

4. J.I. Packer, ed. *Alive to God* (Downers Grove, IL: InterVarsity, 1992), p. 171.

5. Richard Baxter, cited in Packer, *Alive to God*, p. 167.

6. Mark Hitchcock, *101 Answers to Questions About the Book of Revelation* (Eugene, OR: Harvest House, 2012), iBooks edition.

Appendix B: Why a Literal Approach Is Best

1. Donald Campbell, "The Interpretation of Types," *Bibliotheca Sacra*, July 1955, p. 250.

Other Great Harvest House Books by Ron Rhodes

BOOKS ABOUT THE BIBLE

40 Days Through Genesis
The Big Book of Bible Answers
Bite-Size Bible® Answers
Bite-Size Bible® Charts
Bite-Size Bible® Definitions
Bite-Size Bible® Handbook
Commonly Misunderstood Bible Verses
The Complete Guide to Bible Translations
Find It Fast in the Bible
The Popular Dictionary of Bible Prophecy
Understanding the Bible from A to Z
What Does the Bible Say About…?

BOOKS ABOUT THE END TIMES

8 Great Debates of Bible Prophecy
40 Days Through Revelation
Cyber Meltdown
The End Times in Chronological Order
Northern Storm Rising
Unmasking the Antichrist

BOOKS ABOUT OTHER IMPORTANT TOPICS

5-Minute Apologetics for Today
1001 Unforgettable Quotes About God, Faith, and the Bible
Answering the Objections of Atheists,
Agnostics, and Skeptics
Christianity According to the Bible
The Complete Guide to Christian Denominations
Conversations with Jehovah's Witnesses
Find It Quick Handbook on Cults and New Religions
The Truth Behind Ghosts, Mediums, and Psychic Phenomena
Secret Life of Angels
What Happens After Life?
Why Do Bad Things Happen If God Is Good?
Wonder of Heaven

THE 10 MOST IMPORTANT THINGS SERIES
The 10 Most Important Things You Can Say to a Catholic
The 10 Most Important Things You Can Say to a Jehovah's Witness
The 10 Most Important Things You Can Say to a Mason
The 10 Most Important Things You Can Say to a Mormon
The 10 Things You Need to Know About Islam
The 10 Things You Should Know About the Creation vs. Evolution Debate

QUICK REFERENCE GUIDES
Halloween: What You Need to Know
Islam: What You Need to Know
Jehovah's Witnesses: What You Need to Know

THE REASONING FROM THE SCRIPTURES SERIES
Reasoning from the Scriptures with Catholics
Reasoning from the Scriptures with the Jehovah's Witnesses
Reasoning from the Scriptures with Masons
Reasoning from the Scriptures with the Mormons
Reasoning from the Scriptures with Muslims

LITTLE BOOKS
The Little Book About God
The Little Book About Heaven
The Little Book About the Bible

AVAILABLE ONLY AS EBOOKS
The Book of Bible Promises
The Coming Oil Storm
The Topical Handbook of Bible Prophecy